THE ELECTION OF 1988

Reports and Interpretations

GERALD M. POMPER

ROSS K. BAKER

WALTER DEAN BURNHAM

BARBARA G. FARAH

MARJORIE RANDON HERSHEY

ETHEL KLEIN

WILSON CAREY MCWILLIAMS

CHATHAM HOUSE PUBLISHERS, INC.
Chatham, New Jersey

THE ELECTION OF 1988
Reports and Interpretations

CHATHAM HOUSE PUBLISHERS, INC.
Post Office Box One
Chatham, New Jersey 07928

PUBLISHER: Edward Artinian
ILLUSTRATIONS: Adrienne Shubert
JACKET AND COVER DESIGN: Lawrence Ratzkin
COMPOSITION: Chatham Composer
PRINTING AND BINDING: BookCrafters, Inc.

LIBRARY OF CONGRESS CATALOGING-IN-PUBLICATION DATA

The Election of 1988

    Includes bibliographies and index.
     1. Presidents—United States—Election—1988.
2. United States. Congress—Elections, 1988. 3. Elections—United States. I. Pomper, Gerald M.
JK526 1988b   324.973'0927   89-752
ISBN 0-934540-77-2
ISBN 0-934540-76-4 (pbk.)

Manufactured in the United States of America
10 9 8 7 6 5 4 3 2 1

Contents

Figures

Tables

Preface

Nations, as much as individuals, often face difficult, even unpleasant decisions. Hamlet expressed a recurring tough choice, either to "bear those ills we have" or to "fly to others that we know not of." Individuals must decide whether to keep or to change their residences, jobs, or lovers. In 1988, the United States faced a similar social choice, whether to continue the existing political regime by electing George Bush as President or to set off in a new, uncertain direction by the election of Michael Dukakis.

The nation made its decision uncomfortably; a decided majority wished for other alternatives. The 1988 campaign was widely characterized as one of the meanest and least edifying in modern history. But the contest began with higher aspirations, voiced by Dukakis's praise of the ennoblement of public life and Bush's call for a "kinder, gentler nation." Ultimately, the campaigners reneged on these inspiring promises. Disillusioned, only half of their fellow citizens voted.

In this volume, the fourth in a series begun in 1976, seven political scientists recount and analyze the 1988 election. We hope we do so honestly and fairly. But, regardless of our individual political preferences, we also write with little joy in a campaign in which Americans lost the opportunity to consider, debate, and determine their collective life. We can hope, perhaps, that our analysis of the election will contribute to an improved political discourse in the future.

Contributors to this book include:

Ross K. Baker, professor at Rutgers University and author of *House and Senate*

Walter Dean Burnham, Frank C. Erwin Professor at the University of Texas at Austin and author of *Critical Elections*

Barbara G. Farah, survey manager, marketing research, *The New York Times* and contributing author of *Political Action*

Marjorie Randon Hershey, professor at Indiana University and author of *Running for Office*

Ethel Klein, associate professor at Columbia University and author of *Gender Politics*

v

WILSON CAREY McWILLIAMS, professor at Rutgers Unversity and author of *The Idea of Fraternity in America*

GERALD M. POMPER, professor at Rutgers University and author of *Voters, Elections, and Parties*

We gratefully acknowledge the help provided by many persons. Marlene Michels Pomper, who edited the previous volumes in this series, continued to provide valuable informal advice. Carrie Calvo was not only an able research assistant but also a cheerful critic. Kathleen Frankovic provided quick, friendly, and informative access to the surveys she ably directs for CBS News. Irene Glynn, Charlotte Drinkwater, and our ebullient publisher, Edward Artinian, transformed our drafts into professional writing.

We have benefited from the advice, in 1988 and earlier, of M.J. Aronoff, Susan Abrams Beck, Kevin Canada, Dennis Hale, Sadie Goldhawn, Kenneth Goldstein, Charles Jacob, Marc Landy, Maureen Moakley, Diana Owen, Henry Plotkin, Florence Riley, Stephen Salmore, Gordon Schochet, Nancy L. Schwartz, and John K. White. Important financial aid was provided by the Eagleton Institute of Politics and the Research Council of Rutgers University. Laughlin and Patty McDonald were gracious hosts during the Democratic convention. Edith Saks, as always, was efficient and supportive in coordinating a nationwide collaboration.

Each election is but one moment in a continuing American history. For some Americans, however, their personal histories ended before the 1988 balloting. We dedicate this volume to those loved ones whose votes no longer can be counted, but whose remembered voices will always count greatly to us.

January 1989   GERALD M. POMPER

1

The Reagan Heritage

WALTER DEAN BURNHAM

Ronald Reagan in "Political Time"[1]

Ronald Reagan was the most ideological President, and the leader of the most ideological administration, in modern American history. As he continually re-iterated from his first inaugural address in January 1981 to his very last radio address before leaving office, Reagan believed that he came to power in order to carry out a mandate for very large scale change in American politics. The true extent and success of the "Reagan revolution" will remain matters for debate for quite a time to come. But few would deny that he made more of a difference — not only in changing the terms of debate but in changing the playing field itself — than all but a few Presidents in this century. One need think only of the incomprehension, puzzlement, or laughter that would follow a writer's attempt to join the word "revolution" with the name of Richard Nixon, Gerald Ford, or Jimmy Carter. With Reagan, we are on significantly different ground. It is almost as if Reagan had stepped from the pages of the super-libertarian Ayn Rand's best-selling novel *Atlas Shrugged* and had begun securing enactment of as much of her capitalist-utopian program as he could. That was quite a bit; and if in the end he was unable to produce the full Sign-of-the-Dollar millennium that she preached, it was not for want of trying.

Such Presidents are rare. The messy, divided-power, incrementalist, and compromise-prone American political system works against such leadership. In order to understand something of the circumstances that made the Reagan Presidency possible, then credible, then successful, a very long time perspective is necessary. Stephen Skowronek has made a path-breaking attempt to provide an analytic framework in which presidential "success" is systematically linked to the time-bound contexts of presidential action.[2] Presidents may be born free and equal, but their freedom of action varies enormously with the situational context in which they function. Utilizing Skowronek's schema, we can ask two questions: First, is the existing structure of regime commitments resilient or vulnerable? Second, is the individual President under review in affiliation or opposed to these regime commitments? This gives us four kinds of President-context associations. Most Presidents, most of the time, are affiliated with resilient regime commitments. Those Presidents in opposition to regime commitments have frequently looked like leaders of a "guerrilla raid"; their hold on power while in office and their subsequent reputation for effectiveness have tended to be poor.

Then there is the other set of cases: incumbents who preside over a crumbling political order with increasingly vulnerable regime commitments, and those who come to power to carry out an extensive transforming agenda. Such "back-to-back" cases presuppose the existence of "political eras" that emerge out of a previous general regime crisis, become institutionalized and successful in their political arrangements, then themselves become increasingly vulnerable and crisis ridden over time. Taken as a whole, the American political order is noteworthy, particularly in comparative terms, for its profound long-term stability. But as economy and society change, they come to need recomposition and revitalization from time to time. Out of this comes the dynamics of repudiation and revitalization. As a new order emerges out of these crises, the policies and agendas that are dominant are shaped by a new ideological balance that regulates political traffic for a considerable time. Around it a network of policy is formed within government, and alliances develop between the dominant political leadership and key beneficiary groups in the economy and in civil society. Once upon a time, though not lately, the majority support the regime enjoyed from the electorate was mediated effectively enough by partisanship to produce relatively unified control of policy-making institutions in our divided-power constitutional order.

While a regime thus created will last a long time, it will inevitably decay as both its ideology and policy agendas become increasingly ineffective in dealing with emergent collective stress. As the resultant crisis unfolds, it becomes increasingly associated in the public mind, and among key organized interests, with the regime itself. Decline in its legitimacy and the shredding away of its bases of coalitional support will result. Repudiation of the last President in this sequence will go far beyond the personal level; it will involve rejection of the Old Order itself. Thus we have our historical back-to-back pattern of rejected Presidents immediately followed by "great" or at least conspicuously successful chief executives: John Adams to Thomas Jefferson (1800); John Q. Adams to Andrew Jackson (1828); James Buchanan to Abraham Lincoln (1860); Grover Cleveland to William McKinley (1896); Herbert Hoover to Franklin Roosevelt (1932); and, one is tempted to add, Jimmy Carter to Ronald Reagan (1980).

The plight of Presidents in the first half of these pairs is particularly difficult. They may choose to turn their backs on the commitments and coalitions
that brought them to power or to remain steadfast to them and risk going down
with the ship. Under stress in 1979–80, Jimmy Carter attempted the first strategy
—unsuccessfully of course, but sufficiently to fuel a vigorous intraparty challenge for the nomination from Senator Edward Kennedy (D-Mass.). Buchanan
and Hoover are prime examples of the go-down-with-the-ship syndrome. No
matter. All were overthrown, and with systemic consequences that went far
beyond the usual when the White House changed partisan hands. One is not
in the end surprised at the atmosphere of stark futility and frustration that
dominated such luckless administrations.

How great the contrast when we move to Presidents positioned in the second half of these pairs! Temperamentally and otherwise very different from
one another, they nevertheless were to a striking extent either the creators or
re-creators of their political parties. Coming to power on the ruins of a repudiated regime, they demonstrated the remarkable power of *creative repudiation*
as an instrument for revitalizing the political order.[3] The smash-up of existing
commitments in a crisis setting gives such Presidents exceptional freedom of
action, exceptional freedom to seize and reshape the agenda-setting high ground
of politics, and hence quite exceptional scope to succeed in realizing their power
and policy objectives. And what they did seemed to "work" in the end, even
if many subjects raised at the moment of transition were ignored or changed.
Such figures often convey a strong charismatic tone to their Presidencies (though,
in Abraham Lincoln's case, largely through the apotheosis that followed his
martyr's death). This should not be surprising, for as Max Weber and others
have reminded us, charisma comes into its own when existing institutions break
down. Each of these men presided over a heavily modified "public philosophy."
Each was involved in recruiting new personnel and policy, institutionalizing
the new order. Each was central—both as politician and as mass-belief symbol
—in forging a new majority base of support in the electorate.

By this time, it may come as no surprise to the reader that very much of
the Reagan legacy makes sense to me in terms of this traditional decay-revital-
ization cycle. Large-scale systemic crisis and presidential leadership (both repudiated *and* revitalizing) are midwives at the birth of a new order. Reagan and
his allies did their very best to act out a classic American critical-realignment
script almost to the last iota, just as Carter and his allies acted out theirs. But
was 1980–81 really to be compared with 1860–61 or 1932–33? We shall see.
But first let us discuss the dimensions of crisis that made Ronald Reagan's victory and his subsequent partial achievement of a "new direction in American
politics" possible.

The crisis of post-New Deal interest-group liberalism had been foreshadowed (as is historically usual in such cases) by a mounting intellectual critique of its assumptions. These assumptions were still more called into question by growing evidence that they could no longer deliver the goods. As the decade of the 1970s drew to an end, its legitimacy was in tatters. As Republican campaigners in 1988 never tired of telling us, inflation had reached 13.8 percent by 1980, and the prime rate was over 15 percent. At least as serious from the lenders' standpoint, the real rate of interest they received—the nominal rate less the inflation rate—was perilously close to zero. Productivity was down; for the average employed worker, the "real" standard of living, discounting for inflation, had declined by some 13 percent since 1973.[4]

By 1980, just under three-quarters of the national income was absorbed by employee compensation. In contrast, corporate profits tallied only 8 percent of national income, down dramatically from the nearly 14 percent registered as late as 1965. Worse still, net interest payments exceeded corporate profits for the first time since the depths of the Great Depression. This suggested that we might be moving toward a kind of *rentier* society of the sort found in such historically declining ex-great powers as eighteenth-century Venice or the Netherlands. It now made more economic sense to collect one's interest than to take entrepreneurial risks. Still further, corporate and household debt had risen to historic highs, prompting the business press to sound the alarm about the emergence of the "debt economy." Economic dislocation was made personal for many when long lines appeared at gas stations in 1979–80, and when the prices of gold and silver soared to more than $800 and $50 per ounce, respectively, in the early months of 1980.

If the economy was in difficulty, so was the American geopolitical position. If dollars and cents seemed to be spinning out of control, so did a world order so long unquestionably dominated by the United States. Defeat in the Vietnam war had seemingly led to a "little America" mood in Congress and among the public. This was marked by antagonistic congressional investigations of Central Intelligence Agency (CIA) misconduct, major cutbacks in defense spending, and the end of the military draft. The cold-war consensus had, of course, been shot to pieces in the rice paddies of Vietnam and in high and low places at home. Marxist regimes were spreading in Asia, Africa, and Latin America. The empire itself seemed in jeopardy, and a huge reaction among defense intellectuals, like Richard Perle, accelerated and coalesced as the 1980 election approached. By then, the nation was confronted with the apparently endless hostage crisis in Iran, the Soviet invasion of Afghanistan, and the vivid demonstration by the Organization of Petroleum Exporting Countries (OPEC) that the United States had lost control of a commodity vital to its economy.

The 1970s were marked no less by the emergence of crisis in the culture: Traditional standards of morality and, what was worse, the nuclear family itself, seemed to many to be in danger.[5] Much of this involved the stress building between consumerist hedonism, driven by the advertising industry, propagated through the media, and traditional moral standards. As pure self-interest rots any sense of community and interpersonal bonding, so pure pursuit of consumption pleasures, particularly when linked to sex and drugs, creates apparent hazards to the very foundations of society. The adults who sustain family life must renounce considerable pleasures and gratifications for themselves. Both as an economic and as a moral and social unit, the family requires such renunciation. It is less and less the case that it can be taken for granted; as the late 1980's aphorism put it, it is cheaper to buy a Mercedes than to bring a child into the world and rear it to maturity. (The implication is that the Mercedes is also a lot more fun.) Consumption of narcotics, of course, raises the pursuit of sensate gratification to the highest possible power.

These form part of the "cultural contradictions of capitalism," notably in its high-mass-consumption, heavily advertised phase.[6] A Marxist might conclude that these but reproduce at the cultural level the more primordial contradiction between the two conflicting economic needs for the accumulation of capital for investment and the mass consumption of what the economy can produce (i.e., for the efficient movement of inventory). Americans in the street, of course, have not seen things this way. What many of them have seen is an apparent revolutionary breakthrough of destructive countercultural movements from 1968 onward, and these Americans identify this development with political liberalism.

To all this can be added the continuing, perhaps amplifying, effects of the Supreme Court's 1973 decision *Roe* v. *Wade* (410 U.S. 113), which for the first time concluded that a woman's right to an abortion was rooted in a constitutionally protected right to privacy. This decision outraged many conservative and evangelical Protestants as well as the Roman Catholic church, and contributed mightily to mobilizing counterpressure that is still highly visible today. Reactions to this decision also made possible an alliance of convenience between Catholicism and evangelical/fundamentalist Protestantism for the first time in American history. The creation of politicized groups such as the Moral Majority in the late 1970s was the virtually inevitable consequence of all this. If the Republican party during the 1980s became "Reaganized" anywhere, it was over religious-cultural issues, as a review of the party's 1984 and 1988 platforms makes abundantly clear. If in 1988 George Bush and other Republicans could attempt to gain political points by attacking the American Civil Liberties Union and, indeed, the "L word" (liberalism), they were operating in a "realigned" environment in which such strategy made rational sense. For a significant minority of white Americans, political choice is not confined to economics, foreign policy, or other secular issues; it is quite literally a matter of God against Antichrist.

All these strands of crisis converged in the years of the Carter administration. And one must turn to evaluating Jimmy Carter, briefly, as the latest in a series of repudiated Presidents. There have been as many specific configurations of this phenomenon of repudiation as there have been cases. Each of them particularly repays close study if, as I believe, the success of President Reagan arose in part from a public opinion recoil against the *person* of his failed predecessor, not just his policies. This too requires us to consider the symbolic, even thaumaturgic, dimensions of this office.

Since Robert Bellah published his classic essay on the American civil religion two decades ago, scholarship has gradually become more aware of this vital dimension and its connection with the Presidency and presidential power.[7] As an anthropologist whose chief earlier work was on Tokugawa religion in Japan, Bellah was struck by the extent to which presidential addresses and ceremonies, particularly inaugural addresses and ceremonies, were in part religious exercises. The religion in question was, of course, not denominational but civil; a kind of denatured Judeo-Christian symbolic structure that "bonded" Americans in terms of shared values, including transcendental values.

Bellah had concentrated for his evidence on John F. Kennedy's 1961 inaugural address. But the same themes—God's centrality to the meaning of the American experience, sacrificial death and rebirth, the uniqueness of a people "chosen for freedom," and very much else besides—were carried to near perfection in Reagan's 1981 inaugural address. Revitalization of all traditional values (optimism not least among them) was and is central to Ronald Reagan's understanding of his world. If he was the "great communicator," this was not solely the product of his expert background in the mass media. It was because he knew how to tell Americans in a crisis moment what they desperately wished to believe.

Despite the fact that Bellah's seminal essay was written nearly a generation ago, professional study of presidential power among social scientists has yet to explore this vital dimension of that power as fully as seems called for. Nor does reference to a President as "national cheerleader," or something of the sort, do more than trivialize it. The Constitution's fusion of head-of-state and head-of-government functions in the same person creates not only an elective monarchy but a *pontifex maximus,* a chief priest of the American civil religion. In this respect, a Franklin Roosevelt or a Ronald Reagan is perhaps not so very different from the Emperor Augustus of Rome. When Franklin's cousin Theodore observed that the Presidency was a "bully pulpit," he perhaps spoke more precisely than he realized.

Exercise of the civil-religion function thus appears to be an exceedingly important dimension of presidential power generally. Along with other dimensions of their activity, Presidents have historically differed very widely in their capacity to discharge this role credibly and successfully. And here, as elsewhere, the intersection of their individual personalities and the moments in "political time" when they are in the White House may well account for this capacity to be an effective, credible "priest-king." The bonding imperatives associated with this role quite naturally loom far larger during periods of crisis and acute doubt than in more quiescent times. The civil religion is linked closely to the key values of traditional American political culture: generalized but intense commitments to property, liberty, equality, and religion.

As we have suggested, there is a strong sense in this culture that Americans are a "chosen people" and that America is "chosen" among the nations of the earth to work out some transcendental purpose. There is nothing we cannot accomplish if we have the will to do so. In short, the American collective enterprise *cannot fail*. Thus, Presidents, to be fully successful, must somehow project a credible optimism about the future of this country. This, one suspects, is not merely because Americans as a people are noted for prizing optimism as a virtue but because, without it, the whole enterprise is called into question and dark chaos impends. Of all Presidents, those in the grip of a repudiation crisis are least likely to be capable of projecting credible optimism, whatever their underlying temperament.

Indeed, a striking fact about Presidents in the "structurally repudiated" category is that they convey anything but optimism about the future. Jimmy Carter is the latest case in point, and he has much in common in this respect with his predecessors. As crisis deepened, he oscillated between remaining steadfast in supporting crumbling regime commitments and turning his back on them. In the summer of 1979, he went up to the mountain at Camp David, drastically "changed the guard" among his leading political executives, and came down from the mountain to deliver his so-called malaise speech. In this address, Carter invited the public to perceive that the world and history were closing in on the United States. Americans would do well to accept much more limited expectations about future greatness and prosperity (national and personal) than they had been used to.

This invitation to a revolution of declining expectations produced a noteworthy, downbeat symbolic effect. By itself it probably contributed to Carter's ejection from office the following year. It is very normal for Presidents caught up in the toils of the repudiation process to respond to their impossible, deteriorating position by pessimism, withdrawal, and a circle-the-wagons defensiveness. By doing so, they accelerate the whole process of ejection. Carter was no exception. And by 1980, "ungovernability" was very much in the air.[8]

Ronald Reagan and the Politics of Revitalization

In his remarkable 1981 inaugural address, Ronald Reagan launched his program of traditionalist revitalization on all fronts—a creative repudiation of the immediate past and the political order associated with it. Inflationary economic stress was to be attacked by precipitating an almost classic stabilization crisis—very high interest rates and tight credit and massive recession—right away. As in the past, this was designed to (and did) break the back of inflationary expectations, with the indispensable help of Carter's new chairman of the Federal Reserve System, Paul Volcker.[9] Particularly in the early years, but throughout the 1980s, the post-1979 "critical realignment" in Fed policy produced the highest real rates of interest over a considerable period of time since the Great Deflation of 1865–96. As always in our history, this epochal policy realignment acted as a massive engine of transferring wealth from debtors to people with money to lend, that is, from the many relatively poor to the few quite well off.[10] Needless to say, the explosion of federal deficits and current-account deficits (vis-à-vis the rest of the world) that followed the great Reagan tax cuts of 1981 have acted as a mighty engine for keeping real rates of interest at historically high levels long after inflationary expectations disappeared. This is one significant legacy that Ronald Reagan leaves to George Bush and the United States. It is likely to last as long as other key elements of Reaganomics remain in place.

The political economy realignment went far further than interest rates. As usual, a justificatory economic "model" for what politicians wanted to do anyway was scraped up with the help of Arthur Laffer, Jude Wanniski, and others among professional economists. Supply-side economics was advanced to replace the old, evidently discredited neo-Keynesian "demand-side" models that had guided federal public policy for more than a generation.

The new theory, apparently sincerely believed by its advocates, rested on the proposition that cutting taxes, especially for corporations and the wealthy, would liberate such productive, investment-oriented energies that at least as much gross revenue would be generated in an expanding economy from lower rates than had been realized at the old, higher ones. Additionally, one story about the rational expectations of the Reagan economic team was that it anticipated that it would be possible politically to slash the domestic outlays of the federal government so much that they would balance the enormous increase in defense outlays that was a bedrock goal of the new order. Others, notably

Senator Daniel Patrick Moynihan (D-N.Y.), have claimed that Office of Management and Budget Director David Stockman, Treasury Secretary James Baker, and others knew that no such domestic reductions could be achieved; but they also knew that—like the angel with the flaming sword ensuring that Adam and Eve could not return to the Garden of Eden—the ensuing deficits would provide overwhelming assurance that the Democrats could never return to the fiscal conditions that had supported interest-group liberalism. "Defunding the left" was not merely a slogan for the Reagan team but part of a comprehensive policy realignment project.

However all this may be, we do know some undisputed facts. In 1981, the Reagan forces won a set of crucial victories: a very substantial reduction in income tax rates coupled with budgetary changes curbing funding for "discretionary" domestic programs while substantially increasing outlays on defense. Viewed in the extremely large aggregate, that is, in terms of over-time shares either of the total federal budget or of the gross national product (GNP), the compositional changes involved were by no means as large as were probably intended by the Reagan administration, or as feared by their opponents. Thus, defense as a share of GNP rose only from a low of 4.8 percent (1978-79) to a high of 6.5 percent (1986), the latter remaining below 1972 levels. And the defense share of total outlays rose only from 22.7 percent (1978-79) to 28.1 percent (1987), far below the levels customary from the great cold-war remobilization of the early 1950s through the wind-down years of the Vietnam war in the early 1970s.

Still, apart from the fact that there was no war going on in the 1980s, this was enough virtually to double the dollar amounts spent on defense. And if one adds the pressure of net interest payments, which dramatically escalated in the 1980s, the compositional balance was considerably more altered. More microanalyses duly reveal, as observers have repeatedly pointed out, that an extremely heavy squeeze was placed on such relatively "trivial" items as federal housing subsidies and other discretionary domestic spending programs.[11]

As for the tax cuts, they inaugurated a back-and-forth sequence that was to extend through the so-called tax reform of 1986. But the agenda was broadly set in 1981, and has only been amplified since. A continuous move away from progressivity culminated in 1986 with the creation of three large brackets, with a nominal ceiling of 33 percent. Moreover, one feature of this act, decisive for the new order's purposes, was the indexation of these rates to inflation. The previous regime had depended for raising revenues on "bracket creep," whereby nominal incomes would move into higher tax rates while inflation served to reduce or eliminate the real increase in income involved. Congress was thus able to find resources for funding new programs that voters like, or for expanding old ones. One of the chief aims of the Reagan regime was to end this. In 1986—significantly, with bipartisan support—they achieved this goal.

At the same time, a pillar of liberal ideology for decades, the progressivity of the income tax, was virtually abandoned. The fate of Walter Mondale in 1984 was reflected in 1988 when George Bush gave voters an iron-clad assurance that taxes would not be raised ("Read my lips"), and Michael Dukakis provided a more rubbery ("only in the last resort") version. Barring a huge and preemptive economic crisis, it is not easy to see how politicians will be able to raise revenues through the income tax without running the risk of political suicide. Ronald Reagan has taught a very different lesson to the voters; it is another of his legacies, and a very important one.

Modern capitalist states are prone to "fiscal crises," major gaps between revenues and outlays for desired programs.[12] Interest-group liberals of yesteryear essentially managed partial closure of this persistent tendency toward revenue shortfall and deficit through inflationary "bracket creep" in the federal income tax. In the aftermath of the tax cuts of 1981, there was a basic shift toward an unprecedented policy mix: loose fiscal policy and tight monetary policy, all awash in a tidal wave of red ink. By 1985-86, the United States had become a net debtor in the world economy for the first time since 1914, with the debt financing not investment in productive instruments but financing consumption.

Most Democratic-liberal economists were sure earlier in this decade that this policy mix was not viable and would soon collapse. Like the bumblebee—aerodynamically unstable and therefore "can't fly"—it has not only proved viable so far, but it may very well have been an essential ingredient in a world economic transformation that permits more or less noninflationary, more or less sustained, economic growth indefinitely. As we well know, the 1980s have seen the longest, or perhaps second-longest, expansion in the entire history of the American business cycle. As we also know, the great 508-point stock market crash of October 1987 had essentially zero effect on the larger economy, in sharp contrast to such crashes as those of 1929, 1937, and 1969. The relationships between Wall Street and Main Street have obviously been profoundly changed.

Assuming that these transformations have not brought us to the recession-free promised land, sooner or later a significant general economic downturn will occur under these literally unprecedented policy conditions—quite possibly during the Bush era. Reagan's legacy of the unprecedented makes predictions exceptionally difficult. But in the short run, the economic mix has been a politician's dream. Taxes are cut; programs of chief interest to the better-off half of the citizenry, who do most of the voting, are retained; and we enjoy sustained noninflationary economic growth. In short, the American dream of having one's cake and eating it too comes close to realization. For someone interested in winning the next election, what more could one ask?

As for the Democrats, as a once-dominant policy and governing party they have played out the classic role of victims of critical realignment. First, the party leadership in the House attempted to head off the 1981 tax package by outbidding the new administration and its allies. It failed. A widely publicized quest for "new ideas," led by people around Senator Gary Hart (D-Colo.) followed. Among these were various proposals by Democratic intellectuals to develop an "industrial policy" to cope with the manifest competitive decay of American industry in the world market. These and other moves petered out. In 1984, the "new" selection process resulted in the nomination of Walter F. Mondale—the vice-president of a repudiated regime that even in 1988 continued to have astonishingly high negatives in the polls—as its standard-bearer. With the second-highest election-year growth rate in the postwar period and with no war raging, Ronald Reagan won in a landslide that probably no Democratic candidate could have overcome. But 1984 was also a year in which the myriad sectoral interest groups clustered around the Democratic party were especially conspicuous. Further damage was done to the public image of the Democrats as a party of "special interests" (needless to say, in a business civilization, that special interest known as corporate business enjoys a very different and much preferred position).

By 1988, the nominee was Governor Michael Dukakis of Massachusetts—a man who temperamentally and programmatically has more in common with the liberal Republicans of yesteryear than with Franklin D. Roosevelt or Harry S Truman. In its convention, the party stressed unity, patriotism, and national integration, and it wrote the shortest, most general platform (the "stealth platform") in many decades. Here too we have a legacy left behind by Ronald Reagan. In this setting, it was no matter of wonder that George Bush's campaign agenda came to dominate the early period following the 1988 conventions, and that Dukakis's lead in the polls abruptly vanished. As for the co-responsibility the party bears for such key Reaganizing events as the 1986 tax act, I will say more about this below. As a programmatic, organizing entity, the Democratic party seems about as badly off as the Republicans in the 1940s or maybe even the Democrats in the 1920s.

Little more will be said here about the other dimensions of the 1980 crisis to which Reagan and his allies sought to respond through an integrated conservative revitalization program. If the empire has become too weak, we will strengthen it—by toughness as a style, by cooperating with unsavory but anticommunist regimes, and above all by a massive defense buildup culminating in the Strategic Defense Initiative. If traditional morality has come under attack from a variety of marginalized countercultural forces, we will back the traditional forces on every dimension. If there is a governability crisis in politics, the reintegration around a rightist ideological perspective on domestic and foreign issues will put that right too.

Again, whatever one may think about such a program, in detail or as a whole, it has not been unsuccessful in achieving its objectives, particularly at the symbolic, imagistic level. Every new regime seeks, even more than regimes taking office in "normal" times, to isolate, divide, and marginalize its opposition, to the end that the new order can become so institutionalized that it cannot be displaced short of a general systemwide crisis that it too seems unable to control. Symbolism, not costing much in budgetary or tax terms, can give every appearance of providing nourishment for at least part of the popular culture. There is noteworthy public support for "America as No. 1" in the world, though this support tends to erode if maintaining that position becomes overtly painful and expensive (as it did in Vietnam and Korea). The mainstream culture supports, at least as an ideal, traditional religious and family values. If candidates in 1988 almost literally wrapped themselves in flags and pledges of allegiance, there was a good reason for this smaller but telling segment of the Reagan legacy. If indeed the drug problem swelled during the 1980s and other signs of social rot could readily be found, a tough law-and-order stance could continue to do much to reduce the public's anxieties about such deplorable things that nobody seems able to control.

Changes in policies tend to consolidate the winning coalition by enriching and otherwise helping its members while they impoverish and weaken its opponents. But it is at least as important for the institutionalization of a new regime to achieve control through the appointment of key personnel in the state apparatus. Here, without much question, the Reagan legacy is likely to be particularly long lasting—not of course with political appointments, who can always be ousted if by some chance the opposition wins a presidential election, but through the federal *courts*. Here the evidence extends far beyond "mere" partisanship; it has always been the case in this century that the vast majority of federal judicial appointments have come from the President's party. Reagan's judicial appointments were different: They came from the ideological right, not just from the ranks of Republican-affiliated lawyers. By the end of his eight years, Ronald Reagan had appointed more than half of all federal judges; his appointees on the Supreme Court—including William Rehnquist, originally appointed to the Court by Richard Nixon, as chief justice—numbered four.

One of the great news stories of 1987 was the defeat of one of Reagan's nominees, Judge Robert Bork, for the vacancy created by the retirement of Justice Lewis Powell. (A minor postcript was provided when Reagan's next selection, Judge Douglas Ginsburg, withdrew following the revelation that he had once smoked marijuana.) Essentially, this defeat reflected both the limitations and the continuing strength of the "Reagan revolution"; only the limitations received much attention from commentators in the media and elsewhere. The sources of Bork's defeat were several. A crucial intervening event was the recapture of the Senate by the Democrats in the 1986 election, which of course altered the political balance. Connected with this were Robert Bork's own failings; from a political point of view, he had had altogether too much to say about "original intent" and other matters during his career as a law professor. In this climate, a remarkably well organized and successful anti-Bork media campaign was waged by a wide coalition of interest groups, law school professors, and others. This campaign, to some extent with Bork's help, was able brilliantly to portray him as "outside the mainstream," and he was resoundingly defeated, the first such case since 1970.

Bork's defeat was a setback for the Reagan judicial program and a notable victory for his liberal opponents. But life moved on, and Reagan selected in the person of Judge Anthony Kennedy a jurist whom the Senate did confirm. Quite promptly, the Court moved to reconsider a 1976 decision that permitted minority suits against private corporations over discrimination issues.[13] As the 1988-89 term began, speculation became rife among the Court's attentive professional and political publics that Reagan might at last have appointed enough of its members to permit a considerable shift to the right in its doctrines. One needs only to add one point more: The last justice *ever appointed* by a Democratic President and confirmed by the Senate was Thurgood Marshall, appointed by Lyndon Johnson in 1967; politically, an eternity ago. Very shortly thereafter, a huge realignment directed against the Warren Court got under way.[14]

Such reflections remind us, as they should, that the present, normally Republican era in presidential politics really began in 1968, not in 1980. To the extent that we seek chronological convergence between electoral change and transformations in the Supreme Court's position in the political order, at least as much can be said for realignment occurring in the late 1960s as in the 1980s. Be that as it may, there seems good reason to suppose that the liberals' victory over Bork may in the end prove similar to the Duke of Marlborough's victory at Blenheim (1703), which the poet Robert Southey parodied:

> And everybody praised the duke,
> Who this great fight did win.
>
> "But what good came of it at last?"
> Quoth little Peterkin.
> "Why, that I cannot tell," said he;
> "But 'twas a famous victory."

Toward a New American State?

Let us recapitulate the argument as it has developed thus far. Ronald Reagan won in 1980, not merely against an ill-starred incumbent but against and on the ruins of a failed regime. This old order had in fact begun notably to crumble some twelve years earlier in a combined reaction against the Vietnam war, the civil rights revolution, and important elements of the Great Society's programs as these were perceived by the white electorate. In this regard, Jimmy Carter's 1976 victory by the narrowest of margins, in circumstances where Republicans had unusually poor structural assets and Gerald Ford himself had great weaknesses, should almost be read as a fluke. The artifact of a power vacuum within the ruptured Democratic coalition, Carter displayed a singular lack of a coherent national agenda and equally singular ill luck, and thus intensified this vacuum. By doing so, he played out a variant on a very old script indeed—the repudiated President who goes down with an old order.

To oversimplify to a degree, this old order was that of "demand-side" or "Fordist" political economy, predicated on mass production and consumption by Americans of (mostly) American goods, and on sustained noninflationary growth in the American economy and standard of living. Neo-Keynesian political economics and the politics of interest-group liberalism were in the ascendant, as—except for Dwight D. Eisenhower—were Democrats in the White House and Congress. The essential geopolitical and geoeconomic conditions for this regime were progressively destroyed during the tumultuous years that extended from the escalation of the Vietnam war in 1965 through the first and greatest oil crisis of 1973-74.

The Democratic coalition, hugely disrupted in 1968 and 1972, was temporarily reforged in 1976; but this on an aleatory, fragile, and incoherent basis unable to withstand further major shocks. Such shocks were duly supplied in abundance during the Carter years. The period ending sometime around 1983 witnessed the greatest world revolution in prices since the influx of Spanish gold and silver from the New World in the sixteenth century. The upheavals arising from this and other convergent crises created the opportunity for an ideological right to come to power for the first time in many decades—and, as the brilliant career of Margaret Thatcher in Britain and other changes in the 1980s have made very clear, not just in the United States.

There is anything but clarity among analysts as to the precise nature of the politico-economic regime that is rising on the ruins of this older postwar order; there seems little or no agreement even on nomenclature.[15] Some have suggested various neoconservative or neomarket labels for it, others refer to an era of "flexible accumulation." Clear it is that the world market has become vastly more integrated, while the strength of nationally based labor movements has been rapidly waning, along with whatever residual credibility socialism still has in the advanced capitalist world. The Reagan revolution, like its counterparts elsewhere, was aimed at a conclusive discrediting of this older social harmony, welfarist, demand-side order and its replacement as far as feasible by the organization of society and economy through the capitalist marketplace.

In waging political war to consolidate the new political order, Ronald Reagan and his intellectual and political elites demonstrated the extraordinary capacity of high ideological focus to substitute for extremely long hours and crushing attention to detail. Reagan, thus armed, could demonstrate that the American Presidency was nowhere near the "impossible job" that professional observers of the 1960s and 1970s had said it was. In addition to other dimensions, this incredibly complex office also has vital religious functions to perform. And, for long, Reagan used these functions masterfully to reassure a disturbed majority that the old ways were still the best ways and that we could return to traditional bliss through the exercise of political will.

The "revolution" had its evident limits. The revolutionaries had hoped for a much more extensive dismantling of the federal government's domestic functions than they could politically achieve. The early and rapidly abandoned trial balloons about social security made that point. It was ratified after the 1982 elections when the opposition recovered enough courage, determination, and numbers to accept a deadlock on the budget over large-scale agreement on the administration's terms. For another thing, the promise of balanced budgets was replaced by the reality of sustained peacetime deficits large enough to double the size of the national debt in less than a decade.

It is well not to make too much of these limitations and, perhaps, unexpected macro outcomes, at least at the level of politics itself. The presidential "creators" of new regimes typically have failed to solve the problems that brought them to office, at least in terms of the campaign appeals they used. Everyone recalls that Franklin D. Roosevelt campaigned on a balanced budget platform in 1932 and that the depression was terminated by the outbreak of war nine years later, not by the New Deal. As for the Civil War following Abraham Lincoln's election in 1860, Lincoln himself said but the truth in his second inaugural address when he remarked that "nobody could have anticipated a result so fundamental or so astounding." What happens in these realignments is often not success in disposing of the crisis source that gave birth to them but success in capturing the intellectual high ground, in authoritatively defining the agendas of politics, and in organizationally building the revolution by institutionalizing it. To a very striking extent, this is just what Reagan and a now thoroughly Reaganized Republican party have been able to do at the decisively important levels of presidential and, increasingly, judicial politics.

The large question remains whether this synthesis rests on viable foundations. Partly, this is a question of estimating future developments in a political
economy moving literally through uncharted waters; and this in a developing,
rapidly integrating geoeconomic regime that as yet has no name. For example,
how does one cope with an economic recession superimposed on pyramided
corporate and household debt—and, moreover, with massive deficit relationships in the American current-accounts balance with the rest of the world? It
is hardly surprising that some economists, contemplating such a "day of reckoning,"[16] have simply concluded we cannot afford to have such a recession and
so we should not allow one to occur. Similarly, does the possibility of a global
implosion of the financial system lurk in the enormously overhanging debts
of developing countries like Mexico? It may well be that these problems—also
the legacy of Ronald Reagan—will, along with others, mark the administration of George Bush. But one must repeat that the economy is itself being recomposed rapidly and fundamentally. Relative decline in the standard of living
for many or most Americans seems a probable long-term trend. Whether it can
be as skillfully and illusionistically managed as it has been across the 1980s is
one of many questions for which we do not have any well-bounded answers.

There are, however, some specifically political issues connected with the
long-term viability of the "new direction in American politics" that Ronald
Reagan has left us. The careful reader will have noted that a rather strong case
has been made here for some kind of realignment. Certainly a great many elite
actors on both sides of the partisan aisle have acted out their parts in ways
that much resemble traditional realignment scenarios. But the reader will also
have noted that one key element has been omitted up to this point, and for
good reason: It does not exist.

This is the part of realignment that involves *general, comprehensive* partisan shifts across the vertical and horizontal boundaries of the constitutional
system connected with large-scale and durable shifts in electoral behavior. Traditional realignments, in whichever partisan direction, at whatever time, or over
whatever issues, uniformly entailed the capture of control *by a single party* of all
branches of the federal government and (usually) a preponderant majority of
state legislative seats and control of state governments too. As well, all of them
were marked either by very high turnout rates or (as in 1828 or the 1930s) by
sharply increased levels of participation from very low bases in the preceding
era. Both were features of a system of action in which critical realignment deeply
engaged the public at large, and in which its elites, policy consequences, and
new majority coalitions were solidly anchored in the electorate itself.

It has been obvious for some time that nothing of the sort currently exists[17] (see figures 1.1, 1.2, and 1.3). Whenever Republicans sit in the White House

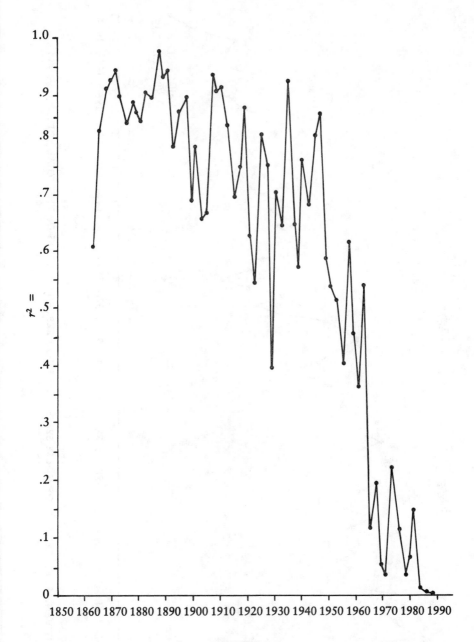

FIGURE I.I

EMERGENCE OF INCUMBENCY EFFECTS IN CONGRESSIONAL ELECTIONS:
RELATION BETWEEN INCUMBENT-HELD AND OPEN-SEAT DISTRIBUTIONS,[a]
NON-SOUTHERN SEATS, 1864-1988

a. Proportion of variance in open-held distributions explained by incumbent-held distributions; 12 cells arrayed in terms of Democratic percentage of the role by district.

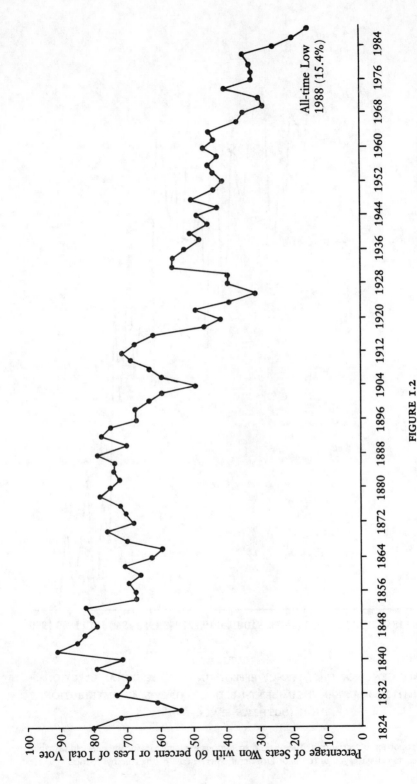

FIGURE 1.2

DECAY IN COMPETITIVENESS: PERCENTAGE OF HOUSE SEATS WON BY 60 PERCENT OR LESS OF THE TOTAL VOTE, 1824–1988

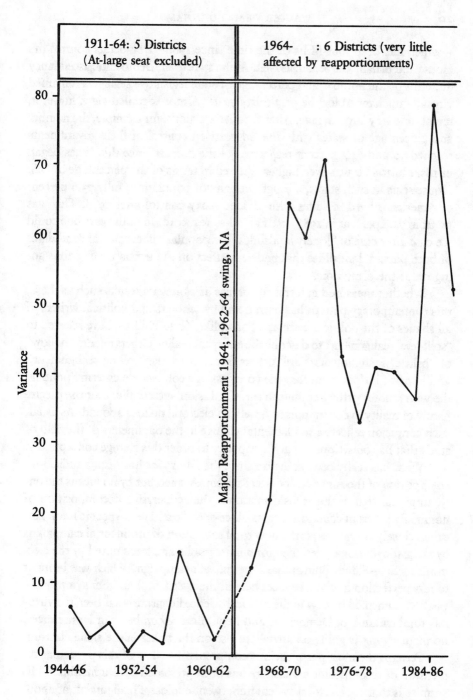

FIGURE 1.3

THE RISE OF INCUMBENCY EFFECTS IN CONGRESSIONAL ELECTIONS[a]

a. Spread (variance) around mean, biennial House district swing, Connecticut, 1944-46 to 1986-88.

—which has been four-fifths of the time since 1968—Democrats control the House and usually the Senate as well. At the state level, Democratic ascendancy in terms of the number and percentage of state legislative seats has remained virtually unchanged for the past thirty years. A more detailed view, however, reveals one very large change: After the 1986 elections, for example, the number and percentage of states with *divided* partisan control of their governments reached 30 and 61.2 percent respectively—the highest since this series began in 1834. In 1988 it was even higher. Viewed in terms of the percentage of U.S. House seats in such states, a rough measure of population, fully 73.6 percent of Americans lived in states with divided party control after 1988. This was up from 71.8 percent in 1986, itself an all-time record. In both years one could see case after case of "lonely landslides" for popular gubernatorial candidates of both parties, landslides that had zero effect on the legislative elections going on at the same time.

Whether measured in terms of surveys or aggregate results such as these, this contemporary pattern has been noted by scholars and political writers of all shades of the political compass. Some, like Kevin Phillips, have referred to "split-level realignment" to describe the emergent reality. Others refer to "hollow" or "brittle" realignments.[18] Still others favor terms like "rolling realignment," and in truth it does seem that the youngest age cohorts are entering political life with a noteworthy Republican tilt. Confusion and conflict over the precise nature of reality in contemporary American electoral politics abound. As usual, such confusion reflects a fundamental change in the parameters of the field of study that has outstripped analytic capacity to order this change conceptually.

What has really been going on since the late 1960s has been a radical *recomposition* of the American political system. A chief, but by no means the only, empirical sign of this transformation is the accelerating decomposition of nominally partisan coalitions across office-specific and level-specific lines. Another, closely connected, is the now total saturation of presidential campaigns by imagistic messages, designed for a mass public and transmitted by the electronic media—Sidney Blumenthal's "permanent campaign," which was brought to rare perfection in all three races held in the 1980s. Still another symptom—vastly documented by now in the political science literature—has been the virtually total triumph of Democratic and Republican incumbents in House races, no matter what is going on anywhere else on the ticket in the same election.

Perhaps the most perspicacious comprehensive view of this particular dimension of recompositional change has been presented by Blumenthal.[19] His surmise is that the electoral system underwent explosive realignment at about the time many were looking for it (i.e., in the years around 1968-72), but in a different vector than they were anticipating. For this realignment cut athwart and partly melted the old party-in-electorate bonds, as the electorate broke apart into ideologically polarized interest groups along a number of dimensions. At the same time, the technology of "engineering consent"—a development already under way and of the deepest concern to V.O. Key, Jr., in the years just before his death in 1963—was now perfected.[20] Since then, Blumenthal argues, one has moved into a sixth electoral era, marked by "permanent campaigns" and campaigners, of whom Ronald Reagan is the archetypal example. Partisan bonds across the divided powers our Constitution mandates are heartily eroded in such a system. Parties, as such, remain significant at the "center"—within the Beltway (the area encompassed by the District of Columbia)—and, indeed, are becoming more vigorous, competent, and ideologically polarized at that level. But one of the curiosities of this regime is that it is entirely possible for parties to be growing stronger at one level and decomposing at another, and to be doing both at the same time.

Such a formulation has its attractions. It calls attention to the true magnitude of decompositional transformation that hit the party system, and most especially the Democrats, twenty years ago. It reminds us that the contemporary presidential Republican era really began twenty years ago—Jimmy Carter's 1976 election against a weak, nonelected incumbent presiding over a repudiated regime was something in the nature of an "accident," disastrous to his party in the end. It did not begin with Ronald Reagan in 1980; nor did the techniques and entrepreneurial organizations of the "permanent campaign." As in a number of areas, Reagan vastly deepened trends that were already under way, itself accomplishment enough. The emergence of the "permanent campaign" also appears chronologically linked to the end of American ascendancy in the world economy in the 1969-73 period and the beginning of a "time of troubles" in that domain that very likely is still with us. "The permanent campaign" is the chief electoral dimension of the interregnum state that emerged from the cosmic smash-ups of the late 1960s.

The interregnum state that has emerged on the ruins of the older political order is, in policy terms, an uneasy, incoherent mixture of interest-group liberalism and free-market (and, increasingly, social-issue) conservatism. It is also deeply blocked and deadlocked as a political regime. The coexistence of conservative Republican Presidents with a continuing flow of entitlement programs marked the strange 1969-77 era, punctuated as it also was by the Watergate affair. The most conservative Democratic President for his time since Grover Cleveland—Jimmy Carter—attempted a mini-right turn of his own as the foundations of the post-New Deal order crumbled under his feet.[21] Ronald Reagan professed rare purity in his ideological commitment to capitalist and socially traditionalist revitalization, but his "revolution" achieved only a limited if very substantial part of its ultimate goals for lack of support broadly based across the *whole* policy system. For better or for worse in the short or longer run, the explosion of debt and deficit was a fruit of this partial blockage of his revolution. Though perhaps in the end debt and deficit will continue to do important work in furthering its course on a different front than anyone imagined in 1981, as Senator Moynihan fears, the ultimate costs and the magnitude of unintended consequences are likely to be very large.

One can perhaps obtain some sense of what might have happened by evaluating, very crudely, what the partisan balance in the House of Representatives might have been like in the wake, say, of Reagan's 1984 landslide, had party bonds remained as strong as in earlier periods of this century's history. We begin with the actual party balance, 254 Democratic and 181 Republican seats, and with the distribution by the partisan candidates for both President and representative winning them. Nationally, Walter Mondale (D) carried 66 districts electing a Democrat, and 1 other (in Manhattan) electing a Republican. Ronald Reagan (R) won 180 districts that also returned Republicans, and 188 that elected Democratic representatives at the same time (this latter—a victorious candidate winning fewer of his congressional party's districts than his opposition's—is also a first). Keeping the 66–1 on the Democratic presidential side intact, we concentrate on these 368 districts that Reagan carried in 1984, and evaluate what the results might have been in earlier periods. In table 1.1, we calculate the distribution of these 368 seats as if they were divided in proportion to split-district results in other elections.

One could provide any of a large number of long-term measurements, but they all convey the same message: Incumbents are so overwhelmingly reelected that House elections have become, as it were, frozen in concrete. Far from being reversed in a 1980s "realignment," these trends produced in 1984 and 1986

TABLE 1.1

HYPOTHETICAL AND ACTUAL CONGRESSIONAL ELECTION RESULTS IN 1984

Year or Period	Mean % of Split Results	Districts Carried for: President House				Total "House"		"Majority"
		D D	D R	R D	R R	D	R	
1984	43.4	66	1	188	180	254	181	73 D
1900-1908	3.9	66	1	16	352	82	353	271 R
1916-24	7.4	66	1	31	337	97	338	241 R
1928-48	13.6	66	1	59	309	125	310	185 R
1952	19.1	66	1	83	286	148	287	139 R
1956-68	27.7	66	1	120	248	186	249	63 R
1972-80	35.4	66	1	153	214	219	215	4 D

the highest proportion of noncompetitive contested congressional elections since the available series began in 1824. It becomes difficult, in fact, to imagine how this trend could increase much further, for it seems to be approaching some absolute limit. Since most of these incumbents are Democrats, House control has not changed party hands since 1954; it seems very unlikely to do so in an immediately foreseeable future.

What does all this matter? There are at least two answers to this question. First, one should consider the extent to which divided control blurs accountability for what happens in Washington. This is an especially serious problem for the presidential out-party, the Democrats. For one thing, since government must be carried on, a great deal of business must be secured on a bipartisan basis. The real deadlock that exists cannot be permitted to become so dominant that paralysis sets in. An important consequence is that the presidential out-party becomes co-responsible for what happens. Additionally, as measures such as the tax reform of 1986 and the welfare reform of 1988 disclose, congressional Democrats are also willing in substantial numbers to support policies that in effect continue certain aspects of the Reagan revolution. The tax change of 1986 was comprehensive, important, and executed in the teeth of a public opinion outside the Washington Beltway that was either indifferent or hostile. In the end, the really important players were the Democratic chairman of the House Ways and Means Committee, the Republican chairman of the Senate Finance Committee, and (cheering them on just offstage) President Reagan and Secretary of the Treasury James Baker.

The process itself is an interesting example of insider politics in the Reagan phase of the interregnum state.[22] Whatever one may think of the results, the public must remain in a state of some mystification about it all. And partisan clues would tell it little or nothing. This very major change in the tax regime was a "DemoRepublican" measure. Whatever one may say about the circumstances producing this convergence on "revenue neutrality" and a new abandonment of the old ideal of progressivity, the 1986 measure clearly extended the Reagan revolution's policy agenda. Democrats played a large, indeed decisive, role in this extension. In this, as in the entire posture of the 1988 Dukakis presidential campaign, the party's leadership reflected the kind of politics of defeat and marginalization that have classically affected victims of earlier realignments. But precisely because this out-party has remained in the ascendancy in the House of Representatives (and, since 1986, in the Senate as well), its *co-responsibility* for the enactment of the "hegemonic party's" policies is vastly larger than in any previous period. The presidential out-party's problems of defining itself and projecting a credible alternative to the many who have not notably benefited from the new order have thus been deeply intensified.

The interregnum state that has emerged on the ruins of the traditional partisan regime over the past two decades seems chiefly to be associated with ideological polarization among activist partisan and candidate organization cadres; massive decay of partisan electoral linkages to the population; and a much greater freedom of politicians at the center to carry out various policy coups—some the result of conflict, some the result of cooperation—with perhaps less regard for public opinion than has typically been the case in the past. By no means accidentally, this state's electoral politics is also associated with a vast movement toward abstention within the electorate, particularly among its lower classes.[23] As a number of scholars have recently been noting, the substantive meaning of elections is changing in the process, while their legal form remains the same.[24] This change seems clearly in the direction of more or less drastically reducing the organized capacity of the adult citizenry to have much substantive influence over what happens to it through political choices made by their elected leaders.

This transformation may perhaps be convenient for the power groups that can win ascendancy against fragmented, marginalized, and demobilized opposition forces in the society. But it is bought at a certain price. Blumenthal and others have noted that while superior performance of the "permanent campaign's" routines wins elections readily enough, the "governing problem" remains and is probably intensified. Jimmy Carter was adept at utilizing the new electoral techniques at a moment of political vacuum to come from virtually nowhere and win the Presidency. He lacked the political experience and the personal temperament to work effectively with a Congress dominated by "his" political party. One somehow doubts that Carter could have reached the top of the greasy pole of presidential politics in any political era before the 1970s. The governability crisis of his day was overwhelmingly obvious and was then and later frequently commented upon. As for Ronald Reagan, he left office in a blaze of popular support, the highest since the 1940s. This was a tribute to his success as symbolic revitalizer, and to the plain fact that his administration ended in conditions of peace and prosperity. But this triumph was strikingly *personal*. The incompleteness of his "revolution"—and the major policy problems that have been left for George Bush to handle—reflect the fact that the governability crisis very much remains with us.

It does so because it is embedded in structural realities of the American constitutional order, realities that no amount of permanent campaigning can overcome. The history of this experiment in formally divided powers, from earliest times to the present, yields a continuing lesson. It is not viable as a framework of government unless it is furnished with political parties.[25] These have in times past not only penetrated and mobilized the citizenry; they have acted for elites as a counterweight to the massive thrust of the constitutional power centrifuge. With varying degrees of adequacy, they have served as bridges over the walls of federalism and separation of powers. When and to the extent that they do not exist, or have become displaced as entrepreneurial organizers of American politics, an instant governability crisis results.

In *The Federalist Paper, No. 51,* James Madison argued that it was essential to liberty that "ambition must be made to counteract ambition"; this was the whole point of separating powers. As electoral coalitions become increasingly dissociated along office-specific lines, as at present, the Madisonian order is not *bridged* any longer; it is strikingly *reinforced.* Ronald Reagan demonstrated that it is still possible to utilize a combination of crisis, ideology, and personal charisma to achieve noteworthy policy change. But this was personalized, only partially successful, and rather quickly waned over time. If in fact charismatic leadership reflects the failure of institutions, its removal with Reagan's retirement may well bring all the vexing problems of the contemporary "interregnum state" back into plain view.

Consider, for example, that in the aftermath of the 1988 election, George Bush took office with a Democratic majority of 10 in the Senate and 85 in the House of Representatives. Of the 51 "new" administrations over the past two centuries, this one has—and by a considerable margin—the weakest base of party support in Congress. Consider also that while historically such divided government was relatively rare, it has now become the *norm* since 1968. This gives us a political recipe for the early 1990s that is likely to be a strange mixture of divisive (deadlocked) government in certain key policy areas, and of coalition government in others. The temptation to resolve problems behind closed doors or via the expert-commission route—as with the so-called tax reform of 1986 or the social security commission a little earlier—will be hard to resist. In such a setting, accountability for what happens will very likely operate at an unprecedented discount.

The 1990s Come Next

The overall legacy that Ronald Reagan left behind is thus strikingly ambivalent. Attempting comprehensive and durable realignment old-style, without producing the mobilized public strength and unified control of institutions, would seem to be an exercise in making bricks without straw. Yet if we consider the replacement of the old, largely closed political economy of Fordism by that of flexible accumulation, and the parallel developments in the American political system to which Reagan made such notable contributions, we might conclude that, these days, no old-style electoral connection is required to produce a Right

Turn that could dominate agendas and public policy for years or decades to come. The rise of what some have called the flexible accumulation order is a worldwide phenomenon. It is linked with what may well be the most momentous global transformation of the late twentieth century, the rapid collapse of state socialism and "command economies" into bankruptcy. This bankruptcy is no mere matter of performance gaps or balance-of-payments difficulties; it extends to the foundations of Marxism as a practical guide to the actions of states and complex economies.

In contrast, the salvific virtues of the market have come into their own around the world with a vigor and a lack of effective intellectual contestation that have probably not been seen since the outbreak of World War I three-quarters of a century ago. The political effects have been no less spectacular than have the broader social and economic consequences. Everywhere, efforts are under way to promote free trade and smooth as much as possible the accelerated flow of capital and technology around the planet. Everywhere, the prime strains of adjustment to this new order—and they are very heavy—are concentrated among the lower sectors of the labor force. These, unlike capital, are immobile and territorially based in national states. But their organized capacity to protest through parties and electoral efforts has waned with remarkable speed and thoroughness. To reiterate the point, this is an era in which Marxism-Leninism really has become the God that failed; an era as well in which neo-Keynesian liberal economics, oriented to social harmony through mass consumption based on mass production in a closed economy, no longer seems a viable or persuasive guide to public policy. Whatever the notable gaps, injustices, or inconsistencies of market ideology, what else really remains as a feasible ruling ideology in the advanced capitalist world in general and the United States in particular?

It is hard to overestimate the damage that this sea change has inflicted on the Democratic party. As a presidentially viable force, this party ultimately lived and seems to have died—at least for the time—by a political economics for which the new order has little or no room. The magnitude of the change in the rhetorical high ground of politics that unfolded during the Reagan years is merely hinted at by George Bush's success in marginalizing the opposition with the "L word" and by inviting the public to "Read my lips. No new taxes."

And one can review the past twenty years of Democratic presidential nominations: in 1968, an "old politics" nominee who was shipwrecked by a flamingly unpopular war and white reaction to the civil rights revolution; in 1972, a "new politics" nominee who was solidly rejected by core elements of his own party; in 1976, a kind of "no politics" nominee who stressed nonideological competence; in 1980, the first elected sitting President to be defeated in forty-eight years; and in 1984, the vice-president of this repudiated regime. With Michael Dukakis in 1988, the nomination process gave the country a Democratic nominee who, like Carter, stressed "competence" rather than "ideology," and thus had little or nothing to offer segments of the electorate who had once been core New Deal voters. Neither revenant liberal Republicanism (1976, 1980, 1988), close alliance with labor leaders and other core Democratic-affiliated groups (1968, 1984), nor "new politics" (1972) have turned the trick. There seems little left for this party to do but wait for a credible leader to arise at a time when things are going seriously wrong for the incumbents.

As we all know, victory has a hundred fathers and defeat is an orphan. George Bush was genuinely vulnerable, at least up to a point. There seems little doubt, postmortem, that the kind of campaign that Dukakis waged lacked organization, a credible theme, and the ability to make the case for change. At the same time, Bush's structural assets—his assets in "political time"—throughout were vastly larger than the mainstream commentaries during the 1988 campaign remotely perceived. This moment may be succinctly described as that of a "third-term election" following two terms of success for the incumbents, and involving the selection by the incumbents either of a consensual nominee (as with Hoover in 1928) or an understudy (as with Martin Van Buren in 1836, William Howard Taft in 1908, and George Bush in 1988).*

Indeed, in many respects the 1980s, as it were, reproduce the 1920s in American political history. The collective agendas of a country wracked by progressive upheavals and participatory demands for inclusion in the process have been exhausted. There was a preceding Democratic administration that disintegrated before one's eyes as misery indices reached acute levels. There was a Republican-led restoration, a revitalization, which flourished in a political vacuum that began anywhere to the left of itself. In 1988 there was even an ethnic candidate who, like Al Smith in 1928, offered managerial competence rather than any serious challenge to the business-saturated mores and policies of the time. Business was very good, at least on the surface, and the world was quite profoundly at peace. As the "normalcy" power configuration rested on the exhaustion of all major alternatives to the business of America being business, so it was remarkably parallel in the 1980s, too.

It may be added that we find two quite specific political parallels. One of these, very importantly ratified by Bush's 1988 victory, is that indeed the majority/presidential party is now Republican. The second is that voter turnout reached historic depths in both the 1920s and the 1980s. In fact, in the

*Something like this was also projected in the 1960, 1968, and 1976 elections; but, in all these cases, for quite different reasons, the "understudies" lost by extremely narrow margins.

non-Southern states in which three-quarters of Americans live, the 54.1 percent turnout rate of 1988 is the lowest in 164 years—lower even than its competitors, 1920 and 1924.

But there are fundamental differences as well, between the structure of the 1928 and 1988 elections. When Herbert Hoover won, so did Republicans elsewhere at all levels from state legislature upward. As he took office in 1929, Hoover had the cheering prospect of a Republican majority of 103 in the House of Representatives. The 1988 election, however, breaks a large number of records in a quite opposite direction. The number of state governments controlled by Republicans is very near all-time lows; the GOP made essentially zero gains in their share of legislative seats. Incumbents in congressional elections have never done so well. Since 1824, never has the proportion of congressional seats won by uncompetitively large margins been anywhere as high as it was in 1988. The coalitional gap between majorities for President, Senate, governors, and the House of Representatives is at historically high levels. And, as we have seen, the Republican deficit of ten seats in the Senate and eighty-five in the House gives the incoming administration notably less political support in Congress than any of its predecessors.

Such things matter, as they have mattered across the 1980s. The Reagan revolution was blocked and displaced because of this institutional entrenchment of opposition forces. It has been displaced in the direction of maintaining aggregate consumption through massive borrowing, since there was no political way of cutting the total expenditures fully enough to bring them roughly into line with the sharply decreased supply of resources following the 1981 tax cuts. Perhaps, had the Republicans had a large majority in Congress as they would have had in earlier years, this could have been done. And had it been done, there certainly would have been a clear public accountability involved.

Taken as a whole, this "mix" of policy probably has accelerated the relative decline of the United States in the global economy. At some point, correcting for it in line with the desires of the Japanese and West Europeans would seem to guarantee an increasing constraint on the capacity of consumers to enjoy the standard of living to which they are accustomed. Meanwhile, expensive problems accumulate. These range from the ever-more-visible homeless to the rapidly accelerating drug problem, and on to the need for replacement of worn-out infrastructure, for cleanup of aging nuclear production/processing plants, for much expanded investment in education and civilian R & D (research and development), and for much, much else besides.[26] These too are the legacies of the Reagan years.

We thus conclude this essay on a deliberately indeterminate note. One can perhaps pose two final questions. First, considering the interregnum state's degenerate electoral linkages across separate powers and between rulers and ruled, How and in what ways can major political conflicts be organized and channeled when and if serious stress arises? In the current conjuncture at home and abroad, it would seem that the most likely source of such stress would be in the economy. The second question is, What would a serious economic recession look like with Reaganomics added as an intervening variable? We simply do not know the answer to either of these questions—in the latter case because there never has been a major recession under conditions of massive federal deficits, top-heavy debt leverage in the corporate sector, and the other unique features acquired by the political economy in the 1980s. We sail on uncharted waters.

One could suppose that if such a recession were to occur, it might trigger a new "politics of upheaval," a 1990s version of the New Deal. In the end, as in the past, both outstanding political leadership and a coherent policy ideology would eventually be required, and someone with the great intellectual gifts of a Keynes to provide it. But as we have suggested earlier, the alternative—a more or less messy but reasonably successful "muddling through"—should not be dismissed by those who would make predictions about the near future. The world economy is vastly more interpenetrated than it was in 1929. It is conceivable that, in the core metropole countries, it may have outgrown Great Depressions. If so, there is no immediately obvious reason why the recomposed political order we have been describing could not continue to stumble along indefinitely.

Still, a form of relatively competent and coherent state management may be required, even under conservative hegemony, to maintain public order and political support, while decline for a large part of the population is skillfully managed and, as far as possible, concealed from open view. As the longer-term effects of the Reaganite policy synthesis work themselves out across the next years, maintaining support while managing decline may well become a truly daunting task even without the sudden trauma of a crash. The institutional and partisan cleavage between George Bush and Congress cannot but complicate such an effort.[27]

One might imagine circumstances under which such a divided, blocked regime could become intolerable to many serious interests that have such weight in governing both this country and the world. Reagan's success has in fact made such a prospect more remote now than in 1980. At the moment it is but a tiny cloud on the horizon. For "regime intolerability" to become more than that would require the eternal American governing problem to become, not merely hopeless, but serious. For the better part of a century, tidy-minded intellectuals have again and again suffered disillusion by assuming that at long last this would occur in their own time. Perhaps time *never* runs out for the United States. Ronald Reagan certainly thinks so; and so do most Americans.

If, on the other hand, things do get serious at some point, perhaps one of President Reagan's most enduring legacies would be to remind his fellow countrymen of the delights of his "golden era," and of how agreeable revitalizing charismatic leadership can be. In that case, as in the crisis that peaked in 1980, the failure of institutions will prompt the search for a new charismatic revitalizer. As always, political entrepreneurs can be depended on to emerge from the crowd and offer themselves to fill the void. Would the country be fortunate enough to find a Franklin Delano Roosevelt, or even a Ronald Reagan, at the end of its search? Who can say?

Notes

1. Stephen Skowronek, "Presidential Leadership in Political Time," in *The Presidency and the Political System,* ed. Michael Nelson (Washington, D.C.: CQ Press, 1984), 87-132.

2. Stephen Skowronek, "Notes on the Presidency in the Political Order," in *Studies in American Political Development,* ed. Stephen Skowronek and Karen Orren (New Haven: Yale University Press, 1986), 1:286-302. Professor Skowronek is in no way responsible, of course, for the uses to which I put his ideas in this essay.

3. Ibid., 301-2.

4. For an overview, see Thomas Byrne Edsall, *The New Politics of Inequality* (New York: Norton, 1984). The other figures here are available in raw form in the public domain, that is, the tabular appendices to recent issues of *The Economic Report of the President.*

5. One of the striking aspects of the Reagan decade is that these dimensions of crisis have shown no signs of abating, as the vast success of works such as Allan Bloom's *The Closing of the American Mind* (New York: Simon and Schuster, 1987) and the explosive growth of the drug problem, among other things, make clear. As the 1988 campaign has also made clear, this fact in no way detracts from the success of conservative appeals directed to these anxieties.

6. Daniel Bell, *The Cultural Contradictions of Capitalism* (New York: Basic Books, 1976).

7. Robert N. Bellah, "Civil Religion in America," *Daedalus,* Winter 1967; reprinted in *Daedalus* 117, no. 3 (Summer 1988): 97-118.

8. See Nathan Glazer and Irving Kristol, eds., *The American Commonwealth 1976* (New York: Basic Books, 1976); and Lloyd Cutler, "To Form a Government," *Foreign Affairs,* 59, no. 1 (1980): 126-43. The list goes on and on.

9. Volcker, it is worthy of note, was reappointed by Ronald Reagan for a second four-year term in 1983. He had hoped for yet another term in 1987, but Reagan chose Alan Greenspan. After all, an election year was pending. The Moor had done his work, the Moor could go.

10. See William Greider, *Secrets of the Temple: How the Federal Reserve Runs the Country* (New York: Simon and Schuster, 1987). If Greider's account is accurate, it would seem that Carter really had no idea of what he was buying when he appointed Volcker in 1979. The dominant issue, in an atmosphere of some panic, was to placate Wall Street, whose candidate Volcker was (pp. 1-47).

11. Perhaps the most accessible midterm account of the Reagan administration is Edsall, *New Politics of Inequality;* there are many others. See *The Changing American Economy,* ed. David Obey and Paul Sarbanes (New York: Blackwell, 1986), with a number of first-rate contributions by eminent academics and journalists.

12. James O'Connor, *The Fiscal Crisis of the State* (New York: St. Martin's Press, 1973).

13. *Runyon* v. *McCrary,* 427 U.S. 160 (1976).

14. Bruce Allen Murphy, *Fortas: The Rise and Ruin of a Supreme Court Justice* (New York: Morrow, 1988). Anyone seeking further support for links between judicial realignment and much more comprehensive political realignment in the very late 1960s will find quite a bit of ammunition for that view in this powerful book.

15. Two interesting cuts at the problem come from Europe: Claus Offe, *Disorganized Capitalism* (Cambridge, Mass.: MIT Press, 1985); and Scott Lash and John Urry, *The End of Organized Capitalism* (London: Polity Press, 1987). The latter in particular is a penetrating and fully comparative account which, though perhaps overlong in analyzing the liquidating Fordist Old Order, asks a great many of the right questions.

16. Benjamin M. Friedman, *Day of Reckoning: The Consequences of American Economic Policy under Reagan and After* (New York: Random House, 1988). This is a brilliantly executed "popular" account of the mess by a leading academic economist. It should be noted that Friedman is studiously agnostic about whether the excesses he describes at length will help trigger anything like the Great Depression. After all, there are many possible ways of going to hell, and 1929 was only one of them. The point is that the bill for this gigantic credit-card party will have to be paid by someone, sometime. There are various ways of arranging to do this. Politics after Reagan will be very largely about such arrangements.

17. The amount of convergent data affirming this point is so large and from so many different files that it would swell this essay to unmanageable length to cite them all. Examples are found in figures 1.1, 1.2, and 1.3 on pages 17–19.

18. See one case among quite a few, Martin P. Wattenberg, *The Decline of American Political Parties, 1952-1984* (Cambridge, Mass.: Harvard University Press, 1986), especially the final chapter on the 1984 election (pp. 132-68).

19. Sidney Blumenthal, *The Permanent Campaign* (New York: Simon and Schuster, 1982).

20. See V.O. Key, Jr., "Public Opinion and the Decay of Democracy," *Virginia Quarterly Review* 37 (1961): 481-94; and his posthumously published work, *The Responsible Electorate* (Cambridge, Mass.: Harvard University Press, 1966).

21. The term "Right Turn" should be attributed. See Thomas Ferguson and Joel Rogers, *Right Turn: The Decline of the Democrats and the Future of American Politics* (New York: Hill and Wang, 1986). Whatever one may conclude about the more controversial features of their analysis, their insistence that there has been something profoundly *bipartisan* going on both before and during the "Reagan revolution" is very well grounded in fact.

22. The most comprehensive account of the genesis of this confection is Jeffrey H. Birnbaum and Alan S. Murray, *Showdown at Gucci Gulch: Lawmakers, Lobbyists, and the Unlikely Triumph of Tax Reform* (New York: Random House, 1987).

23. See Water Dean Burnham, "The Turnout Problem," in *Elections American Style,* ed. A. James Reichley (Washington, D.C.: Brookings Institution, 1987), 97-133.

24. This is the thrust of the forthcoming book by the Cornell scholars Benjamin Ginsberg and Martin Shefter, *Reconstituting American Politics* (New York: Basic Books, forthcoming). See also Walter Dean Burnham, "Elections as Democratic Institutions," in *Elections in America*, ed. Kay Lenz Schlozman (Boston: Allen and Unwin, 1987), 27-62.

25. Brilliant accounts of what happens politically under the American constitutional regime when these parties are missing can be found in James Sterling Young, *The Washington Community, 1800-1828* (New York: Columbia University Press, 1966); and Eric L. McKitrick, "Party Politics and the Union and Confederate War Efforts," in *The American Party Systems: States of Political Development,* ed. William Nisbet Chambers and Walter Dean Burnham (New York: Oxford University Press, 1967, 1975), 117-52. Needless to say, a strong partisan focus in the electoral and political institutions of the country is not always a *sufficient* condition for coherence, as Woodrow Wilson reminded us a century ago in *Congressional Government* (New York: Macmillan, 1885). But it certainly is a *necessary* condition for it, judging from a history that goes back to the very earliest times.

26. In confirmation hearings for OMB Director-designate Richard Darman, Senator John Glenn (D-Ohio) estimated the total cost of these items at $365 billion (19 January 1989). One could believe this to be an underestimate.

27. A noteworthy "revolution of declining expectations" about presidential power and effectiveness seemed to emerge when George Bush succeeded Ronald Reagan. In this view, the substantive power of the Presidency itself may well be on the wane. See the extensive and significant article by David Rapp, "Reagan Added Luster but Little Clout to Office," in *Congressional Quarterly Weekly Report* 47 (7 January 1989): 3-12. See also Theodore J. Lowi, *The Personal President* (Ithaca, N.Y.: Cornell University Press, 1985). Such analyses conform to this author's understanding of the characteristics and dynamics of the interregnum state that has risen on the ruins of an older American political order.

2

The Presidential Nominations

GERALD M. POMPER

Somehow, it worked.

Forecasts of the presidential nominations of 1988 predicted disasters ranging from the selection of extremist candidates to prolonged conflicts within the Democratic and Republican parties. The prenominating campaign seemed to be written by comedians who included large elements of farce in the script, from sexual innuendoes to the presentation of a cake to the Ayatollah Khomeini. Observers competed to derogate potential candidates, labeling them "wimps" and "dwarfs."

Eventually, the presidential nominations provided textbook examples of effective American political parties. According to traditional explanations, U.S. parties are primarily interested in winning elections. To achieve victory, they seek politically adept but inoffensive candidates and pursue party unity by conciliating diverse factions, promoting agreement on public policies, and focusing party members' efforts on effective campaigns.[1]

In 1988, the parties did what the textbooks expected. In nominating Michael Dukakis and George Bush, they chose two men who were experienced politicians with extensive records of public service, men who, if not stirring, were at least acceptable to tens of millions of their party's voters. By the end of the conventions, these new leaders had achieved unity among all party factions. As they launched their election campaigns, Democrats and Republicans adopted consensual programs in their competitive efforts to win the November election.

But doing "what was expected" was itself unexpected, for American politics has been greatly transformed in the past two to three decades. In the nominations of such candidates as Barry Goldwater, George McGovern, Jimmy Carter, and Ronald Reagan, the old rules no longer applied. Presidential nominations have changed from selection by party leaders to selection by mass electorates.

Party organizations have been displaced by candidate organizations and the mass media. Moderation in policy has been replaced by ideological conflict. Insurgent "outsiders" have been more likely to win nomination than have established party leaders.[2]

Paradoxically, the presidential nominations of 1988 brought the United States new men who looked like the candidates of an older order. Yet, behind their familiar appearance, these candidates represented changed political parties in a changed American politics.

The Political Setting

The political circumstances of 1988 portended close competition. For the first time in twenty years, an incumbent President would not be on the ballot, so there would be no built-in advantage for one candidate. Democrats were especially grateful that they would not risk a repetition of Ronald Reagan's two sweeping victories in the contests of 1980 and 1984.

But Reagan had changed the contours of American politics, and this contest would be fought on a reshaped landscape. One change concerned the balance between the two major parties. For nearly fifty years, Democrats had enjoyed plurality support in the voters' party identifications, their underlying political predispositions. During the Reagan years, this difference had narrowed, perhaps to the point of insignificance. As the 1988 election year opened, a Democratic advantage in voter loyalty that had stood at 52–27 percent in 1964 had diminished to no more than 40–32 percent.[3] A Republican realignment might be in the offing.

On the simpler measure of actual victory, Republicans might already be considered the majority party. They had won four of the last five presidential elections and had suffered only one clear defeat since the end of the Second World War. A fashionable argument was that the party already held a "lock" on the Electoral College because of the movement of population to Republican areas of the South and West.[4] The election would be hard fought, as Republicans tried to prove their dominance and Democrats to demonstrate their survival.

The party competition had already begun in the off-year elections of 1986. Recovering from their overwhelming defeat in the 1984 presidential contest, the Democrats showed new strength. They won a net total of eight Senate seats, to take control of both houses of Congress. Particularly satisfying were their five victories in the South, which in recent years had been their weakest area in national elections. Nevertheless, Republicans could take comfort in winning eight new governships and holding losses in the House to only six seats, far below the normal off-year decline of the President's party.[5]

Issues had changed as well, bringing the parties closer together ideologically. The Reagan economic program had three related elements: reducing the domestic activities of the national government, increasing military spending, and lowering taxes. By 1988, the combined effect of these policies was continuing massive deficits in the federal budget, with important consequences for the nation's economic position in the world. The immediate political significance was that presidential candidates were severely restricted in their programmatic appeals. No expensive new programs could be advanced, no candidate would suggest new taxes, and even the once-extravagant Democrats focused on the budget deficit.

In foreign policy as well, party differences had narrowed. Reagan had come into office as the hero of anticommunist Republicans, who rejoiced in his denunciation of the Soviet Union as the "evil empire." Then his ideological purity was stained by the attempted trade with Iran of weapons for hostages. Furthermore, his most conspicuous actions were a series of summit meetings with the new Soviet leader and the ratification of the treaty banning intermediate-range nuclear force missiles (INF), which actually destroyed American—and Soviet—weapons. With defense spending stabilized, and a Republican President advocating cooperation, not conflict, with the Soviet Union, there would be no ideological division on foreign policy issues.

Differences between the parties remained on social, or "life-style," issues. Much of the emotional fervor of the Reagan era had come from the unsettling consequences of social movements, particularly among women and blacks. Heated issues had persisted to 1988, and would boil over in the fall election campaign. In some instances, the defenders of traditionalism had won, as in the defeat of the Equal Rights Amendment. In other cases, the Reagan years showed that even a conservative administration could not reverse many of the social changes of the past two decades. Despite Reagan's own personal opposition, at least verbally, the right to abortion remained in the Constitution. Despite formal opposition by the Justice Department to affirmative action, the courts continued to enforce programs in behalf of racial minorities and women.

One of the most significant events of the prenomination period was the Senate's rejection of Judge Robert Bork as a justice of the Supreme Court. Bork had achieved enormous prestige among conservatives by his careful, often brilliant advocacy of a strict adherence to the original wording of the Constitution. Opposing the use of the courts in behalf of abortion, civil rights, and women's rights, he had become both the symbolic champion of traditionalists and the symbolic enemy of modernists.

The rejection of a presidential nominee to the Supreme Court is highly unusual. When Bork was nominated, it seemed likely that he would be con-

firmed and that his confirmation would create a conservative majority on the
Supreme Court that would last for decades beyond the Reagan administration.
Instead, the drawn-out debate over the nomination showed that life-style issues
were politically charged. Bork was strongly rejected, in opinion polls and in
a Senate vote of 58–42 that included all but one southern Democrat and five
Republicans among his opponents. The vitriolic conflict foreshadowed the later
bitterness of the presidential campaign.

As a close election loomed between Republicans and Democrats, the prospects also increased for hard battles within each party. Since each party had
a real prospect of success, ambitious politicians of all stripes began to see themselves as potential White House tenants. As the lists of contestants grew longer,
without clear leaders, even more aspirants were tempted to make the race, and
media reporters and politicians freely added still more names to the list of possibilities. By the end of 1987, the cluttered scoreboard included six declared Republican candidates and eight Democrats (including one who had withdrawn
and then reentered). At least eight other Democrats and five other Republicans
gained some serious attention before deciding not to seek the nomination.[6]
One of them, New Jersey Senator Bill Bradley, quipped that his reason for not
running was to make sure that somebody was left to answer rollcalls in the
Senate.

With multiple candidates, the two-party races were already confusing. Further confusion was added by new nominating rules, which meant that the candidates would be fighting their battles over uncertain terrain. Some of the territory, to be sure, was known. As had been true since 1968, the convention
delegates needed for nomination would be won principally in direct primary
elections or party caucuses in the individual states. In the Democratic party,
as in 1984, another large group of convention votes (15 percent) would be cast
by "superdelegates," that is, Democratic party officials and officeholders. The
selection of these delegates would begin in February, with local caucuses in
Iowa and a presidential primary in New Hampshire. It would end with June
primaries in the larger states of New Jersey and California.

The great unknown territory for the candidates was "Super Tuesday" on
March 8, when delegates would be selected from twenty states. Most of these
contests would take place in the South and therefore could create a special
regional effect on the race. Super Tuesday, in fact, had been devised for this
very purpose. Southern Democrats, along with others, had learned that presidential nominations were greatly affected by early events, such as the New
Hampshire primary, which gave initial victors "momentum" toward victory.
The southerners were anxious to see this momentum turned to the advantage
of the South and more moderate party candidates. By scheduling all southern

primaries on the same early date, they hoped to increase the possibility of the nomination of a candidate either from the region or supportive of its interests.

Whatever the wishes of its creators, however, other outcomes were possible on Super Tuesday, from the victory of a candidate with early momentum to a deadlocked convention. Most likely, Super Tuesday would again demonstrate the "law of unintended consequences," and the actual effects would be quite different from the planned results.[7]

Democrats: Diversions and Decisions

The Democratic contest began with a clear leader. It ended with a clear leader too, but the party's choice was a very different man.

As attention turned to nominating politics in 1987, the focus was on candidates who had established themselves in the 1984 election. Senator Gary Hart, the 1984 Democratic runner-up, was the leading preference among Democratic voters. Considerable support was also evident for the Reverend Jesse Jackson, who had run the first serious presidential campaign by a black leader in 1984. Many Democrats, especially party leaders, favored Mario Cuomo, governor of New York, who had delivered a stirring keynote address to the 1984 Democratic convention.[8]

Then the fun began. Hart, though married, was discovered to be involved sexually with a Miami model, Donna Rice. Comedians literally transformed his campaign into a joke. (Among the more printable quips was Johnny Carson's suggestion that Hart's campaign slogan was, "He's back in the saddle again.") Hounded by reporters, and despite some public support,[9] Hart withdrew from the race. He reentered in December and briefly led opinion polls again, but he no longer had any significant chance of nomination.

Cuomo withdrew his name from the list of possible nominees in February, almost casually, at the end of a radio broadcast in New York. Nevertheless, speculation continued that he would reconsider entering the race at a later date, or might even be drafted by a deadlocked party. Cuomo's decision not to run had the significant effect of bringing Michael Dukakis into the race. As governor of Massachusetts, Dukakis began to attract support in the Northeast that otherwise might have rallied to Cuomo.

As the year went on, others entered or declined. Delaware Senator Joseph Biden did both. After announcing his candidacy in June, he was discovered to have plagiarized speeches from Neil Kinnock, the head of Great Britain's Labour party, and to have exaggerated his academic achievements. Hart's affair had made personal morality a focus of press attention, and Biden's errors were magnified by the limited amount of hard news available. Biden, too, felt compelled to withdraw.

The shuffling of candidates concluded, the Democrats entered 1988 with six aspirants: Jackson, Dukakis, former Arizona Governor Bruce Babbitt, Senator Albert Gore of Tennessee, Representative Richard Gephardt of Missouri, and Senator Paul Simon of Illinois. Of these, Jackson was the most interesting. In 1984, he had established himself as a national figure, a stirring speaker, and the undisputed leader of blacks, a key group within the Democratic coalition. In 1988, he aimed at least to establish himself as the leader of the left, progressive wing of the party, both white and black. Jackson was not likely to be the winner. It seemed doubtful that a majority of Democrats would support any black candidate, or any candidate without governmental experience, and virtually certain that they would not support a candidate with Jackson's relatively extreme views. Yet, because of his special constituency, and because his campaign was fueled by inspiration more than money, Jackson would certainly remain in the race, whatever his prospects. Neither the other candidates nor the press knew what to make of a candidate who could not win but would not lose, this "horse of a different color."[10]

With the race structured, all the candidates faced the basic strategic needs of any campaign: to gain attention, to develop a theme, to form a winning coalition. In 1988, these basic strategies were inevitably shaped by Super Tuesday. Each candidate had to find answers to the same questions: How can I get *to* Super Tuesday as a viable candidate? How can I get *away* from Super Tuesday as a viable candidate?

Except for Jackson, the first task facing the Democratic candidates was to gain attention. In the modern nominating process, the way to get attention is to do well in the initial contests in Iowa and New Hampshire. Since these are relatively small states, candidates can seek support on a more personal level. Money is always useful, but personal contact can offset large expenditures on media advertising. Success in these early contests can bring a candidate "momentum," increased attention in the media, financial contributions, and new popularity as voters begin to pay attention.[11] Carter in 1976 and Hart in 1984 had demonstrated the enormous impact of these early tests. For the unknown candidates of 1988, they would be even more important preliminaries to the main bout of Super Tuesday.

Of the six Democrats still active at the beginning of the year, two failed to "make the cut": Babbitt and Simon. Gephardt came in first in Iowa, and Dukakis easily won the primary in his neighboring state, New Hampshire. Gore, the only southerner in the race, disregarded the early contests and focused directly on Super Tuesday. Jackson, too, had a strong southern base among black voters, and his candidacy continued unaffected by his vote in the preliminary states.

The voters of Super Tuesday, and of later contests, now faced a different set of choices, for "in nominating campaigns preferences are dynamic, subject to significant change as a result of learning and momentum."[12] Jackson's appeal was strong and sure, but essentially confined in the South to black voters. The true dynamics of the contest on March 8 involved the three remaining white candidates. Gore made regionwide appeals, attempting to use the southern tilt of Super Tuesday to build a base of national support. He and Dukakis shared a common interest in defeating Gephardt, and their television ads focused on inconsistencies in the congressman's positions.

Dukakis had no obvious base in the region, but he had other advantages. The breadth of Super Tuesday turned the day into a mass election, not a local one; under these circumstances, the Dukakis treasury and organization could be most effective. He used these resources to best advantage by focusing on areas of potential support—Florida, Texas, suburbs, and non-southern states that were also holding contests on Super Tuesday.

In the balloting, three candidates split the vote almost equally, but none scored a decisive breakthrough. Jackson secured his base in the Deep South, and in Virginia, where black voters predominated in the Democratic party. Gore won five upper South and border states. Dukakis also won five states, two in the South and three in the Northeast, as well as the caucuses in Washington State.

The clear loser was Gephardt, who won only his home state of Missouri. Along with Simon, he could remain in the race only if the tides now flowing could be reversed. The dynamics of momentum had probably reduced the race to Jackson, Gore, and Dukakis. Moreover, a closer analysis of the returns already suggested a Dukakis victory. While Jackson had mobilized his black base, and Gore his white southern base, neither had demonstrated much of an appeal beyond these core groups.

Dukakis certainly had not swept the field—he actually was third in total popular votes on March 8—but he had held his own in unfamiliar territory and had begun to assemble the broad coalition crucial to election victory. He led among self-identified Catholics, women, college-educated voters, Hispanics, liberals, and former Reagan voters. His weaknesses were few: black and lowest-income voters, monopolized by Jackson; self-identified conservatives, who would have little effect on the nomination; and fundamentalist Protestants.[13]

The significance of Super Tuesday can be seen in tables 2.1 and 2.2. These tables show both the results of individual contests and the accumulation of votes and delegates over the weeks. Included in table 2.2 is a politically signifi-

TABLE 2.1

Date	State	Total Vote	Dukakis N	%	Jackson N	%	Gore[a] N	%
8 Feb	IA*	126,000	27,846	22.1	11,088	8.8	0	.0
16 Feb	NH	123,360	44,163	35.8	9,622	7.8	8,388	6.8
23 Feb	MN	100,000	33,300	33.3	19,800	19.8	1,000	1.0
	SD	71,606	22,341	31.2	3,867	5.4	6,015	8.4
1 Mar	VT	50,791	28,341	55.8	13,053	25.7	†	
8 Mar	AL	405,642	31,234	7.7	176,860	43.6	151,710	37.4
	AR	497,544	94,036	18.9	85,080	17.1	185,584	37.3
	FL	1,273,298	520,779	40.9	254,660	20.0	161,709	12.7
	GA	622,752	97,149	15.6	247,855	39.8	201,772	32.4
	KY	318,721	59,282	18.6	49,720	15.6	145,974	45.8
	LA	624,450	95,541	15.3	221,680	35.5	174,846	28.0
	MD	531,335	242,289	45.6	152,493	28.7	46,226	8.7
	MA	713,447	418,080	58.6	133,415	18.7	31,392	4.4
	MS	361,811	30,030	8.3	160,644	44.4	120,483	33.3
	MO	527,805	61,225	11.6	106,617	20.2	14,779	2.8
	NC	679,958	138,031	20.3	224,386	33.0	235,945	34.7
	OK	392,727	66,371	16.9	52,233	13.3	162,589	41.4
	RI	49,029	34,222	69.8	7,452	15.2	1,961	4.0
	TN	576,314	19,594	3.4	119,297	20.7	416,675	72.3
	TX	1,766,904	579,545	32.8	432,891	24.5	356,915	20.2
	VA	364,899	80,278	22.0	164,569	45.1	81,372	22.3
	WA*	104,000	45,760	44.0	35,984	34.6	2,496	2.4
15 Mar	IL	1,500,928	244,651	16.3	484,800	32.3	76,547	5.1
20 Mar	PR	364,899	83,562	22.9	105,821	29.0	52,545	14.4
26 Mar	MI	212,668	61,674	29.0	113,777	53.5	4,253	2.0
29 Mar	CT	241,395	140,250	58.1	68,315	28.3	18,587	7.7
5 Apr	WI	1,014,782	483,036	47.6	286,169	28.2	176,572	17.4
19 Apr	NY	1,575,186	801,770	50.9	584,394	37.1	157,519	10.0
26 Apr	PA	1,507,690	1,002,614	66.5	411,599	27.3	45,231	3.0
3 May	DC	86,052	15,403	17.9	68,841	80.0	688	.8
	IN	645,708	449,413	69.6	145,284	22.5	21,954	3.4
	OH	1,376,135	862,837	62.7	378,437	27.5	30,275	2.2
10 May	NV	169,008	106,306	62.9	43,435	25.7	2,535	1.5
	WY	2,148	254,175	78.9	45,101	14.0	11,597	3.6
17 May	OR	388,932	220,913	56.8	148,183	38.1	5,445	1.4
24 May	ID	51,370	37,706	73.4	8,065	15.7	1,901	3.7
7 June	CA	3,089,164	1,878,212	60.8	1,087,386	35.2	55,605	1.8
	MT	120,962	83,101	68.7	26,733	22.1	2,177	1.8
	NJ	640,479	404,783	63.2	210,718	32.9	17,933	2.8
	NM	188,610	115,052	61.0	52,999	28.1	4,715	2.5
14 June	ND[d]	3,405	2,891	84.9	514	15.1	†	

NOTES: * indicates that the state held a caucus, not a primary; † indicates that the candidate or the "uncommitted" line was not listed on the ballot. a. Gore suspended his campaign on 21 April.

THE DEMOCRATIC PRIMARIES

| Gephardt[b] | | Simon[c] | | Others and Uncommitted | | Total | Cumulative | | |
N	%	N	%	N	%	Vote	Dukakis %	Jackson %	Others %
39,438	31.3	33,642	26.7	13,986	11.1	126,000	22.1	8.8	69.1
24,425	19.8	21,095	17.1	15,790	12.8	249,360	28.8	8.3	62.9
7,100	7.1	17,900	17.9	20,900	20.9	420,966	30.3	10.5	59.2
31,149	43.5	4,010	5.6	4,225	5.9				
3,911	7.7	2,641	5.2	2,844	5.6	471,757	33.0	12.1	54.9
30,018	7.4	3,245	.8	12,575	3.1	10,282,393	26.9	26.0	53.1
59,705	12.0	8,956	1.8	63,686	12.8				
183,355	14.4	28,013	2.2	126,057	9.9				
41,724	6.7	8,096	1.3	26,156	4.2				
29,004	9.1	9,243	2.9	25,179	7.9				
66,192	10.6	4,996	.8	60,572	9.7				
41,975	7.9	16,471	3.1	31,349	5.9				
72,772	10.2	26,398	3.7	30,678	4.3				
19,538	5.4	2,171	.6	29,307	8.1				
305,071	57.8	21,640	4.1	19,001	3.6				
37,398	5.5	8,159	1.2	36,718	5.4				
82,473	21.0	7,069	1.8	21,993	5.6				
2,010	4.1	1,373	2.8	2,059	4.2				
8,645	1.5	2,882	.5	9,221	1.6				
240,299	13.6	35,338	2.0	123,683	7.0				
16,056	4.4	6,933	1.9	15,691	4.3				
1,040	1.0	3,848	3.7	14,872	14.3				
34,521	2.3	634,893	42.3	24,015	1.6	11,783,321	27.6	26.8	45.6
10,947	3.0	66,412	18.2	45,612	12.5	12,139,499	25.5	26.9	47.6
27,222	12.8	4,466	2.1	1,276	.6	12,352,167	25.6	27.4	47.0
966	.4	3,138	1.3	10,139	4.2	12,593,562	26.2	27.4	46.4
8,118	.8	48,710	4.8	13,192	1.3	13,608,344	27.8	27.5	44.7
3,150	.2	17,327	1.1	12,601	.8	15,183,530	30.1	28.4	41.5
7,538	.5	9,046	.6	33,169	2.2	16,691,220	33.4	28.3	38.3
258	.3	744	.9	86	.1	18,799,115	36.7	28.3	38.3
16,788	2.6	12,268	1.9	†					
†		15,137	1.1	90,825	6.6				
4,901	2.9	2,028	1.2	9,633	5.7	19,290,271	37.7	28.0	34.3
†		2,255	.7	9,020	2.8				
6,612	1.7	4,667	1.2	2,723	.7	19,679,203	38.0	28.2	33.8
†		1,387	2.7	2,312	4.5	19,730,573	38.1	28.2	33.7
†		43,248	1.4	24,713	.8	23,769,788	42.1	29.2	28.7
3,387	2.8	1,573	1.3	3,871	3.2				
†		†		7,045	1.1				
†		2,829	1.5	13,014	6.9				
†		†		†		23,773,193	42.1	29.2	28.7

b. Gephardt withdrew from the race on 28 March. c. Simon suspended his campaign on 7 April.
d. No Democratic candidates filed to be on the ballot; these results are write-in votes.

TABLE 2.2
ACCUMULATING DEMOCRATIC PARTY DELEGATES

Week Ending	State	New Delegates	Total Selected	% of Total	Dukakis % of Majority	Dukakis % Needed of Remainder[a]	Jackson % of Majority	Jackson % Needed of Remainder
13 Feb	IA	58	124	2.9	1.7	50.6	.4	51.3
20 Feb	NH	18	142	3.4	2.1	50.6	.4	51.5
5 Mar	MN							
	SD							
	ME							
	VT							
12 Mar	WY	50	192	4.6	3.0	50.8	1.3	51.7
	AL							
	AR							
	FL							
	GA							
	HI							
	ID							
	KY							
	LA							
	MD							
	MA							
	MS							
	MO							
	NV							
	NC							
	OK							

Date	States							
	RI							
	TN							
	TX							
	VA							
	WA							
26 Mar	IL, PR, MI	1236	1378	33.1	21.9	58.4	19.0	60.5
2 April	CT, WI	349	1727	41.4	25.4	63.7	24.5	64.5
9 April	NY	91	1818	43.6	31.1	61.1	30.4	56.7
23 April	PA	191	2009	48.2	35.3	62.5	33.9	63.8
30 April	DC	500	2509	60.2	51.0	61.7	40.3	75.0
7 May	IN, OH	220	2729	65.5	60.7	57.0	40.9	85.8
14 May	NE, WV	296	3025	72.6	71.7	51.8	44.4	101.6
21 May	OR, ID	88	3113	74.7	75.9	47.7	45.2	108.6
11 June	CA, MT, NJ, NM	79	3192	76.6	78.9	45.2	46.7	114.2
		622	3814	91.6	108.1	53.9		275.5

a. Remaining delegates include uncommitted superdelegates.

cant figure: the proportion of delegates needed in the remaining contests in order to clinch the nomination. After Super Tuesday, these data show the dramatic narrowing of the race and, in later contests, Dukakis's progress to victory.

For the next month and a half, the basic question was whether the candidates could expand their base. Gephardt's final test came in Michigan, a test he failed despite his strong opposition to foreign imports, notably cars. The congressman then formally withdrew. Simon briefly revived his campaign in his home state of Illinois, where he led the field. But in the Wisconsin primary that followed, his uncompromising liberal stance brought him less than 5 percent of the vote in one of the most liberal states in the nation. He then "suspended" his campaign.

As candidates were eliminated, Jackson's candidacy expanded enormously. After winning a third of the vote in his home state of Illinois, finishing second behind Simon, he won a spectacular victory in Michigan, gaining over half the total vote. Clearly he was now much more than a black candidate, and the press, for the first time, saw him as a true prospect for the nomination. The ardor cooled slightly when Jackson was held to 28 percent in the Connecticut and Wisconsin balloting, finishing behind Dukakis. Still, these were impressive performances, since neither state has a large black population.

Closer analysis reveals that Jackson's base, although growing, was still limited. The Michigan results were impressive largely because they were unexpected. Although called a primary, the process in Michigan was more akin to a caucus, since it was run by the party, not the election authorities. Turnout was quite small: 212,000, in a total electorate of 6.8 million. No polls were available, but an examination of precinct returns suggested that a majority of the vote had been cast in black precincts.[14]

Jackson also won significant white support, yet here too the overall figures were misleading. Jackson sought to create a class-based coalition, allying lower-income, working-class whites with his cohesive black foundation. In fact, his white support was distinctly tilted toward the upper socioeconomic groups, those with middle or higher income and those with a college education.

Table 2.3 details the primary results, among whites, in the four critical states of Texas, Illinois, New York, and California. Jackson did show some appeal to the youngest voters and white liberals, but his support dropped among core groups of white Democrats: those of median income, high school graduates, and ideological moderates. Moreover, even among groups where Jackson did relatively well, Dukakis did better. Jackson had significantly increased his support among whites over 1984, but he was not drawing much better among whites than other black candidates (e.g., Mayor Tom Bradley of Los Angeles) had done in local elections.[15]

TABLE 2.3

WHITE DEMOCRATIC VOTE FOR DUKAKIS AND JACKSON
(PERCENTAGE OF STATE PRIMARY VOTES)

	Dukakis				Jackson			
	Tex.	Ill.	N.Y.	Calif.	Tex.	Ill.	N.Y.	Calif.
Age								
18-29	22	22	56	66	6	6	25	29
30-44	24	24	62	57	10	10	22	37
45-49	23	23	69	73	5	5	15	21
60+	21	21	79	81	5	5	6	14
Income								
Under $12,500	32	32	69	72	4	4	16	23
$12,500-25,000	19	19	71	73	7	7	16	24
$25,001-35,000	18	18	68	67	5	5	12	29
$35,001-50,000	23	23	71	74	10	10	15	21
Over $50,000	25	25	64	66	6	6	18	26
Education								
Less than high school	23	23	71	61	9	9	12	16
High school graduate	25	25	77	64	4	4	9	12
Some college	22	22	68	70	5	5	15	24
College graduate	23	23	62	68	10	10	21	27
Graduate degree	20	20	64	58	11	11	18	35
Ideology								
Liberal	20	20	61	56	14	14	28	42
Moderate	26	26	72	78	5	5	9	17
Conservative	20	20	77	75	3	3	5	11

SOURCE: CBS News poll.

Jackson's overall support expanded or shrank in an inverse relationship to the size of the electorate. He did best where few voters turned out, in the party caucuses, and did worst in the more participatory primaries. Because his supporters were intensely devoted, they were more willing than others to spend the considerable time involved to participate in a party caucus. As a result, Jackson was the leader in almost a third of the states (6 of 19) holding party caucuses. By contrast, he ran first in only a sixth of the constituencies (6 of 36, including the District of Columbia) holding primaries.[16] The effect of the different mechanisms can be seen in four states—Vermont, Texas, Idaho, and North Dakota—that held both caucuses and primaries. In the four caucuses, Jackson won 36 percent of the aggregate vote and carried Texas and Vermont—

all with only 40,519 votes. In the primaries in the same states, Jackson received far more total votes, over half a million, yet he won less than 29 percent of the aggregate vote and carried none of the four states. This is the difference between small and intense politics and mass politics.

A decisive test now loomed. In New York, Jackson had a large base in the black population, a fourth of the party electorate, the largest in any non-southern state. He faced overwhelming opposition from a group of equivalent size, Jewish voters, who were suspicious of his connections with anti-Semitic spokesmen and his position on Israel.

The crucial vote would be that cast for Gore. After his showing on Super Tuesday, Gore had not attracted any new support and had to do well in New York to maintain his financial and political standing. In what had become large-ly a two-man contest between Dukakis and Jackson, Gore faced the problem of any third candidate, the argument that a vote for Gore, by denying Dukakis a clear victory, would in effect be a vote for Jackson. Gore was further handi-capped by the endorsement of New York City's mayor, Edward Koch. The outspoken mayor's support turned out to be an embarrassment for Gore, as Koch appeared to be appealing to antiblack sentiment in his attacks on Jackson.

Dukakis benefited from both a dislike of Jackson and a perception of Gore's irrelevancy. More positively, the Massachusetts governor was regarded more favorably on a personal level than his opponents, he represented the mainstream of his party, and he bore no scars from the primary battle itself. These steady if undramatic attributes brought Dukakis a clear victory—an absolute majori-ty of the total vote and the leading position in virtually every demographic and philosophic category among whites. Judging his political philosophy, 61 percent of liberals found it "about right," neither too liberal nor too conserva-tive; they were joined by 63 percent of moderates and 58 percent of conserva-tives in this Goldilocks prescription. Although supported only by one of twen-ty blacks, Dukakis lost only 3–2 among Hispanics; and he won pluralities, com-bining blacks and whites, among union members, Catholics, and persons with no more than a high school education. He thereby showed a potential for re-uniting the historic Democratic majority coalition.[17]

The New York primary, in effect, settled the Democratic nomination. If Jackson could not assemble a plurality in this state, with its large black popu-lation and liberal white constituency, he could not do so anywhere. With a vote of only 13 percent among white Catholics and only 16 percent among whites with incomes below $25,000, Jackson's efforts toward a populist alliance had evidently failed. Gore, clearly no longer a contender, quickly withdrew. From that point, momentum took over. Dukakis won every one of the thirteen re-maining primaries except the District of Columbia, and his delegate totals

TABLE 2.4

GROUP VOTING IN THE DEMOCRATIC PRIMARIES

	Proportion of Primary Voters	Dukakis	Jackson	Others
Total votes	22.7 million	9.7 million	6.6 million	6.4 million
% of vote	100	43	29	28
Men	47	41	29	30
Women	53	43	30	26
White	75	54	12	35
Black	21	4	92	4
Hispanic	3	48	30	20
18-29 years	14	35	38	27
30-44	31	37	36	26
45-59	25	42	30	28
60 and older	30	53	19	29
Liberal	27	41	41	19
Moderate	47	47	25	28
Conservative	22	38	23	38
Democrat	72	43	33	24
Independent	20	44	20	34
Catholic	30	60	18	22
White Protestant	36	43	10	47
Jewish	7	75	8	17

NOTE: This table, which constructs a Democratic primary electorate for the nation, combines vote totals and exit poll percentages from 33 primary states where delegates were selected from February to June. Vote totals are from secretaries of state. Sources of exit poll percentages: 10 from New York Times/CBS News, 14 from CBS News alone, 5 from ABC News, and 1 from NBC News. No exit polls were available in Montana, Oregon, or Washington D.C.

SOURCE: *New York Times*, 13 June 1988.

were further enhanced by the support of superdelegates. On June 7, he became the first front-running Democrat since 1964 to win the California contest, gaining 60 percent of the vote.

Table 2.4 summarizes the results in all the Democratic primaries. Dukakis carried pluralities of almost every group of Democrats except blacks. Even his slightly poorer performance among the youngest and liberal voters was probably due to Jackson's dominance among blacks. The Massachusetts governor was now not only the certain nominee but also the consensual choice of both his party's voters and his party's leaders.

The Democratic preconvention contest meant more than a personal triumph for Dukakis. It also was a dynamic process that brought policy consensus within the party and improved Democratic chances of electoral victory in the fall. This dynamic process was evident in the structure of the competition between the candidates, in policy issues, and in the changing popularity of the contenders.

Achieving consensus was aided, first, by the structure of the competition. Although Democratic voters are split among liberals, moderates, and conservatives, the ideological spectrum among the candidates was actually quite limited. The more liberal wing of the party lost potential candidates such as Cuomo, Biden, and Hart. Eliminating Simon, Jackson became the sole representative of this faction. At the other end, the conservative wing of the party was completely absent.

The final three-way contest between Gore, Dukakis, and Jackson might be represented as a choice among the conservative, moderate, and liberal elements of the party. These convenient labels are actually misleading, for there never was a truly conservative Democrat in the race in 1988. Indeed, although there are still large numbers of conservative Democratic voters, there are few of that ideological variety among Democratic officials. Gore might be considered relatively more conservative because of his support of some weapons systems, but his voting record on core Democratic issues—civil rights, feminism, and domestic spending—is generally liberal.

Dukakis was truly a moderate, yet he found it necessary to underline his more liberal positions. To reassure ideological voters in party primaries, the Massachusetts governor pointed to his opposition to U.S. military interventions and his membership in the American Civil Liberties Union. Jackson, for his part, was clearly a liberal, but his more extreme positions were on issues of foreign policy, which he deemphasized in 1988. On domestic issues, Jackson's positions were notable principally because he stated explicitly what most Democrats believed implicitly. With little basic disagreement, the prospects for party unity were always good.

Consensus in the party also developed on issues. The themes of the candidates had been developed from the first contests and had been honed through a series of debates. Each candidate had a particular stress, of issues and of personal appeal, that would bring him a different coalition. Despite their differing emphases, however, the more important feature of the process was the emergence, often implicit, of common Democratic positions on the major issues. Rather than increase division within the party, the nominating process brought agreement. The party unity that would be formalized at the party convention was actually forged in the debates and contests held earlier in the year.

A composite Democratic appeal might read as follows: "We look to a progressive national party, . . . the party of civil rights, and social progress and human rights" (Gore). "We have to do what our governors have done. . . . That is, use government appropriately, use it efficiently, and make sure that when you use it, you're using it in the context of fiscal responsibility" (Gephardt). "The next American frontier is a vibrant, growing economy that provides good jobs at good wages for every citizen in the land" (Dukakis). "The incentive must be to reinvest in America; retrain our workers; reindustrialize our nation; research for . . . reconversion during a peacetime economy" (Jackson). "We have to see to it that all young people in our country have the chance for a quality education" (Simon). "My concept is workplace democracy, which says we're going to get moving, become productive, by listening to workers, by sharing the profits rather than cutting wages" (Babbitt).[18]

The third development in the Democratic contest was the change in the popularity of the candidates, illustrated in figures 2.1 and 2.2. The figures show how many Democrats had any opinion on Dukakis and Jackson, and the proportion who were favorable, undecided, and unfavorable. Opinion on the two candidates changed, but in different ways. Jackson was always well known, but at the beginning of his campaign, he was regarded quite negatively. As time went on, opinion about him changed; he had more positive than negative ratings by the end of active competition, and he grew even more in later public estimation. Dukakis started with limited recognition. Over time, he gained more attention, and almost all of it was positive. For both candidates, unusually, the campaign improved their popularity, leaving the party in good spirits and with a highly regarded leader.[19]

Democrats: Toward the Election

Electoral considerations now became predominant. To win the Presidency, Dukakis and the Democrats had two different, possibly conflicting needs. They had both to consolidate their base and to extend beyond their base. Consolidation required the enthusiasm of liberals and blacks. Extension required the support of moderates and Democrats who had voted for Reagan. Policy programs were part of these conflicting requirements. How, for example, could the party both promise the social programs wanted by its left wing and avoid the tax increase opposed by most voters?

More directly, Jesse Jackson personified the problem. Jackson spoke for the Democrats' core constituency, blacks, who could provide as much as a sixth

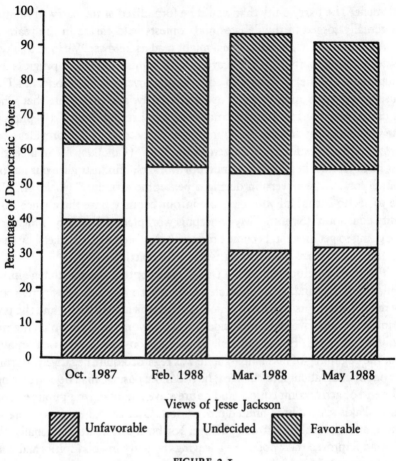

FIGURE 2.1
THE POPULARITY OF JESSE JACKSON AMONG PARTY IDENTIFIERS

of the votes needed to win the White House. Moreover, with nearly a third of all the votes cast in the primaries, Jackson could fairly claim to be the conscience of party liberalism, white and black. Yet neither blacks nor liberals alone could elect a President. Jackson remained personally unpopular among the moderate majority of all voters. Particularly critical in the election would be "Reagan Democrats," as numerous as blacks in the total electorate. Two-thirds of this swing group opposed placing Jackson on the party ticket.[20]

The vice-presidential nomination focused the problem. In recent decades, American parties have granted the presidential nominee the prerogative to choose his running mate. Jackson began an open campaign to pressure Dukakis for the position, on the basis of his second-place showing in the primaries.

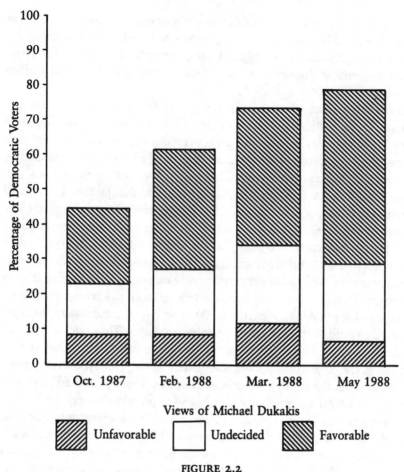

Views of Michael Dukakis

Unfavorable   Undecided   Favorable

FIGURE 2.2

THE POPULARITY OF MICHAEL DUKAKIS AMONG PARTY IDENTIFIERS

Actually, there was little tradition behind this claim, and opinion polls demonstrated that Jackson would hurt the Democratic ticket. Yet his large constituency could not be ignored.

In the weeks preceding the Democratic convention, Dukakis made several moves to increase his electoral support. For vice-president, he selected Senator Lloyd Bentsen of Texas, a moderate who would broaden the party's appeal toward the center and right of the country. Jackson and his supporters were not only disappointed by the choice; they were angered by Dukakis's failure, whether inadvertent or purposeful, to notify Jackson in advance of the decision.

At the Atlanta convention, Dukakis acted to mollify Jackson and his supporters. The runner-up was accorded considerable personal attention and was praised repeatedly. Indeed, for the first two nights of the convention, Jackson was far more visible than the incoming party leader. When the runner-up delivered a stirring speech to the delegates, the governor's majority stowed its own banners and instead displayed Jackson placards stapled by Dukakis's staffers onto wooden posts.

More substantively, the runner-up was given new institutional power within the party. Jackson clearly intended to renew his candidacy; modifications in delegate-selection rules improved his chances in future elections. New seats were added to the Democratic National Committee for Jackson supporters, and he was promised financial aid in the fall campaign. Even with these concessions, the fact remained that Dukakis was in command and that Jackson had no real alternative but to support his party. Rules changes might have a marginal effect on future contests, but Dukakis, if elected, would certainly dominate the party.

Jackson's challenge to Dukakis at the convention was ideological more than personal; the platform became the focus of that challenge, and eventually another means to establish party unity and broaden its electoral appeal. On some issues, Dukakis accepted Jackson's position, such as a strengthened condemnation of South African apartheid. On other issues, compromise language was found to meld liberal aims with moderate programs. Thus, Jackson wanted a specific pledge to double federal spending on education. The adopted platform called for "significantly increasing" these funds. Finally, on two issues, the convention balloted. By 2–1 votes, Dukakis's delegates defeated proposals to increase taxes on upper-income groups and to promise "no first use" of nuclear weapons. The Jackson forces had the satisfaction of presenting their case. The Dukakis group had the different satisfaction of showing the television audience that they were not wild liberals. As can be seen in table 2.5, the vote on these proposals closely correlated with each state's support of Dukakis or Jackson.

The party platform demonstrated that electoral victory was the predominant consideration. In recent conventions, the Democratic platform has been elephantine, as the party committed itself to hundreds of programs. While platforms have always been important indicators of party direction,[21] the Democrats went so far as to leave themselves open to attack as the servants of "special interests." To counter this image, Party Chairman Paul Kirk pushed for a relatively short and relatively vague platform. The size of the platform was reduced considerably, to less than 5000 words; it had been about 35,000 words four years earlier.

Although shortened, the platform still advanced the two goals of party unity and electoral victory. Its title, "The Restoration of Confidence and the Revival of Hope," echoed the campaign themes of Dukakis and Jackson. In fewer than fifty compound sentences, the party dealt with hundreds of policy questions. Although not vapid, the platform emphasized party goals instead of endorsing specific legislation. To lessen controversy, it sometimes used evasive language; for example, support for "reproductive freedom" replaced "a woman's right to abortion."

A reader of the platform could certainly understand the party's basic message: Activist government would address social needs through acceptable but undeclared means. Thus a Democratic administration would "commit itself . . . to the principle that no one should be denied the opportunity to attend college for financial reasons," but no budget cost was suggested. The party simultaneously championed "maintaining a stable nuclear deterrent sufficient to counter any Soviet threat" and a "halt [to] all nuclear weapons testing," without suggesting that there might be problems in reconciling these two pledges.[22] The effects of the Reagan years were evident in the emphasis on the private sector and the absence of promises of new spending, and in the appeals to middle-class voters. The heart of the Democrats remained on their left—but in 1988 they would not wear their heart on their sleeve.

Dukakis brought the convention to its climax with his acceptance speech on the final night. Discounted in advance as a poor speaker, the governor roused his audience, and his speech was interrupted by appplause twice as often as Jackson's masterful effort. Nevertheless, Dukakis presented no striking new programs, nor did he provide any content to his promises of "the next American frontier" and "a new era of greatness." The values he stressed were uncontroversial: economic opportunity, pride in ethnic traditions, good jobs at good wages, honesty among public officials, community concern.

Asserting that "this election is not about ideology, it's about competence," he sought to picture himself and his party as the embodiment of mainstream opinion. Praising both Reagan and Jackson, the Dukakis speech combined Reagan's American patriotism and Jackson's social idealism. Without once mentioning a budget expenditure and while barely citing a legislative bill, he convinced his audience that the Democrats could fulfill the ancient Athenian oath: "We will transmit this country greater, stronger, prouder and more beautiful than it was transmitted to us."[23] That promise was enough to convince the Democrats that they had found the way to victory.

Republicans: Decisions without Diversions

The Republican choice of a nominee was both quicker and simpler than the Democratic. The party had a simpler process, for it had been less concerned with repeatedly changing its methods of nomination. The political situation,

TABLE 2.5, DEMOCRATIC CONVENTION ROLL-CALL VOTES

| | Presidential Balloting | | | | | Balloting on Platform | | | | | |
| | | | | | | Plank on Fair Tax | | | No-First-Use Plank | | |
	Totals[a]	Dukakis	Jackson	Others[b]	Abstained	Y	N	A[c]	Y	N	A[c]
AL	65	37	28	0	0	14	35	16	19	38	8
AK	17	9	7	1	0	5	7	0	8	8	0
AZ	43	28	14	0	0	15	21	0	15	25	0
AR	48	31	11	0	1	11	27	0	9	25	0
CA	363	235	122	0	0	104	240	0	119.09	192.63	1
CO	55	37	18	0	0	20	31	0	20	32	0
CT	63	47	16	0	0	16	42	0	21	39	1
DE	19	9	7	2	1	8	11	0	8	11	0
FL	154	116	35	0	0	33	89	0	33	100	0
GA	94	50	42	0	0	30	43	0	36	43	0
HI	28	19	8	0	0	8	19	1	8	19	1
ID	24	20	3	0	0	3	18	0	3	18	0
IL	200	138	57	0	0	28	75	0	40	62	7
IN	89	69.50	18	0	0	18	68	0	19	66	1
IA	61	49	12	0	0	11	48	0	21	38	0
KA	45	30	15	0	0	12	29.50	0	14.50	28.50	0
KY	65	59	6	0	0	6	43	0	6	46	0
LA	76	41	33	1	0	23	11	1	26	13	0
ME	29	17	12	0	0	11	15	0	11	14	0
MD	84	59	25	0	0	21	58	0	21	58	1
MA	119	99	19	0	0	20	79	0	23	86	1
MI	162	80	80	0	2	78	77	0	78	77	0
MN	91	57	29	3	0	36	45	0	42	46	0
MS	47	19	26	0	0	24	15	1	27	16	0
MO	88	50	37	0	0	31	49	0	33	50	0
MT	28	22	5	0	0	5	21	0	7	19	0
NE	30	22	8	0	0	7	23	0	7	23	0
NV	23	16	5	0	0	5	15	0	6	15	0

State											
NH	22	22	0	0	0	0	22	0	1	21	0
NJ	126	107	19	0	0	19	39	68	19	64	43
NM	30	22	8	0	0	7	19	0	7	20	0
NY	292	194	97	0	0	90	181	0	108	173	0
NC	95	58	35	0	2	36	51	1	37	51	0
ND	22	17	3	0	1	2	11	0	5	11	0
OH	183	136	46	0	0	46	131	0	48	132	0
OK	56	52	4	0	0	4	44	0	4	46	0
OR	54	35	18	0	0	18	31	0	18	34	0
PA	202	179	23	0	0	22	177	0	22	179	1
RI	28	24	3	0	1	3	15	2	4	16	0
SC	53	22	31	0	0	29	19	0	30	23	1
SD	20	19	1	0	0	2	16	0	2	17	0
TN	84	63	20	0	4	12	54	0	15	57	0
TX	211	135	71	1	0	72	123	0	72	121	0
UT	28	25	3	0	0	3	18	0	5	20	0
VT	20	9	9	1	2	10	9	0	11	9	1
VA	86	42	42	0	0	37	46	0	41	44	0
WA	77	50	27	0	0	27	46	0	29	42	1
WV	47	47	0	0	0	0	44	0	1	43	0
WI	91	65	25	0	0	24	59	0	25	59	0
WY	18	14	4	0	0	4	12	0	6	10	0
DC	25	7	18	0	0	13	6	0	16	8	0
PR	57	48.50	8	0	0	3	53	0	8	48	0
VI	5	0	5	0	0	5	0	0	5	0	0
Samoa	6	6	0	0	0	0	6	0	0	6	0
Guam	4	4	0	0	0	0	4	0	0	4	0
Abroad	9	8.25	0.50	0	0	0.50	8.50	0	1	8	0
TOTALS	4162	2876.25	1218.50	0.50	9	1091.50	2499.00	90	1220.59	2474.13	67

SOURCE: *Congressional Quarterly Weekly Report* 46 (23 July 1988): 2033.

a. Totals may not add due to absences. b. Details on the votes for other candidates: Alaska, Lloyd Bentsen, 1; Delaware: Joseph R. Biden, Jr., 1; Louisiana: Richard A. Gephardt, 1; Minnesota: Richard H. Stallings, 1; Texas: Gephardt, 3; Vermont: Gary Hart, 1. c. Abstained.

too, was straightforward for the Republicans. As the party in power for the past eight years, it would necessarily campaign on the basis of that record, restricting the range of debate among potential candidates.

The structure of the Republican competition was also plain. Since the New Deal, the party had consisted of two basic groups: a largely eastern moderate-to-liberal faction, and a more conservative faction based in the Midwest. These alignments had been evident in many past contests, from Eisenhower vs. Taft down to Bush vs. Reagan.[24] But by 1988, this long-standing division was invisible. Reagan's victories had completed the transformation of the Republicans to a coherently conservative party with no significant liberal elements. Every aspiring candidate in 1988 claimed to be Reagan's authentic heir and the authentic spokesman of Republican conservatism.

Divisions within this limited ideological range still remained, and were represented by the six announced candidates, who stressed different elements of the Reagan heritage. Jack Kemp, a New York congressman, and Delaware Governor Pierre DuPont focused on the Republican economic program of limiting government, tax reduction, and increasing opportunities for private business. Alexander Haig, former secretary of state, concentrated more on assertive foreign policy leadership.

Particularly interesting were the three more prominent candidates. The clear leader was Vice-President George Bush. Emphasizing the virtue of "loyalty," Bush was the person who had been closest in government, at least physically, to Reagan. Previously considered relatively moderate, Bush now adopted for his own all Reagan programs, including the tax cuts he once called "voodoo economics," opposition to abortion, and increased military spending. A year before the election, opinion polls confirmed his leading position, as he won the endorsement of 43 percent of Republican voters. Robert Dole, party leader in the Senate, emphasized his legislative competence and service to the administration. Although an orthodox Republican, Dole appeared relatively moderate because he would at least consider the possibility of tax increases. He was the only Republican besides Bush to receive significant support in the polls, although he trailed Bush by a 2–1 margin.[25]

The Reverend Pat Robertson was the great unknown in the Republican race. His focus was on a different element of the Reagan legacy, its traditionalist stance on questions of personal life style. As a television evangelist, Robertson had won a large following by his stress on these issues. As a mirror image of Jesse Jackson among the Democrats, he raised similar questions about the appropriateness of introducing moral issues into politics, as well as personal questions about his lack of direct government experience. The parallel might be carried further if Robertson could attract new followers into politics by mobilizing

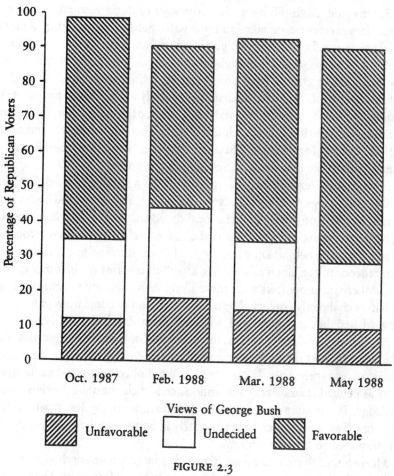

FIGURE 2.3

THE POPULARITY OF GEORGE BUSH AMONG PARTY IDENTIFIERS

his touted "secret army." Evangelical Protestants were relatively new to politics. If they could be coherently mobilized by Robertson, they might transform Republican politics as dramatically as Jackson had affected the Democrats.

Bush was clearly the man to beat, but his opponents could not find any hard stick to beat him with. Since they all praised the Reagan record, how could they convince Republicans not to vote for the second-highest official in the administration? Surely they could not claim more extensive experience or superior paper credentials. One possible argument was that Bush would be a weak candidate in a likely close race. Yet the polls did not prove any of the Republican alternatives to be noticeably stronger, nor were the Democrats likely to nominate a candidate of great personal appeal.

For his side, Bush did have the advantages of name recognition, of experience in a previous campaign, and of a well-financed organization. Among Republican voters, he began with high ratings and as figure 2.3 shows, he maintained this position steadily throughout the campaign. The front-runner did carry a certain suspicion from conservatives, who remembered his earlier criticism of Reagan. As vice-president, particularly in the year before the first primaries, he made a number of overtures to the party's right wing. For example, Bush gave a testimonial speech for William Loeb, an extremely conservative New Hampshire publisher. These actions brought derision from the press, but they consolidated Bush's position within the party.

In the earliest tests, Robertson appeared to be a significant candidate, despite low poll ratings. In early caucuses in Michigan, Robertson and his temporary ally, Kemp, won nearly half the local delegates. As the 1988 contests began, the conservative evangelist startled observers when he finished second in the Iowa caucuses, behind Dole but ahead of Bush. Analysis of the results lent some credence to the claim of a "secret army." In contrast to the other candidates, Robertson supporters were more likely to be first-time primary voters who had been directly contacted by a candidate, and to come from groups not typical of Republican voters, such as union members and Catholics.[26]

But Robertson's base was actually quite limited. Even more than was true for Jackson, support for Robertson would be much less significant in the broader arenas of mass primaries. In New Hampshire, Robertson's standing declined rapidly as he made extravagant and undocumented claims of his foreign policy knowledge. In the state's primary, he ran fourth, receiving less than a tenth of the vote. Two weeks later, he fared poorly in South Carolina, where he had been presumed to be very strong.

Momentum, the feared engine of presidential nominations, had sputtered and died after Iowa, then received a jump-start in New Hampshire. Dole's campaign failed to take advantage of his initial victory, while Bush rallied in the last week. The vice-president reversed his fortunes from a 37–19 percent defeat in Iowa to a 38–28 percent victory in New Hampshire. The overall impact of these two early contests was to scrub the second string (DuPont, Haig, and Kemp), virtually eliminate Robertson, and make Super Tuesday a direct confrontation between Bush and Dole.

In that single day, Bush won the presidential nomination. He won every one of the sixteen Republican primaries, and indeed won handily in all but the two states bordering Dole's Kansas home. Bush not only carried every state; he also was preferred by almost every significant demographic and philosophical group. Bush's greatest advantage, simply put, was Ronald Reagan. Bush gained 62 percent of the votes of those who approved of Reagan's performance as

President, but trailed Dole, 37 to 43 percent, among those critical of the incumbent President.

The fortunate fact for Bush was that, on Super Tuesday southern Republicans overwhelmingly (by 83–13 percent) liked the Reagan record, in fact liked it better than Republicans in any other region.[27] His ultimate election prospects uncertain, Bush might not be the right man for the party, but he had found himself in the right place at the right time. This decisive impact is evident in tables 2.6 and 2.7, showing the great increase both in Bush's popular vote and pledged delegates on this date. Super Tuesday, created to influence the Democratic nomination, had instead determined the Republican choice. Summarizing state results, table 2.8 records the broad support that Bush received from party voters.

Only a dramatic surprise could now stop Bush. When he won the Illinois primary the following week, defeating Dole in the Midwest, all opposition disappeared. By the first of May, the vice-president had mathematically won the presidential nomination. He could then devote himself to the relatively simple task of completing the unification of a party that bore few scars from the brief preconvention struggle.

Republicans: Toward the Election (of 1980)

The Republican convention in New Orleans had but one essential purpose: to boost Bush's presidential campaign. Trailing Dukakis in opinion polls, sometimes by large margins, the vice-president needed to convert the enthusiasm and ideological fervor of his party into a national electoral majority.

Although it was 1988, the implicit strategy adopted by Bush was to use the convention to relive the 1980 election. This scenario was evident both in the way Bush promoted intraparty unity and in the way the Republicans attempted to extend their appeal to the total electorate.

In the 1980 election, conservative Republicans had become the dominant faction in the party, a position that was no longer debatable after the Reagan years. In New Orleans, the party took every opportunity to reiterate that ideological stance, and Bush took every personal opportunity to conciliate the right wing in his party and to identify himself as the spokesman of a party united on conservative principles.

The platform provided one instance. Six times the length of the Democratic manifesto, the party program deliberately and specifically supported hundreds of conservative positions. These included a pledge not to increase general taxes but to reduce capital gains levies, higher military spending and deployment of the Strategic Defense Initiative ("Star Wars") antimissile system, opposition to abortion, and support of school prayer.

TABLE 2.6

Date	State	Total Vote	Bush N	%	Dole[a] N	%	Robertson[b] N	%
8 Feb	IA*	108,838	20,244	18.6	40,597	37.3	26,774	24.6
16 Feb	NH	157,625	59,267	37.6	44,765	28.4	14,817	9.4
23 Feb	SD	93,405	17,373	18.6	51,560	55.2	18,307	19.6
1 Mar	VT*	47,832	23,582	49.3	18,654	39.0	2,439	5.1
5 Mar	SC	195,292	94,717	48.5	40,230	20.6	37,301	19.1
8 Mar	AL	213,515	137,717	64.5	34,803	16.3	29,679	13.9
	AR	68,305	32,103	47.0	17,691	25.9	12,910	18.9
	FL	901,222	559,659	62.1	191,059	21.2	95,530	10.6
	GA	400,928	215,699	53.8	94,619	23.6	65,351	16.3
	KY	121,402	71,991	59.3	27,922	23.0	13,476	11.1
	LA	144,781	83,684	57.8	25,626	17.7	26,350	18.2
	MD	200,754	107,002	53.3	65,044	32.4	12,848	6.4
	MA	241,181	141,091	58.5	63,431	26.3	10,853	4.5
	MS	158,872	104,856	66.0	26,849	16.9	21,448	13.5
	MO	400,300	168,927	42.2	164,523	41.1	44,834	11.2
	NC	273,801	124,306	45.4	107,056	39.1	26,832	9.8
	OK	208,938	78,143	37.4	72,919	34.9	44,086	21.1
	RI	16,035	10,407	64.9	3,624	22.6	914	5.7
	TN	254,252	152,551	60.0	54,918	21.6	32,036	12.6
	TX	1,014,956	648,557	63.9	141,079	13.9	155,288	15.3
	VA*	234,142	124,798	53.3	60,877	26.0	32,077	13.7
15 Mar	IL	858,256	469,466	54.7	308,972	36.0	58,362	6.8
20 Mar	PR	3,973	3,858	97.1	107	2.7	4	.1
29 Mar	CT	104,171	73,545	70.6	21,043	20.2	3,229	3.1
5 Apr	WI	359,294	295,340	82.2	28,384	7.9	24,791	6.9
26 April	PA	870,549	687,734	79.0	103,595	11.9	79,220	9.1
3 May	DC	6,720	5,887	87.6	470	7.0	269	4.0
	IN	437,655	351,875	80.4	42,890	9.8	29,885	6.6
	OH	794,904	643,872	81.0	94,594	11.9	56,438	7.1
10 May	NE	204,049	138,753	68.0	45,503	22.3	10,407	5.1
	WV	122,346	109,255	89.3	†		10,522	8.6
17 May	OR	274,451	200,075	72.9	49,127	17.9	21,133	7.7
24 May	ID	68,275	55,439	81.2	†		5,872	8.6
7 June	CA	2,193,579	1,816,283	82.8	282,972	12.9	92,130	4.2
	MT	85,907	62,884	73.2	16,752	19.5	†	
	NJ	242,272	242,272	100.0	†		†	
	NM	88,744	69,398	78.2	9,318	10.5	5,325	6.0
14 June	ND	39,434	37,068	94.0	†		†	

NOTES: † indicates that the candidate or the "uncommitted" line was not listed on the ballot. * indicates that the state held a caucus, not a primary. Vermont and Virginia votes were only advisory with delegates selected in later caucuses.

THE REPUBLICAN PRIMARIES

Others & Uncommitted		Cumulative		
N	%	Total Vote	Bush %	Others %
21,223	19.5	108,838	18.6	81.4
38,776	24.6	266,463	29.8	70.2
6,071	6.5	359,868	26.9	73.1
3,157	6.6	407,700	29.5	70.4
23,044	11.8	602,992	35.7	64.3
11,103	5.2			
5,601	8.2			
54,073	6.0			
25,259	6.3			
7,891	6.5			
9,121	6.3			
15,860	7.9			
25,806	10.7			
5,719	3.6			
22,417	5.6			
15,333	5.6			
13,581	6.5			
1,090	6.8			
14,747	5.8			
70,032	6.9			
16,390	7.0	5,456,376	54.6	45.4
21,456	2.5	6,314,632	54.6	45.4
4	.1	6,318,605	54.6	45.4
6,459	6.2	6,422,776	54.9	45.1
11,138	3.1	6,782,070	56.3	43.7
†		7,652,619	58.9	41.1
94	1.4			
14,443	3.3			
†		8,891,898	61.9	38.1
9,386	4.6			
2,569	2.1	9,218,293	62.4	37.6
4,116	1.5	9,492,744	62.7	37.3
6,964	10.2	9,561,019	62.9	37.1
†				
6,357	7.4			
†				
4,703	5.3	12,171,521	67.3	32.4
2,366	6.0	12,210,955	67.5	32.5

a. Dole withdrew from the race on 29 March. *b.* Robertson suspended his campaign 16 May.

TABLE 2.7
ACCUMULATING REPUBLICAN PARTY DELEGATES

Week Ending	State	New Delegates	Total Selected	% of Total	Bush % of Majority	Bush % Needed of Remainder
13 Feb	IA	37	129	5.6	4.1	50.8
20 Feb	NH	27	156	6.8	5.3	50.8
27 Feb	NV					
	MN					
	SD					
		18	174	7.6	5.3	51.2
5-12 Mar	AK					
	VT					
	SC					
	AL					
	AR					
	FL					
	GA					
	KY					
	LA					
	MD					
	MA					
	MO					
	MS					
	NC					
	OK					
	RI					
	TN					
	TX					
	VA					
	WA					
		785	959	42.1	61.8	32.9
26 Mar	IL					
	PR					
		96	1055	46.3	69.1	28.7
2 April	CT	35	1090	47.8	71.3	27.4
9 April	CO					
	WI					
		47	1137	49.9	77.9	22.0
23 April	NY	163	1300	57.0	92.3	8.9
30 April	PA	77	1377	60.4	100.4	
7 May	DC					
	IN					
	OH					
		165	1542	67.7	113.7	

TABLE 2.7
(continued)

Week Ending	State	New Delegates	Total Selected	% of of Total	Bush % of Majority	Bush % Needed of Remainder
14 May	NE					
	WV					
		55	1597	70.1	117.9	
21 May	OR	32	1629	71.5	120.8	
28 May	ID	52	1681	73.8	125.1	
11 June	CA					
	MT					
	NJ					
	NM					
		245	1926	84.5	146.5	

In its title, "For Our Children and Our Future," the party platform pointed toward "change and progress." Some new programs were included in regard to child care and education, such as tax credits, while maintaining the Republican preference for private rather than governmental action. Still, the manifesto was largely a reiteration of past party programs, with much of the language directly replicated from the previous conservative years, 1980 and 1984. In the few disputes that arose over the platform, the conservative thrust was further underlined: The commitment to Star Wars was restated four times, while proposals to permit abortion in cases of rape or incest were decisively rejected. The party would not dilute, and Bush would not dispute, this conservative ideology.

The vice-presidential nomination provided a second instance. Bush faced a small campaign to designate a right-wing running mate, but had complete freedom to make his own selection. His strategic choice was whether to select a person who would consolidate his backing within the party or, like Dukakis, to use the vice-presidency to extend his appeal to different voting groups. Bush chose the first, intraparty strategy.

The vice-presidential nominee was J. Danforth Quayle, a second-term senator from Indiana. Aside from his good looks and youth, Quayle had little apparent electoral appeal of his own, came from an uncompetitive state, and was unknown even to such Republican leaders as California Governor George Deukmejian. Quayle's appeal was within the party, for he had a solid conservative record. From the antimissile program to abortion to civil rights, and even on the popular program to require notice of plant closings, Quayle had supported Reagan's positions. That orthodoxy sustained Quayle even when con-

TABLE 2.8

VOTING IN REPUBLICAN PRESIDENTIAL PRIMARIES

(PERCENTAGE VOTING FOR GEORGE BUSH)

	New Hampshire	Southern States	Illinois
Sex			
Men	36	61	54
Women	40	55	50
Age			
Under 30	35	58	41
30-44	33	48	49
45-59	41	60	57
60 and over	47	66	56
Partisanship			
Republican		60	56
Other		53	43
Ideology			
Conservative	39	56	54
Other	37	61	49
Education			
High school graduate or less	46	61	57
Some college	36	55	54
College graduate	34	58	47
Religion			
Protestant		58	51
Catholic		65	56
Fundamentalist	22	30	32
Income			
Below $25,000	40	55	51
$25,001-35,000	35	57	54
$35,001-50,000	37	59	54
Over $50,000	38	59	48
Attitude toward Reagan			
Approve	43	62	57
Disapprove	17	37	35
TOTAL	38	57	55

troversy arose over his military service during the Vietnam war. His designation demonstrated that the conservative dominance of the party established in 1980 would continue under Bush's leadership.

The Republicans also returned figuratively to the 1980 election as they attempted to extend their appeal to the general electorate. In traditional political fashion, they praised their own policies of the past eight years, claimed success for what was now called the Reagan-Bush administration, and contrasted their party record to the alleged defects of the previous Carter years. Invoking any politician's favorite theme, Republicans championed Bush as the capable heir to a record of peace and prosperity.

Yet Republicans would not limit their campaign to their record or their candidate. They attempted to make a deeper, ideological appeal. Conservatism, rather than peace and prosperity, would be the dominant electoral theme of the Republican convention. The Republicans believed that the 1980 and 1984 elections were not only victories for Reagan but endorsements of a world view. The ideological platform, the coherently conservative ticket, the programmatic rhetoric were parallel efforts to maintain a presumed newly dominant coalition. Conservatism would not only unify the party; it would also be the means to hold the White House.

As they presented their case to the national television audience, Republicans emphasized the ideological difference between the parties. Opening the attack, Reagan denounced the Democrats for avoiding the "L word," and condemned them as "liberal, liberal, liberal." The refrain was reiterated by other speakers, such as keynoter Tom Kean, the governor of New Jersey, who derided Democrats as a party of "pastel patriotism" that tried to "hide its true colors," and Pat Robertson, who revealed that Dukakis was "a card-carrying member of the American Civil Liberties Union." The repeated warnings about frightening liberalism led cartoon character Mike Doonesbury to mock outrage: "This is irresponsible! There are *children* still up at this hour!"

As George Bush accepted his nomination, he restated the party's themes. In a forceful address, he minimized Dukakis's emphasis on competence as "a narrow ideal," while stressing "the beliefs we share, the values that we honor." Invoking the common American values of patriotism, family, and religion, the Republican nominee reiterated the convention themes: past accomplishments and conservative policies of economic growth through the private sector, military strength, and traditional life styles. While suggesting some new policy proposals, he also made an absolute pledge against increased taxation, implying, like his opponent, that programs never cost money.[28] In a significant keynote to his campaign, he concluded with the Pledge of Allegiance.

The Choices and Theories of 1988

The nominating contests of 1988 eventually presented the American electorate with a meaningful choice. That choice was not as extreme as partisan campaigners presented it, but it was still real. Michael Dukakis and George Bush were neither the ogres nor the saints portrayed at the party conventions. Democratic and Republican policies diverged, but the next President would neither trample on the masses nor destroy American business.

The Reagan years had demonstrated both the possibilities and the limits of American politics. Priorities could be changed, spending could be increased or decreased, courts could be moved through systematic appointments, arms control could be advanced, and national interests abroad could be redefined. America was certainly different in 1988 than it had been in 1980—even if the country was not clearly "better off " after those eight years.

Yet it was also true that even a self-consciously conservative administration could not remake the nation, much less the world. The welfare state remained, the mutual dependence of government and business remained, federal spending grew, formal equality of blacks and women continued to advance, international power continued to spread beyond the Soviet and American blocs. Whatever the voting results, in the spring primaries or in the fall election, the new President would still be severely limited by the unrelenting facts of limited budgetary resources, international trade deficits, national rivalries, and rising but unfulfilled expectations within and outside the United States.

The limits of American politics were revealed by the party candidates of 1988. Both men pointed to the same problem areas—education, family stability, arms control. In their acceptance speeches, they invoked the same themes—economic growth, community, public service, American exceptionalism. They even seemed to be similar persons. The new party leaders were not dynamic personalities, but each was experienced, intelligent, and relatively capable when compared to their intraparty rivals. "Maybe we didn't want to fall in love in 1988," suggested pollster Paul Maslin. "Instead, we opted for the political equivalent of 'safe sex.' "[29]

Yet, Dukakis and Bush were different; in their origins, their careers, their voter and leadership coalitions, their policy interests, Dukakis and Bush offered the voters a distinct choice between leaders. Most fundamentally, the candidates were appropriate representatives of distinct political perspectives. Dukakis might emphasize the personal quality of leadership, but the question remained: Leadership *for what?* Bush might emphasize the personal quality of experience, but the question remained: Experience *in what?* Beyond their individual traits, the candidates and their parties differed in particular programs and basic values.

Democrats, and Dukakis, believed in an activist government that would advance social and economic equality. Republicans, and Bush, believed in limiting government to advance individual liberty. This basic difference in orientation could be seen even in interpretations of the simple prologue to the nation's basic charter: "We the people . . . do ordain and establish this Constitution." Democrats read these words as a grant of power to be used to "promote the general welfare." To Republicans, these words emphasized the subordination of government in the effort to "secure the blessings of liberty." The party difference was evident as well in delegates' opinions. By a 7–2 margin, Democrats preferred "bigger government providing more services"; by a 29–1 margin, Republicans preferred "smaller government providing fewer services."[30]

The parties and candidates differed on other values. Republicans were more concerned over individual moral behavior and would use the power of government to strengthen traditional values, for example by prohibiting abortion. Democrats were more tolerant of distinct life styles and more pluralist in composition and values, for example in support of affirmative action programs. In foreign relations, as exemplified by differences over policies toward Nicaragua and military spending, Democrats emphasized international cooperation, while Republicans placed greater stress on assertive nationalism.[31]

The parties' differences were not absolute, and they shared in the American consensus that combined elements of all these values. But their focus and direction were significantly different. Dukakis and Bush would be equally limited by factual reality as President, and the necessities of campaigning within a diverse country might cause them to hide some differences. When one of them would need to act as President, however, he would start from different values and give a different response. There was a choice in 1988.

The nominations of 1988 also rested upon theories of politics and political science in regard to the nature of political parties—and, indeed, of voter behavior. Do voters respond on the basis of past loyalties and memories, or in the light of present conditions; do they judge on programmatic promises for the future, or do they focus on the qualities of individual leaders? These alternatives would be tested by the fall election results.

The nominating process also raised questions about the role of political parties. Theories of parties have seen them in essentially two different ways: as promoters of policy programs developed by the membership, and as groups of politicians seeking public office. The first theory emphasizes party democracy and ideological unity. Through membership participation, the party would fulfill the ideal defined by Edmund Burke: "a body of men united, for promoting by their joint endeavors the national interest, upon some particular principle in which they are all agreed."[32]

The second theory sees political parties as "rational-efficient" organizations primarily interested in winning office. To gain power, they follow public opinion and design popular programs. Thus, "Parties formulate policies in order to win elections rather than win elections in order to formulate policies."[33] Instead of being ideological, parties are pragmatic and flexible in their approach, adopting whatever policies will win them the backing of an electoral majority.

Through most of U.S. history, the parties have acted more in accord with the second theory, changing their policies as electorally necessary. This flexibility (or, as some might call it, lack of principle) was possible because parties were led by relatively small groups of politicians devoted to the pursuit of office. Recent reform movements, however, have changed the character of the parties, with important practical consequences for presidential nominations. The United States has changed from a system in which nominations were made mainly by leaders of "rational-efficient" parties to a system in which nominations are determined largely through persuasion of party members by candidate organizations and the media.

Different candidates result from different processes. When the choice of a party leader is made by politicians seeking office, they are more likely to place emphasis on qualities of electoral appeal, even if the result is the nomination of a bland but inoffensive candidate. If left to party members, the choice is more likely to be a person tested on the basis of adherence to the ideology of the most fervent members of the mass party. The party may nominate a true believer, but may damage severely its chances of victory.

This potential conflict particularly affected the Democrats for a number of elections. Candidates such as George McGovern or Walter Mondale met the ideological tests of party voters, but were unacceptable to the general electorate. In 1988, Jesse Jackson was the purer ideological candidate. If he were not black, or if the nomination had been decided only in caucuses of devoted party members, he might have been nominated, and then decisively defeated in the general election. Indeed, that result momentarily seemed possible after Jackson's surprise victory in the limited Michigan primary.

In the end, the Democrats did choose a candidate with a possible appeal to moderate voters, but the nomination process did not ensure the party this happy result. Instead, that process required Dukakis to prove his liberal credentials. As he would soon discover, an ideology that raised cheers among thousands of party activists in Iowa and New Hampshire could also arouse fear among millions of uncommitted voters throughout the nation.

The Republicans, in 1988, also showed the conflict between ideology and pragmatism within the party. Robertson won initial support because of his forthright conservatism, before revealing the personal liabilities that ended his campaign. Yet George Bush, too, had to give hostages to ideology, by his repeated efforts to demonstrate conservatism. The vice-president eventually won his party's nomination easily, not on the basis of his electability, but after proving his ideological purity. Even at the convention he dominated, Bush continued to stress conciliation with the right wing of his party rather than a broader appeal.

These dynamics of the nominating process carry serious implications for the workings of American democracy. Effective popular control of government requires that voters have a significant choice before them in elections. But effective democratic government requires that there be considerable basic agreement between the parties and from one administration to another. By emphasizing the ideological acceptability of candidates to their mass memberships, the contemporary nominating process may both give the voters a choice and give them a choice they would rather refuse.[34]

Despite its reasonable results in 1988, the present nominating system retains significant flaws. The system does not allow the reluctant but able candidate to be drafted, as the experience with Cuomo shows. Providing a large number of superdelegates will not provide an opening for leadership by party elites, who were terrified of the possibility of a bargained nomination in 1988. Voters themselves give little weight to the problem of choosing an electable candidate, emphasizing instead personal qualifications and issue positions.[35] No solution is apparent, but the problem is real and continuing.

Choosing its leadership is the most important task of a democracy. Writing the American Constitution over two hundred years ago, the framers found it particularly difficult to develop a means to select the President, and settled on an ambiguous solution. That process remains as difficult to perfect today as it was to create in 1787. Now that the Presidency affects the life of the entire planet, we must think anew.

Notes

1. The classic theoretical explanation is Anthony Downs, *An Economic Theory of Democracy* (New York: Harper & Row, 1957); and the classic defense is E.E. Schattschneider, *Party Government* (New York: Rinehart, 1942), chap. 1.

2. For analysis of these changes, see Howard Reiter, *Selecting the President* (Philadelphia: University of Pennsylvania Press, 1985); for a particularly critical analysis, see Nelson Polsby, *Consequences of Party Reform* (New York: Oxford University Press, 1983).

3. Trends in party identification are derived from *Public Opinion* 8 (October/November 1985), and, for later years, from the CBS News/New York Times poll.

4. See Stuart Rothenberg, "A New Look at the Lock," *Public Opinion* 10 (March/April 1988): 41-54.

5. For reports and data on the 1986 elections, see *National Journal* 18 (8 November 1986): 2670-2721.

6. Democrats include Senator Bill Bradley of New Jersey, Senator Dale Bumpers and Governor Bill Clinton of Arkansas, Governor Mario Cuomo of New York, Senator Edward Kennedy of Massachusetts, Senator Sam Nunn of Georgia, Governor Chuck Robb of Virginia, and Congresswoman Patricia Schroeder of Colorado. Republicans include Senator William Armstrong of Colorado, presidential Chief of Staff Howard Baker, former UN Ambassador Jeane Kirkpatrick, former Senator Paul Laxalt of Nevada, and Governor James Thompson of Illinois. A fuller list is provided in *Congressional Quarterly Weekly Report* 45 (7 November 1987): 2732.

7. Harold Stanley and Charles Hadley predicted these effects in advance. See "The Southern Presidential Primary," *Publius* 17 (Summer 1987): 83-100.

8. CBS News/New York Times poll, 14 May 1987.

9. *Los Angeles Times,* 10 May 1987.

10. C. Anthony Broh, *A Horse of a Different Color* (Washington: Joint Center for Political Studies, 1987).

11. In a major work, Larry Bartels analyzes the method and meaning of momentum. See his *Presidential Primaries and the Dynamics of Public Choice* (Princeton: Princeton University Press, 1988).

12. Ibid., 303.

13. CBS News/New York Times poll, 8 March 1988.

14. *Congressional Quarterly Weekly Report* 46 (2 April 1988): 853-57.

15. For an overall analysis, see Martin Plissner and Warren Mitofsky, "The Changing Jackson Voter," *Public Opinion* 11 (July/August 1988): 56-57.

16. *Congressional Quarterly Weekly Report* 46 (9 July 1988): 1894-95. The territories and Puerto Rico are excluded.

17. CBS News/New York Times poll, 19 April 1988.

18. The quotations are from articles in the *New York Times* from 4 to 19 January 1988, and from William Schneider, "A Consumer's Guide to the Democrats in '88," *Atlantic* 259 (April 1987): 37-59.

19. Data are from the CBS News polls of designated months. In July, Jackson's ratings improved further, to 44–19–24 among Democrats. As Republicans began to concentrate their fire on Dukakis, his popularity became less firm within his own party, with ratings of 40–36–6, then grew in August to 56–29–7. Bush also slipped among Republicans in July, to ratings of 46–25–11, then recovered even before the party convention, to 58–26–10.

20. Los Angeles Times poll, 18 July 1988.

21. Gerald M. Pomper with Susan S. Lederman, *Elections in America,* 2d ed. (New York: Longman, 1980), chaps. 7, 8.

22. Democratic National Committee, *Report of the Platform Committee,* 2, 6.

23. *Congressional Quarterly Weekly Report* 46 (23 July 1988): 2052-54.

24. Warren Miller and Kent Jennings, *Parties in Transition* (New York: Russell Sage Foundation, 1986), chap. 3; Frank Munger and James Blackhurst, "Factionalism in the National Conventions, 1940-1964," *Journal of Politics* 27 (May 1965): 375-94.

25. CBS News/New York Times poll, 27 October 1987.

26. Ibid., 8 February 1988.

27. Ibid., 8 March 1988.

28. *New York Times,* 19 August 1988, A14.

29. Quoted by Paul Taylor, *Washington Post National Weekly,* 19 June 1988.

30. *New York Times.* Delegate Survey, 14 August 1988, 32.

31. Value dimensions in public opinion have been developed for 1988 opinion surveys by the Gallup Organization for the *Los Angeles Times-Mirror.* See *The People, Press, and Politics* (Los Angeles: Times Mirror, 1987).

32. The categorization of party theories is from William Wright, *A Comparative Study of Party Organization* (Columbus, Ohio: Merrill, 1971), chap. 1. The first theory is advocated in two classic works: Robert Michels, *Political Parties* (New York: Free Press, 1962; orig. pub. 1911); and Committee on Political Parties, "Toward a More Responsible Two-Party System," *American Political Science Review* 44 (September 1950).

33. Downs, *Economic Theory,* 28. Also see Joseph Schlesinger, "On the Theory of Party Organization," *Journal of Politics* 46 (May 1984): 369-400.

34. John H. Aldrich, "A Downsian Spatial Model of Party Activism," *American Political Science Review* 77 (December 1983): 974-90. For a British comparison, see Patricia Sykes, *Losing from the Inside* (New Brunswick, N.J.: Transaction Books, 1988).

35. CBS News poll, October 1987.

3

The Campaign and the Media

MARJORIE RANDON HERSHEY

It was 24 July 1988, three days after Michael Dukakis accepted his party's nomination to run for President. His acceptance speech had been electrifying. With it, he took command of a convention that Jesse Jackson had captivated for three days. "Michael Dukakis brought it off," announced the editorial page of the *Washington Post,* using terms such as "stirring," "formidable," and even "genius." "The question after [the Democratic convention in] Atlanta," the *Post* concluded, "is whether [Vice-President] George Bush can get *his* act together."[1]

In a brief story in the same day's edition of the *Post,* however, lay a small seed of doubt about Dukakis's "formidable" prospects. Bush, the reporter wrote, was planning a major assault charging that Dukakis was soft on crime. The attack would focus on Dukakis's support for weekend furloughs for prison inmates, a program the Massachusetts governor had inherited from his predecessor. One beneficiary of this program, a black man named Willie Horton who had been convicted of first-degree murder, had escaped to Maryland while on weekend pass, brutalized a white man and raped his fiancee. Bush would use Willie Horton as the symbol of his claim that Dukakis was not tough enough on crime.

The Dukakis campaign was preparing itself aggressively for the charge, said the *Post,* quoting several Democratic state attorneys general. "Bush will try and create problems—pushing a few emotional buttons on crime," said Iowa Attorney-General Tom Miller. But Dukakis had an "impressive" record of reducing the crime rate in Massachusetts, Miller pointed out. That record would surely render Bush's attacks weak and ineffective.[2]

By 8 November, as Bush's campaign manager Lee Atwater had planned, Willie Horton had become almost as much of a household name as Michael Dukakis.

The Strategic Environment of the Campaign

Political campaigns are planned and executed within an environment: a set of existing national conditions, institutions, and personalities. That environment puts constraints on campaigners' choices. The challenge for the campaigners is to call attention to and make use of those elements of the environment that help their cause, and to downplay or redefine the elements that threaten their success.

In these terms, there were two presidential campaigns in 1988: the one that took place from the end of the primaries until the Republican convention in August, and the one that began during the convention and lasted until election day. In the first campaign, the Presidency seemed to be Michael Dukakis's to lose; in the second, it was George Bush's to win. The two campaigns faced the same strategic environment. A big difference between them was the media campaign that reshaped the image of George Bush.

Almost all the elements of the strategic environment in 1988 favored a Republican victory. Ronald Reagan, with whom Bush closely associated himself, continued to be popular with voters. In the summer of 1988 the world was, relatively speaking, at peace.

Perhaps most important, Bush had been in office at a time of economic recovery. The economic statistics—all but the size of the federal deficit, that is—were looking better than they had in the memory of large numbers of voters. The economy seemed particularly robust to young voters, whose experience in national politics was limited to the Reagan and Carter years. In November 1980, at the close of Jimmy Carter's term, unemployment stood at 7.5 percent; in June 1988, the unemployment rate was 5.3 percent, the lowest in fourteen years. Inflation was under control; the consumer price index rose 13.5 percent in 1980, but only 4.0 percent from August 1987 to the time of the Republican convention in August 1988. "If you cranked all this into a computer," one Republican political analyst said in August, "it would tell you the Republicans can't lose."[3] In fact, in election years since the Second World War when the nation was prosperous and at peace, the incumbent party has rarely lost.

Another powerful environmental force working for Bush was the so-called Republican lock on the electoral college. The general election is in reality a set of fifty state elections held on the same day. Under these rules, the Republican party has built a clear and continuing advantage in recent presidential races. Although more voters consider themselves Democrats than Republicans, Republican nominees won four of the five presidential elections leading up to 1988, three of them by impressive margins.

The magnitude of the Republican advantage can be seen in the figure on the inside front cover of this book. Twenty-three states cast their electoral votes for the Republican candidate in every one of those five presidential races. These states, most of them west of the Mississippi, have a combined total of 202 electoral votes, only 68 short of the number George Bush needed to win. Another thirteen states, with 152 electoral votes among them, went Republican in four of the five races.

The only voting unit to go Democratic in all five elections was the District of Columbia, with its 3 electoral votes. A mere six states voted Democratic in a majority of the five races: Hawaii, Maryland, Massachusetts, Minnesota, Rhode Island, and West Virginia. So, if recent history serves as a guide, the Democrats came into 1988 favored in areas with only 50 electoral votes.[4]

It was not always this way. During the era of President Franklin Roosevelt (1932-48), the Democratic party won 82 percent of the electoral votes. In the period from 1968 to 1984, Democratic presidential candidates were held to 21 percent. The decline occurred in every region of the country, but most dramatically in the South and West. In the southern states, the Democratic percentage of the electoral votes dropped from 95 percent in the Roosevelt era to 22 percent in the recent period, and from 94 percent to an incredible 4 percent in the West.[5] Dukakis strategists, reading these numbers, could be forgiven if they were tempted to consider another line of work.

The electoral college works for the Republicans in another way as well. It overrepresents states with small populations. And in recent electoral history, since the South and West became Republican strongholds, Republican presidential candidates have swept the small states.

One reason for this Republican dominance is that the most potent symbolic issues in recent American politics have favored Republican presidential candidates.[6] Partly as the result of changes in the national Democratic party's leadership and appeals since the early 1960s, Republicans at the national level have been able to put their political copyright on symbols such as family, strong national defense, tough punishment of criminals, and even displays of patriotism.[7]

The strategic environment, in short, gave powerful advantages to the Republican candidate. How, then, could anyone have expected George Bush to lose? One answer is that despite all the good economic news, there was a lingering sense of unease about the staying power of the economic recovery, made more palpable by the events of mid-October 1987. Many Americans took their first plunge into the stock market in 1987, enticed by the dizzying rise in stock prices. The Dow-Jones industrial average, which began the year with a value of 1927, soared to an all-time high of 2722 in late August. Just two months later, the bottom dropped out. The Dow fell more than 500 points in a single day, resulting in the loss of $500 billion in capital—on paper, at least. It was the worst stock market crash since the Great Depression. Months later, the market seemed to be back on an upward, if bumpy, climb. But for many people, the romance of the heady economic recovery had chilled. The darker suspicion remained that present prosperity might contain the basis of its own undoing. The media focused increasingly on two worrisome economic indicators: the biggest trade and federal budget deficits in the nation's history. The U.S. trade deficit rose sharply in August 1988, and was expected to surpass $120 billion by the end of the year. The budget deficit cast an even bigger shadow. In the words of one writer, "In part because politicians in Washington doubled the national debt to a once-unimaginable $2.7 trillion in the 1980s, the world's biggest lender nation has become the biggest borrower, leaving control of its destiny exposed to the whims of foreign creditors."[8]

The Democrats hoped that voters would be swayed by their concerns about an uncertain economic future, by the fear that the two big deficits could lead to economic disaster for their children, rather than by their satisfaction with the recent past. The same hope had driven the Democratic presidential campaign in 1984. But it required the nominee to make a persuasive argument; the impact of the deficits was not nearly as easy for voters to see or imagine as was the tangible, daily effect of lower inflation and unemployment. And it was a hope that flew in the face of research showing that people tend to vote retrospectively: on the basis of their evaluation of the incumbent administration's recent record, not its likely future.[9]

Perhaps the biggest reason why Democrats were optimistic about winning the Presidency, however, despite all the environmental forces working against them, was their confident expectation that the Republican candidate would self-destruct. Bush's support in his own party appeared to be broad but shallow. In contrast to Ronald Reagan, Bush inspired little emotional fervor, little depth of ideological commitment. One measure of Bush's apparent weakness was that although he was the logical Republican nominee—the second-in-command to one of the most popular Republican Presidents of all time, with a substantial campaign war chest and a big lead in the polls over his rivals for the nomination —he still drew five opponents in the early primaries and caucuses.

Part of the problem was that George Bush had served seven years in the vice-presidency. The office gave him widespread name recognition and a certain amount of media attention, largely in ceremonial situations. But it also put him in the President's shadow. It is difficult for vice-presidents to demonstrate the independence and toughness that Americans normally value in a presidential candidate. That may help explain why the last person elected President directly from the vice-presidency was Martin Van Buren in 1836. Adding to the difficulty was the contrast between the larger-than-life figure of Ronald Reagan, viewed by some supporters with a reverence that bordered on the religious, and the wimpy, preppy, insubstantial, occasionally silly image that dogged Bush.

Even after Super Tuesday, when he effectively captured the Republican nomination, George Bush remained an elusive figure to most voters. He had not staked out any particular issue as his own, nor could he call any particular constituency in the Republican party "his people." He was New England born and raised, with a home in Maine, yet he referred to himself as a Texan, the state to which he had moved in the 1940s but in which he now maintained as "residence" only a rented hotel suite. He was a scion of wealth, a Yale Phi Beta Kappa and fraternity man, who complained that media people were not reporting his love for country music and pork rinds. He claimed to be a true conservative, yet as recently as 1980 he had campaigned as a relative moderate. In a word, he did not seem authentic. As one speaker at the Democratic convention put it, deriding Bush's claim to be a Texan, the vice-president was "all hat and no cattle."

Bush had other political handicaps as well. He was viewed as too far removed from the lives of working people to be able to understand their concerns. His role in the Iran-*Contra* scandal was suspicious but not yet clear. There were accusations that Bush had worked with and helped Panama's strongman General Manuel Antonio Noriega, even though he knew of Noriega's drug-smuggling activities to the United States.

Then there were Bush's idiosyncracies as a public speaker. Several of his more off-the-wall comments had been widely quoted, including his speculation that Bush supporters in Iowa had failed to show up for a straw poll because they were attending debutante parties. In the words of Dukakis's pollster, "George Bush simply doesn't seem presidential to a majority of American voters."[10] After two Reagan campaigns, Bush looked like easy pickings.

For the Democrats to capitalize on Bush's apparent weaknesses, they needed a strong and attractive candidate. One of Michael Dukakis's great strengths was that he was perceived to be a moderate Democrat, unlike three of his recent predecessors who had gone down in flames in presidential elections as self-described liberals. But part of the credit for Dukakis's image as a moderate was due to Jesse Jackson. When he emerged as Dukakis's main rival in the primaries, Jackson's ideology and flamboyant personal style made the Massachusetts governor look moderate by contrast—a perception that Dukakis encouraged.

Dukakis made every effort to claim the label "conservative" for himself. He compared his record as a budget balancer in Massachusetts with the Reagan administration's succession of deficits. He argued that because he wanted to conserve natural resources, as against Bush's earlier enthusiasm for offshore oil drilling, it was he, Dukakis, who was the true conservative.

The effort was less successful once Jackson was out of the presidential race and Dukakis was being compared with the obviously more conservative George Bush. As columnist George Will said in early June, "The premise of the Bush campaign is that many people west of the Berkshires think that only two things come from Massachusetts, liberals and lobsters, and pretty soon they're going to wake up and say, 'That's not a lobster.' "[11]

Another of Dukakis's strong points during the nomination season would also turn on him later. Like George Bush, even after the primaries ended, Dukakis had not yet defined himself clearly to large numbers of Americans. He was viewed favorably in May by almost three times as many people as had unfavorable impressions of him, but those favorable ratings were buttressed by very little information about his record or his proposals.[12] That may have helped him gain support in the primaries. But it left him vulnerable to being defined by his Republican opponent, rather than by his own efforts.

Two things were clear about Dukakis's style as a campaigner. For one, his approach to his audiences was cool, unemotional, cerebral, even bland, to the extent that a *Newsweek* writer termed him "the Mr. Spock of politics, a totally rational alien bemused by the passions around him."[13] He preferred immersion in the details of government programs to the sweaty excitement of working a campaign crowd. His aides felt that their boss's managerial temper was a real advantage. Voters had had enough of charisma after eight years of Ronald Reagan, they argued. Now the public wanted competence.

Second, Dukakis marched to his own drummer. He did not believe in attack politics. Even when he seemed to be losing the nomination race in Illinois and Michigan, he resisted making major changes in his campaign. He would not adopt a style with which he was uncomfortable.

This was the strategic environment. Yet in this "first campaign," media coverage paid little attention to the many Republican advantages in the presidential race. Media coverage characteristically ignores the stable elements of the campaign environment. It focused instead, as the media normally do, on the strange and unexpected: in this case, a moderate Democratic nominee, of quiet confidence and nonideological approach, leading his Republican opponent in all the polls.

Candidates' Game Plans: Learning from 1984

Every campaign is fought with the last election in mind. Even before an election is over, reporters and participants begin to try out explanations as to why the likely winner will prevail and the likely loser will fail. Once the returns are in, a more intense effort takes place to explain what the voters meant. These explanations might be constructed from voting returns or exit poll data, or simply from insiders' beliefs about what worked and what didn't. Soon after election day, a small number of these constructed explanations emerge as the most plausible. After much repetition in the media, these explanations take on the dignity of "established fact" and guide campaigners in the next race for that office as they make their strategic decisions.[14]

The most widely repeated "established fact" about the 1984 presidential race was that Walter Mondale, the loser by a landslide, was crippled by his proposal to raise taxes. As Mondale ruefully admitted in 1988, "I taught a whole generation of politicians how to handle the tax issue: to not mention it."[15] The entire cast of the next campaign had learned that lesson perfectly. The word "taxes" never passed Michael Dukakis's lips without being followed quickly by the words "last resort." George Bush took the logical next step. In a one-liner he would repeat almost daily during the fall, Bush said in his acceptance speech at the Republican convention, "Read my lips: NO . . . NEW . . . TAXES."[16]

Another accepted explanation for the 1984 Reagan landslide was that Mondale and the Democrats were seen as captives of special interests: organized labor, blacks, feminists, gays. The flip side of this explanation was that the Democrats had turned their backs on the middle class, on "mainstream" white America. A majority of this group, including large numbers who considered themselves Democrats, voted for Reagan in 1984. As a result, these so-called Reagan Democrats and the groups to which they belonged—ethnic, working-class voters; moderate-income families who felt they were barely getting by economically; members of the baby-boom generation who were not well-off enough to call themselves Yuppies—became the prime targets of the Dukakis campaign.

Beginning with his acceptance speech at the Democratic convention, Dukakis aimed his appeals at the Reagan Democrats. In many ways it was a Reaganesque approach: one that stressed values rather than specific policy proposals. The Democrats, wrote David Broder, "know from their polling that at the end of the eight-year Reagan cycle, a theoretical majority supports 'change.' They also know that a majority disappears if the direction of change gets specific enough to have substantive, ideological content."[17]

So the values Dukakis expressed were those of character, leadership, and integrity. He aimed to contrast doubts about Bush's abilities and leadership skills with his own experience as a competent chief executive. He intended to hit hard at Bush's ties to the Iran-*Contra* and Noriega scandals, and to refer

also to the "sleaze factor," the long series of Reagan appointees who had enriched themselves at public expense or otherwise been guided by questionable
ethical standards.

He linked himself to the values of family and community by telling the
story of his immigrant father's voyage to the United States and his effort to
bring his children into the American dream of opportunity and upward mobility.
Dukakis's references to issues, too, involved concerns of the struggling middle
class: the problems families face in paying for housing, health care, day care
and college costs for their children. He charged that under Reagan, the rich
have gotten richer, the poor poorer, and the middle class has been squeezed.
Dukakis would use these themes to voice the anxieties many Reagan Democrats
felt about the future, even if they believed themselves to be coping in the present.

Many in the party's liberal wing would have called for extensive government spending to help remedy these problems. But in a time of massive deficits,
hints of more government social spending would raise the specter of new taxes.
Dukakis took a different road. He avoided making a lot of promises. He would
make the federal government the agent of several new programs for low- and
middle-income families, but it would be business and state and local governments that would pick up most of the tab. This partnership approach had been
used frequently by Dukakis in developing programs as governor of Massachusetts.

With these appeals, Dukakis hoped to win back the Democrats who had
strayed from their party in recent presidential elections. The choice of Texas
Senator Lloyd Bentsen as his vice-presidential running mate was integral to that
strategy. Bentsen was substantially more conservative than Dukakis. Media reaction to his nomination often focused critically on the issue differences between the two men. They held contrasting views on the Reagan tax cuts, gun
control, the death penalty, aid to the *Contras* in Nicaragua, mandatory school
prayer, the MX missile, and Reagan's "Star Wars" proposal. But that was the
point: The choice of Bentsen was a message to southern whites and other conservative Democrats that Michael Dukakis was attentive to their concerns.

Bentsen's nomination was a message to George Bush, too. It challenged
Bush personally: Bentsen had beaten Bush eighteen years earlier in one of Bush's
two tries for elective office. It prompted media references to another "Boston-
Austin axis"—the fact that Bostonian John F. Kennedy won the White House
in 1960 (from another incumbent vice-president) with a Texas senator as his
running mate. And it forced Bush to put more campaign resources into a region
—the South—that he would otherwise have been tempted to take for granted.

The choice of Bentsen did not indicate that Dukakis would make a quixotic attempt to win back the South for his party. Another of the widely ac-

cepted explanations for the 1984 Reagan victory was that Walter Mondale had unwisely run a fully national campaign, without first having secured his natural Democratic base in the northeastern and midwestern states. The Dukakis campaign planned a more carefully targeted "frostbelt" strategy. The intention was to win most of the eastern states (for about 100 electoral votes), add the big states of the industrial Midwest (for another 100), and pick up the rest of the needed electoral votes in California and other Pacific Coast states. If Bentsen could help gather electoral votes in the South, so much the better.

George Bush faced a very different task. First and foremost, he was down in the polls. In May, Bush was running ten points behind Dukakis. Surveys reported that more people held unfavorable opinions of Bush than had favorable opinions of him.[18] Bush did not have the appeal to middle-income Americans that had fueled Ronald Reagan's electoral success. If Dukakis were able to sustain his lead among Reagan Democrats, Bush would probably lose the election.

But researchers have found that voters do not make their choices solely on the basis of candidate evaluation, nor are they solely driven by partisanship. Instead, voters respond to the political stimuli they receive. If a candidate presents a compelling set of issue appeals, then issues are likely to take on increasing importance in voters' decisions.[19] The right issues, then, could help voters forget their dislike for Bush. The challenge for Bush's handlers was to find the right issues.

Before Memorial Day, Bush staffers assembled two small groups of Reagan Democrats in New Jersey, all Dukakis supporters, to try out a series of possible campaign themes. In these "focus groups," researchers for the Bush campaign presented material on several "hot button" social issues. When the presentation ended, half of the thirty focus group members changed their vote preference to George Bush. The Bush staff felt they had struck gold.[20]

The first of these issues, curiously enough, was the Pledge of Allegiance. As governor, Dukakis vetoed a bill requiring Massachusetts teachers to lead their students in the Pledge daily. The bill was clearly unconstitutional, Dukakis argued.[21] But for many of the focus group members, Dukakis's response was beside the point. For them, the importance of the Pledge as a patriotic symbol overrode more complicated First Amendment considerations. Bush's advisers had gotten their hands on a powerful symbolic issue that opened up some soft spots on Dukakis. It raised concerns that he was an eastern elitist who disdained public demonstrations of patriotism. It reminded some listeners of their suspicion that liberal internationalists, who had opposed American involvement in the Vietnam war and criticized the use of American military force elsewhere, would not defend their homeland as vigorously as would other

Americans. It underscored the hazards of Dukakis's cool and cerebral style: that he was not very skilled at connecting emotionally with an audience.

Another issue that scored heavily with the focus groups was the Massachusetts prisoner furlough program, as represented by the brutal Willie Horton. So did the news that Dukakis had described himself as a card-carrying member of the American Civil Liberties Union (ACLU), a group that has long defended unpopular causes in the legal system. So did Bush's contention (though inaccurate) that Dukakis opposed every new weapons system.

The outlines of a strategy were emerging from this meeting: one that could promise a Bush breakthrough among the much-sought-after Reagan Democrats. Its purpose was to define Dukakis to the voters before he was able, or willing, to define himself. The definition would be that Dukakis was a liberal in the mold of Walter Mondale, Jimmy Carter, and George McGovern. He would be labeled an economic liberal, favoring higher taxes and bigger government, to tie him to the economic miseries of the Carter administration. Don't risk the current economic prosperity, Bush's campaign would argue, by electing a liberal.

Dukakis would also be defined as a liberal on defense. Because he favored a nuclear freeze in the early 1980s and opposed some new weapons, he would be described as even more antimilitary than previous Democratic presidential candidates. Bush would charge that Dukakis was naive in foreign policy matters, too willing to trust the Soviets. Reagan used that appeal with apparent success in 1984, claiming the Democrats are "so far left, they've left America."

Even more, the Bush staff intended to define Dukakis as a social liberal: overly concerned with the rights of criminals, unconcerned with other people's fears of crime, happy to defend any group or belief, no matter how objectionable to the majority. These symbolic, populist themes had been used very effectively by Republican candidates since the late 1960s as a means of separating blue-collar voters from their Democratic ties and encouraging them to vote against their likely economic interest—one of many examples of the muting of class divisions in American politics.

In view of Dukakis's positive ratings in the polls, it was clear that this strategy would require the Republicans to go on the attack. That was a risky decision. Conventional wisdom teaches that candidates who use negative or attack messages are often seen by voters as unpleasant, lacking a positive program, and therefore unworthy of support. That is why candidates who find themselves behind are likely to use surrogates—political allies who are not running for anything—to spread the negative message. But Bush's advisers felt that their candidate was in a unique position to benefit by waging his own relentless attack. Not only would such a strategy call attention to Bush's definition of

Dukakis, it would also help erase the image, prevalent in media coverage, that Bush was a wimp, a lap dog, a weak man in Reagan's shadow. The Democrats would now find, Bush claimed, that they had engaged a couple of pit bulls.

The Bush assault on Dukakis began in May. In this "first campaign," the plan did not seem to be working as well as Bush's strategists had hoped. George Will wrote in July, "In the two months he has spent pointing at Dukakis and exclaiming, 'Eeeeek!—a liberal!,' the percentage of Americans identifying Dukakis as a liberal has risen from 27 to 28 percent."[22] Dukakis's lead in the polls had not shrunk much, nor had voters' attitudes toward Bush improved.

Nevertheless, some change was taking place. By July, some polls were measuring a decrease in favorable opinions of Dukakis and an increase in unfavorable opinions (see chapter 4). In addition, Bush's charges and his no-new-taxes pledge had the advantage of cementing his appeal to the "hard right" in the Republican party, which had long suspected Bush of being a pragmatist rather than a true conservative. That allowed the vice-president to campaign free from sniping on his right flank. It also gave him the freedom to take more moderate positions, intended to preempt Dukakis, on issues such as education, day care, and the environment.

Taking advantage of that freedom, Bush honed the second of the two personas that would characterize his general election campaign. In his acceptance speech at the Republican convention, he sounded the theme of a "kinder, gentler nation." It was meant to reassure voters, women in particular, who were finding the new George Bush alarming.

Bush's advertising was carefully designed to convey these two simple messages. One was to paint Michael Dukakis as an out-of-the-mainstream liberal with a soft spot in his heart for criminals, high taxes, and unilateral cuts in national defense. The other was to show George Bush as a gentle family man who could be trusted. "And every day, there's a photo opportunity and sound bite to reenforce the first message and a photo op and sound bite to reenforce the second. And everything they do fits into one of those two messages."[23]

It was a meticulously planned strategy. And it was a measure of Bush's trust in his handlers that he did not deviate from it, even in the weeks between the two parties' conventions when Dukakis was running way ahead.

By the opening of the Republican convention, the renaissance of George Bush was under way. Once Ronald Reagan had given his valedictory and left the convention for home, as a Republican consultant put it, Bush "shed his vice-presidential skin."[24] His astonished advisers found him to be more aggressive, more self-confident, more relaxed, more purposeful. He would need it; a big storm lay ahead.

QUAYLE UNDER GLASS

The choice of a vice-presidential nominee is important for several reasons. It is the presidential candidate's first big decision after being nominated, so it will be taken as a measure of his judgment. Is the running mate capable of performing well as President if the need should occur? In fact the need has occurred fairly often in American history; of the thirty-nine Presidents from Washington to Reagan, nine were vice-presidents who took office after the death or resignation of their running mate.

But the primary calculation in selecting a vice-presidential candidate is electoral. Can the candidate bring in one big state or demographic group that the presidential candidate is not likely to win without help? The immediate task, after all, is to win; governing comes later.

Indiana Senator Dan Quayle's function on the Republican ticket was to reassure conservatives, appeal to the Reagan Democrats in the baby-boom generation, and enable George Bush, at the age of sixty-four, to talk about the future. Quayle, a mediagenic forty-one-year-old, was introduced by Bush at a press conference as a "man for the future," a phrase repeated by virtually every other Republican leader interviewed at the national convention.

It was the past that proved troublesome for Quayle. He had spent four undistinguished years in the House of Representatives, known largely for the long hours he spent on the golf course, followed by eight somewhat less undistinguished years in the Senate. He had not been identified with much legislation, with the exception of the Job Training Partnership Act that he coauthored with Edward Kennedy, one of the Senate's leading liberal Democrats.[25]

Nor had he been prepared for big-league media scrutiny. Almost immediately after he was introduced as Bush's choice, the story broke that in 1969 Quayle had apparently pulled strings, through associates of his wealthy family, to get into the National Guard and avoid active service in Vietnam. That was certainly the aim of many young men at the time, but it struck some as hypocritical in Quayle's case because of his outspoken support of American involvement in Vietnam and his right-wing views. Quayle at first demurred, then later admitted that calls had been made on his behalf.

Soon after, newspapers reported that Quayle, who had a mediocre record in college, had evidently been admitted to law school because of family connections as well; he lacked the usual academic credentials for admission. Again, his responses to his media questioners were bumbling, often angry, and at times even suggestive of panic.

The specifics of the charges were not as influential as the general impression they created: that Quayle was a lightweight who had gotten where he was because of his privileged background, and who lacked the maturity and judgment expected in someone who could be a heartbeat away from the Presidency. By extension, the stories also cast doubt on George Bush's judgment. Republican consultants were horrified that the growing controversy was deflecting attention away from Bush's long-awaited emergence as an effective candidate. In the words of pollster Harrison Hickman, Bush "did a good job of getting out of Ronald Reagan's shadow. Now he has to find a way to get out of Dan Quayle's."[26]

Bush's campaign responded by assailing the bearers of the bad news. It was a "media feeding frenzy," Bush said, an unfair effort to pillory a young man. To dramatize that claim, Quayle's first press conference after the convention was a carefully crafted media event in his home town, Huntington, Indiana, with about 6000 supporters present to cheer his answers and howl down reporters' questions. Quayle himself charged that media people were impugning the patriotism of millions of Americans who had been National Guard members.

Michael Dukakis's reaction, typically, was low-key. He did not criticize Quayle's qualifications. Characteristically, he emphasized the positive. No one has questioned Lloyd Bentsen's ability to serve as President, he said. Voters should ask themselves whether Bush or Dukakis made the more presidential judgment. Dukakis's staff was euphoric over the controversy. "The election's over," one staffer exulted when the choice of Quayle was announced.

The New George Bush: Attack Politics and the Pledge of Allegiance

But it was far from over. In fact, despite the uproar over Quayle, George Bush's prospects were clearly on the rise by the end of August. The start of the Bush media campaign, dominated by negative ads, trashed the "first campaign" and ushered in the second. After so many weeks of seeming ineffective, he finally succeeded in setting the agenda and campaigning on his issues.

The fall media campaign opened with Bush attacking Dukakis on the Pledge of Allegiance. Bush had ended his acceptance speech by leading his audience in the Pledge. He did so frequently in campaign appearances, saying, "I believe that our schoolchildren should have the right to say the Pledge of Allegiance . . . I don't know what his problem is with the Pledge."[27]

Foreign observers might find it puzzling that the Pledge of Allegiance, so thoroughly accepted by Americans, could ever become a big issue in a presidential campaign. The Pledge falls into the category of "valence issues": those on which a great majority of citizens agree. To most politicians, the best way to deal with a valence issue is to get on the right side of it, quickly and very publicly, and stay there.

But Michael Dukakis was a lawyer, surrounded by lawyers, who were incredulous that any intelligent American would fall for such an appeal. Dukakis therefore made no effort to deal with it as a valence issue. Instead, he responded, lawyer-like, that Bush would not make a very good President if he proposed to sign an obviously unconstitutional bill. Even some conservatives also found the Pledge campaign offensive. Columnist William Safire, for instance, wrote with disdain that Bush "throws red meat to the Yahoos" on this issue.[28]

Bush's advisers, in contrast, were gleeful. Dukakis had taken the bait, leaving the field during the battle of patriotism. According to Gallup polls after a similar exchange in the first presidential debate, voters sided with Bush three to one on the Pledge issue, and nearly one-third had a lowered opinion of Dukakis because of it. Said former Democratic national chair Robert Strauss, "Dukakis made a major mistake— he got into an election debate on the subject. He captured the hearts of seventeen lawyers and lost three million voters."[29]

The largest number of Bush ads, however, dealt with the Massachusetts prison furlough program. The most memorable of these ads showed zombie-like prisoners milling through revolving doors. The voice-over intoned that Dukakis's policy was to allow weekend passes to first-degree murderers who were not even eligible for parole, and that many had escaped while on furlough. Later, independent groups supporting Bush aired several powerful television ads on this issue, including one featuring the victims of Willie Horton's crime spree.

The ads drew criticism for a lack of fairness. Most states have prisoner furlough programs, and murders have occurred as a result, including one in California during Ronald Reagan's terms as governor and in the federal furlough program while Bush was vice-president. Dukakis excluded first-degree murderers from the Massachusetts program after the Willie Horton scandal. Ironically, the crime rate had dropped sharply in Massachusetts since 1982. In addition, neither the Pledge of Allegiance nor Willie Horton was involved with any policy question the federal government deals with. Controlling crime, for instance, is a responsibility mainly of state and local governments.

But Dukakis and his staff failed to see how well these symbolic themes resonated with Reagan Democrats and other target groups of voters. A senior Bush adviser explained, "An election campaign is in part a national tribal ritual, a rite of renewal, and if you don't respond in a way that says you know it, you send a subliminal signal to people that you are really outside the mainstream culture. . . . [On] the ACLU and furlough [issues] . . . Dukakis allowed himself to be defined as the kind of liberal who would use the legal system to protect aberrant behavior, rather than stamp it out."[30]

By reinforcing Reagan Democrats' concerns about liberalism, the ads forced Dukakis to react to Bush's initiatives rather than set his own agenda. The impact was quick to be felt in the polls, as well as in media commentary. Coming from a double-digit deficit in early August, Bush had pulled ahead of Dukakis by the end of that month. For the first time in the campaign, more people had a favorable than an unfavorable opinion of George Bush.[31]

By the second week in September, controlled panic had set in among Dukakis's staff. With the exception of Dan Quayle's nomination, there had been little good news for almost a month. Throughout that time the campaign had been pounded by what one writer called a "Niagara Falls of negative attacks, a 'slur du jour' since August that has pummeled Dukakis's lead. . . . It's about as subtle as the now legendary 1950 Florida Senate campaign when George Smathers accused his opponent of being a 'thespian.' Call it the Big Lie technique."[32]

Dukakis was getting a lot of advice. Most of it was sharply critical of his failure to respond aggressively to the volley of Bush charges. Dukakis had been warned by his pollsters that the "red meat" issues were strongly affecting people in focus groups. Several Democratic senators who had previously run in 1980 and 1982, years when they were the target of negative campaigns, cautioned that unanswered smears are often believed. But Dukakis refused to respond in kind. At his core, Dukakis was a cautious man, a reformer trained in the suburban good-government tradition of Brookline, Massachusetts. He opposed negative campaigning, and he was committed to running on his own issues.

Even if Dukakis had wanted to react with attacks of his own, there is some question whether his staff would have been able to organize as meticulously well planned an effort as Bush's advisers had. The Dukakis staff, like their candidate, was composed mainly of very bright Bostonians with little experience in national politics. They did not make extensive use of the help and advice volunteered to the campaign by seasoned Democrats across the nation. The Dukakis headquarters soon had the reputation of being insular, arrogant, and aloof.

Even worse, the lines of authority within the campaign were unclear. A lot of television ads were written, but until late in September there seemed to be no one person with the authority to decide which would be produced and aired. As a result, there was no step-by-step plan or overarching theme to the Dukakis advertising. First the campaign ran ads aimed at blue-collar and lower-middle-class voters, stating that the much-touted prosperity of the Reagan years had passed them by. Then came a series of more complex ads, which were apparently widely misunderstood, purporting to show cynical Bush strategists packaging their candidate. One Washington Democrat commented, "The bumbling, ineffectual George Bush the Dukakis campaign planned to run against suddenly disappeared. When he disappeared, the whole Dukakis strategy disappeared."[33]

Dukakis's message was also being upstaged by another Democrat. Jesse Jackson, one of Dukakis's greatest advantages in positioning himself as a moderate in the primaries, became another of Dukakis's serious problems in the early fall. The dilemma was how to avoid seeming too close to Jackson and too responsive to his concerns (and thus risk being labeled as "captive of special interests"), and at the same time obtain Jackson's enthusiastic efforts for the ticket among black voters. Ever since the nomination of Lloyd Bentsen, which, to one reporter, hit Jackson and his supporters "like a car bomb,"[34] the question of Jackson's feelings about Dukakis had been an ongoing theme in media coverage. Even after a mid-September meeting held to harmonize their differences, reporters continued to watch closely for signs of estrangement.

The Bush campaign offered a sharp contrast. The top echelon was very experienced—Bush's media adviser, Roger Ailes, had been a master of attack politics since Richard Nixon's 1968 campaign—and after James A. Baker III came on as chairman in late August, highly organized. It was an old story. In every recent presidential election, the Republicans have been able to assemble a professional, battle-tested set of campaign advisers, media people, pollsters, and organizers. " 'They press a button and all the best talent pops up,' said Bob Strauss. 'Our nominee presses a button and we get a bunch of very bright, very intelligent young people who have to reinvent the wheel.' "[35]

Center Stage: The Debates

Michael Dukakis had lost center stage in the campaign when the Republican convention began in August, and had never regained it. Since then, prospective voters had seen him mainly through the distorted lens of the Bush ad campaign. The first presidential debate, held the evening of 25 September in Winston-Salem, North Carolina, promised an audience of 100 million people. To the Dukakis staff, it offered hope: a means of putting his campaign back on track. Dukakis was an articulate and quick speaker; Bush, normally, was not. It was Dukakis's main chance to undo the damage the Republican ads had done, to prove that he was no wild-eyed liberal, and to make his own case on issues.

Bush had a mission of at least equal importance. He needed to flesh out both of his campaign personas: the "kinder, gentler" George Bush and the liberal-bashing pit bull. But he also had to sustain the belief that a new, more presidential George Bush had emerged. To do so meant avoiding the old, gaffe-filled "Bushspeak," showing himself to be on top of issues, and projecting a calm and masterful image. That was more easily done in the controlled environment of a media ad than in response to reporters' questions on live television.

Though the candidates saw these debates as make-or-break events, social scientists disagree as to whether presidential debates have much influence on voters.[36] When a candidate stresses the same themes and demonstrates the same personal style in the debate that he or she has shown throughout the earlier months of the race, then the effect may be simply to reinforce viewers' existing opinions. But there are opportunities for greater impact: when one or both candidates act out of character or say something unintended, when one candidate is not yet well known, and among viewers who were not paying attention to the campaign before. In other words, the debates matter when they teach some voters something new about a candidate.

In this case, the debate offered little new learning. Both candidates succeeded in following their own long-standing scripts, often with only minimal relationship to the reporters' questions. A content analysis of the debate transcripts (see table 3.1 on page 90) shows that Dukakis placed much heavier stress than Bush on the issues of health care, drugs, and housing—issues of great public concern on which Dukakis had long argued that Reagan policies had failed. On health care, for example, the Democrat charged that the Reagan-Bush administration had done nothing to help the 37 million Americans who could not afford health insurance. His own proposal would require most businesses to insure their employees—the kind of government-business partnership he had instigated in Massachusetts. Bush's response, equally characteristic, was that such a requirement would cost business too much and risk losing jobs. A better answer, he said, was to let low-income people pay a fee to join the existing Medicaid program.

Dukakis also hit Bush hard on the issue of the federal deficit, in answer to a variety of questions. Bush, a Reagan convert to supply-side economics, had proposed a tax cut for capital gains — income from assets such as stocks and tax shelters, held mainly by the wealthy. This tax break, he argued, would encourage them to invest more, generate new jobs, and in turn increase tax collections. Dukakis claimed that if Bush said he could cut taxes for the wealthy, fund all the weapons systems the Pentagon asked for, and pay for social programs as well, he'd be "the Joe Isuzu of American politics." The one-liner was new; the theme was not.

With respect to symbolism, Dukakis's answers were studded with references to the themes with which he had begun his campaign: leadership, strength, family, opportunity for the hard-pressed middle class. His record number of

TABLE 3.1

CANDIDATES' USE OF ISSUES AND SYMBOLS IN THE PRESIDENTIAL DEBATES

Number of Mentions	First Debate		Second Debate	
	Bush	Dukakis	Bush	Dukakis
Domestic Policy Issues				
Health care, health insurance	3	22	0	6
Drugs, drug programs	8	24	2	10
Housing, homeless	8	23	0	5
National debt/deficit	2	11	3	12
Education, schools	19	8	3	3
Foreign Policy, Defense				
Weapons, weapons systems	18	19	8	20
Nuclear freeze	4	3	6	0
Unilateral cuts in defense	4	1	4	1
Modernization of weapons	2	0	6	3
Symbols				
Leadership, leaders, lead	3	23	5	11
Children, young people, next generation	12	27	13	21
Strength/strong	4	19	4	11
Family/families	3	20	8	4
Opportunity	3	13	1	7
Pledge of Allegiance	2	2	0	0
Optimistic	1	1	3	1
Furloughs (of prisoners)	5	2	0	0
Republicans	3	0	5	5
Police	3	0	2	0
Experience	3	6	4	2
ACLU (American Civil Liberties Union)	4	0	2	0
Peace	6	1	6	1
Democrats	4	0	11	3
Liberals, liberalism, left	12	0	13	9

SOURCE: Debate transcripts, *Congressional Quarterly Weekly Report* 46 (1 and 15 October 1988): 2743-53, 3005-15.

mentions of "children," "youngsters," and the "next generation" included a series of stories about young people and their families struggling to deal with problems of health insurance, drugs, and college costs.

The symbols Bush stressed, as the data show, were carefully coordinated with those playing in his television ads: prison furloughs, police, the ACLU, peace, and above all, liberalism. Early in the debate, in rebuttal to a question on Dukakis's leadership, Bush asked, "Do we want this country to go that far left?" That line lingered after the debate as the primary message of Bush's "spin controllers"— staff members and allies working to influence the way reporters interpreted the outcome.

Polls and commentary immediately after the debate called it a draw or gave a slight edge to Dukakis. But within two or three days, a consensus had formed that Dukakis was the winner on points. He had kept Bush on the defensive, the consensus said, by detailing particular domestic problems (health insurance, for example) and offering specific programs to address them. He was somewhat weaker in the area of defense.

Yet Dukakis's "victory" in the debate did not translate into a lasting gain in the polls. The main reason was that he had not given most viewers new information about his strengths. And stylistically, he had confirmed one major weakness. His demeanor as he scored these debating points was serious, even grim. His message—that the economic recovery was uneven and the deficit was a threat—could easily be portrayed as one of doom and gloom, an image heightened by what reporters called his "eat your peas" look.

In an age dominated by Reagan's warm, relaxed style, the rather aloof and unemotional Dukakis was not able to touch his audience's feelings, to give them an incentive to approach him in personal terms. Even after one questioner virtually invited Dukakis to demonstrate that his leadership had elements of passion, he came close only in his angry response to Bush's charges about the ACLU. "Of course the vice-president is questioning my patriotism," he flashed back. "And I resent it."

So although Bush was thought to have lost the debate, it was more of an opportunity foregone than a serious blow. But the Republicans' relief was short-lived. The vice-presidential debate lay ahead.

George Bush's George Bush

Ever since the fiasco over his National Guard service, Dan Quayle had been the invisible man of the 1988 campaign. His campaign appearances were confined to small towns and, more important, small media markets. Even then, Quayle was a frequent embarrassment. In the first few weeks after his nomination, for example, he had called the Holocaust "an obscene period in our nation's history," and then, in trying to clarify what he meant, "We all live in this century. I didn't live in this century." A *New York Times* reporter took note of a new button on Capitol Hill that said simply, "President Quayle," and quoted House Democratic Whip Tony Coelho as explaining, "It's the two most feared words in the English language."[37]

The saving grace for the Republicans, Bush's staff thought, was that public expectations for Quayle were so low. All Quayle had to do in the vice-presidential debate was to sound at least minimally coherent—perhaps even to remain vertical would be enough—and he would have done "better than expected." By 5 October, when the debate took place in Omaha, Quayle had been extensively coached. The coaching seemed to pay off initially; Quayle criticized Dukakis and sounded knowledgeable, if overprogrammed, on several issues.

The moment of his demise began innocently enough. One reporter asked Quayle what was the first thing he'd do if something happened to George Bush and he, Quayle, became President. It was a question his handlers had not anticipated. He came back with a canned answer, only partly relevant, on his qualifications to be vice-president—the first of twenty-seven times he used the words "qualifications" or "experience" in the debate. Another reporter on the panel, unsatisfied with Quayle's response, asked the same question again. The same answer reappeared, this time with slight embellishments. As a conservative columnist suggested, "It seemed that someone backstage, armed with a remote-control wand, was operating a compact disc—a very compact disc—in Quayle's skull."[38]

When the question was pressed a third time, Quayle overreached. As he had done in some previous speeches, Quayle commented that he had as much experience in political office as another leader who had become President at a young age: John F. Kennedy. The courtly demeanor of Lloyd Bentsen changed. With cold contempt, Bentsen responded, "Senator, I served with Jack Kennedy. I knew Jack Kennedy. Jack Kennedy was a friend of mine. Senator, you're no Jack Kennedy." Quayle's look of hurt and shock, visible to the millions of watchers, confirmed the perception that his inexperience had been thoroughly exposed by the senior senator from Texas.

After the debate, Bush insisted that Quayle "came through with flying colors." But no one was buying. By margins of two or three to one in postdebate polls, respondents felt Bentsen had turned in the better performance.[39] In fact, several commentators noted longingly that Bentsen could have been a better presidential candidate than his running mate. His criticisms of the Republicans were few but effective; in response to a question about the Reagan prosperity, for instance, Bentsen said, "If you let me write $200 billion worth of hot checks every year, I could give you an illusion of prosperity, too."

The Dukakis campaign, anticipating Quayle's performance, was ready with television ads that began airing right after the debate. One, with the sound of a heartbeat in the background, reminded viewers that one in five vice-presidents goes on to become President.

But again, to the campaign's great frustration, victory in a major event did not produce major improvement in the polls. Part of the problem was that Bush's ads had already done their job. By the time of the vice-presidential debate, Dukakis's unfavorable ratings were almost twice what they had been in early August (see chapter 4). More important was that vice-presidential candidates rarely have much effect on the presidential vote. It was relatively easy to raise people's doubts about Dan Quayle. It was much harder to convince prospective Bush supporters that because of Quayle's inadequacies, they ought to switch to Dukakis.

And interestingly enough, Quayle's weaknesses offered Bush an odd advantage. Quayle made Bush look strong. One writer pointed out, "When Bush stands next to Quayle, he leaves an impression very different from the one created when he is at Ronald Reagan's side. After years as a thoroughly overshadowed second in command, Bush comes across as seasoned and authoritative, compared with Quayle."[40] As several commentators noted, Quayle was George Bush's George Bush.

The Last Debate: The Last Chance

With only a month left before election day, Dukakis tried to stem the Bush tide by offering more specific proposals aimed at the middle class. For example, he suggested letting first-time home buyers use up to $10,000 from their Individual Retirement Account (IRA) as down payment on a home. That fit neatly within Dukakis's effort to appeal to middle-income people who were finding the good life—home, college, security—just out of reach. Bush had earlier recommended letting people invest up to $1000 a year in an "individual savings account," with interest accumulating tax free, to help them afford to buy a home or pay for college. Dukakis ridiculed the idea, holding up a $20 bill before a Pennsylvania audience. "That's his solution for the average American. . . . He says it will make it possible for us to afford a home. Twenty bucks! Pay for college. Twenty bucks!"[41]

Now the pressure was mounting for Dukakis to begin a dramatic surge before it was too late. The only major campaign event remaining was the second presidential debate. The scheduling of that debate accurately reflected the importance of presidential elections in American life; it would take place just as soon as the National League playoff games were over.

The media consensus was that Dukakis would need a decisive victory in the debate, held 13 October in Los Angeles, to have a chance of winning the Presidency. But a "decisive victory" would evidently have to involve more than a superior substantive performance. After all, Dukakis had been regarded as the winner on substance in the first debate, and it had not helped him greatly in the polls. Now, Dukakis would have to reach his audience on an emotional and visceral level: to teach them something new about his character.

The debate's first question, though brutal, gave him a chance to do just that. CNN anchorman Bernard Shaw asked Dukakis, "If Kitty Dukakis were raped and murdered, would you favor an irrevocable death penalty for the killer?" Dukakis might have used his response to express his horror of crime, his love for his family, and his human desire for vengeance, as well as his fervent belief in the rule of a humane law. Instead, he calmly, almost impassively, reaffirmed his opposition to the death penalty. The debate could have ended at that point.

It did not, of course. The candidates put forward their differing views of national defense, with Dukakis emphasizing the broader view that national security must be defined to include a strong economy and a favorable balance of trade, not just more missiles. Bush reaffirmed, and Dukakis derided, his belief that a flexible budget freeze—holding all spending increases to the rate of inflation, with the exception of social security—would bring down the deficit. Dukakis warned that Bush's vague economic proposals, tax cuts, and spending commitments would increase the deficit and therefore that Bush would be likely to raid the social security trust fund to compensate. The two candidates' issue emphases were consistent with those in the first debate (see table 3.1).

But in the end, the verdict was that Dukakis had not made that vital emotional link with his audience. He tried to appear warmer, and he continued to address the themes of leadership, strength, and the next generation more than Bush did. It was Bush, however, who got his message across. Bush seemed more confident and relaxed than he had at any time since his acceptance speech. And he put heavy stress on the symbol that had produced his confidence: the labeling of Dukakis as a liberal. At one point Bush used the word "liberal" three times in a single sentence. Dukakis neither blasted Bush's negative campaigning nor tried to defend liberalism as the proud tradition that had brought the nation social security, unemployment insurance, and Medicare. He simply contended that using labels such as "liberal" was not useful.

After the debate, the media all but declared the race over. The question became whether it would be a Bush landslide or just a Bush win. Strategic changes in the Dukakis campaign seemed to confirm the truth of the story. Key Dukakis staffers were pulled out of states where Bush was running far ahead. Democratic efforts were concentrated on eighteen states, with a barebones 272 electoral votes, where Dukakis was still competitive. The problem, of course, was that in order to win the Presidency, Dukakis could not afford to lose in a single one of those states.

It was at this point of desperation that Dukakis found some of the most effective themes of his campaign. Roused to genuine anger by some mudslinging attacks (for example, a flier produced by the Illinois Republican party claiming that "all the murderers and rapists and drug pushers and child molesters in Massachusetts vote for Michael Dukakis"), he finally agreed that he had to respond. Beginning in the third week of October, Dukakis decried the "lies" and "garbage" that had been thrown at him. Others called the Bush campaign racist for centering on Willie Horton, a black man who had raped a white woman.

Many Democrats cheered, but lamented that the new aggressive style had come too late. Democrats in several states, among them California and Ohio, had long since been running their own media ads rather than those produced by the Dukakis campaign, which they regarded as ineffective. Bush seemed stung by Dukakis's new charges. His negative campaigning was merely "comparative," he said, an effort to get his opponent to be specific on the issues.

Dukakis also took up the cry of economic nationalism. The Reagan administration, he argued, had permitted budget and trade deficits that allowed foreign interests to buy up American assets on the cheap. The result was, he said, that American kids would find themselves working for foreign owners, and American goods would be increasingly undercut by foreign competition.

More effective yet was the populist message "he's on your side." As election day drew near, Dukakis made more and more use of the class-based oratory that he had so carefully avoided in the primaries. In interviews on television news programs and in some of the strongest speeches of the campaign, Dukakis came back to the liberal message that Bush's programs favored the wealthy, not the hard-working middle class. What will the beneficiaries of Bush's tax cuts do with the money?, Dukakis asked. "Hire a second butler? Hire a lifeguard for the pool?"[42] He finally declared himself a liberal, if only for a day, in a fervent closing appeal to traditional Democratic constituencies.

Bush, in contrast, held steadily to the symbolic themes that had characterized his campaign since May. In late October he offered yet another version of that familiar refrain, the Willie Horton furlough issue: "Clint Eastwood's answer to crime is, 'Go ahead, make my day.' My opponent's answer is slightly different. His answer is, 'Go ahead, have a nice weekend.' "[43]

One reason the campaign stayed with these negative appeals was that even after many months of work, George Bush was still not considered a strong enough candidate to win on his own, with positive messages. Another, quite simply, was that the negative campaigning kept working. By late October, even Jesse Jackson's approval ratings were higher than Dukakis's. Even more significantly, the proportion of respondents saying that George Bush was "tough enough" on crime and criminals rose from 23 percent in July to a full 61 percent in late October, while the proportion saying Dukakis was not tough enough rose from 36 to 49 percent.[44] It would be hard to find more convincing proof of the efficacy of attack politics. The campaign did make a difference.

The Campaign, the Media, and Democratic Discussion

It had been a bitter campaign, and even before it ended, media people criticized every part of it, including their own role. There was justice in that.

In a representative democracy, where most people's active participation is limited to choosing among candidates for office, the quality of campaign discussion and debate is vitally important. Citizens depend on the campaigns and the media to offer the kinds of information that make an informed choice possible. The dilemma is that both sources of information have other goals, beyond contributing to democratic discussion, that will inevitably take priority for them. For campaigners, the primary goal is to win. For the commercial media, the primary goal is to attract viewers or sell newspapers. In their pursuit of these primary goals, providing full and useful information may be inconvenient, if not an outright hazard. The 1988 campaign offered a clear example of the high costs of this conflict for a democratic society.

The media have long known that it is difficult to attract viewers and readers with detailed discussions of political issues. Drama, conflict, immediacy, and simple themes are much more likely to entice an audience in entertainment programs, and in newscasts as well. The result is that campaign coverage in the commercial media has long been dominated by the dramatic, streamlined motif of the horse race: reports of who's ahead, who's falling behind, who's doing better than expected.[45]

"Horse-race journalism" hit new heights, or depths, in 1988. Television networks and major newspapers found in 1984 that their polling technology was lagging behind that available to the candidates. By the time of the 1988 campaign, the major media had caught up. But these polls were expensive. To justify their cost, their findings were reported as major news stories frequently and at length. Poll results, then, became a much bigger part of campaign coverage than ever before.

Reporting poll results can add excitement to campaign coverage; it helps increase audience size. But to citizens deciding how to vote, the horse-race data are at best useless. The only people whose voting decisions are informed by polls are those who intend to back a winner, regardless of what the candidate plans to do if elected. At worst, the poll data give an image of firmness to a not-so-firm set of preferences, and may affect some voters' calculations as to whether or not to participate in this one major choice open to them. One writer conveyed these concerns when he suggested that the media "at least wait until a few days before the election to announce the winner."[46]

But the pollsters and various candidate handlers—the media consultants, campaign managers, and advisers—were not prone to such patience and humility. Even more than in previous elections, the handlers and their strategies were the story of the campaign coverage. They happily set forth the details of their strategies to manipulate the public and the media, and reporters fed this "news" to an audience apparently fascinated by its own manipulation. The "spin," the effort by campaigns to control the way they were covered, became a regular feature of reporters' stories.

As table 3.2 shows, almost two-thirds of the campaign coverage in the print media dealt mainly or exclusively with campaign strategy. The wire services maintained heavy emphasis on strategy throughout the fall. Even the prestigious

TABLE 3.2

DO NEWS STORIES EMPHASIZE CAMPAIGN STRATEGY OR POLICY ISSUES?
(GENERAL ELECTION CAMPAIGN, 1988)

Percentage of News Stories Covering	New York Times			Indianapolis Star[a]		
	Sept. 1-7	Oct. 1-7	Nov. 1-7	Sept. 1-7	Oct. 1-7	Nov. 1-7
Campaign strategy only	11	21	33	14	23	13
Mainly strategy, at least some policy[b]	34	39	38	57	35	53
Mainly policy, at least some strategy	34	24	11	17	21	7
Policy only	13	8	6	6	16	7
Neither	9	7	12	6	5	20
N =	(47)	(71)	(72)	(35)	(43)	(30)
Summary						
Campaign strategy, mainly or exclusively	45	60	71	71	58	66
Policy, mainly or exclusively	47	32	17	23	37	14

a. Mainly wire service coverage, including AP, UPI, Knight-Ridder, Scripps-Howard.
b. "Strategy" is defined to include the choice of locations for campaign stops, style and atmosphere of the campaign, staff activities, relative standings of the candidates, fund-raising activities, endorsements, efforts to attract the support of groups, political benefits and costs—as long as no policy issues are mentioned. "Policy" is defined as a reference to any policy issue, even if only the name of the issue is mentioned (including such campaign "issues" as the Pledge of Allegiance) or to the candidates' experience and qualifications. "Mainly strategy" means that half or more of a story's paragraphs are devoted wholly to strategy. If a paragraph includes any mention of a policy issue, it is defined as a policy paragraph.

New York Times, which began the fall campaign by devoting almost half of its coverage to policy issues and candidates' qualifications, had matched the wire services' preoccupation with strategy by November—the time when campaign news would have its biggest audience.

This emphasis has obvious advantages for reporters. It permits them to be investigative without needing to know very much about complex political issues. It is much easier to grasp and convey the making of candidate images than it is to understand and explain the federal budget or national defense. It lets reporters maintain the necessary appearance of impartiality and balance in a way that an in-depth look at the candidates' proposals may not.

It might be argued that an emphasis on campaign strategies benefits voters as well, in two ways. First, it alerts them to the campaigners' plans to influence them. Second, it may be relevant to their voting choice, on the assumption, though questionable, that a candidate who cannot carry out an effective strategy is unlikely to make an effective President.

What this emphasis on strategies and performance is more likely to do, however, is to make both voters and reporters into drama critics, judges of how effective the tactic was, not how much sense the candidate made. Consider an instructive example, in which a former Democratic national chair offered this strange tribute to the opposition candidate's manager, James Baker: "It's masterful. Here he has this vapid, unattractive, know-nothing vice-presidential candidate, who I'm sure was picked over Baker's objections, and he's got him covered up in the alley, in the dark and won't bring him out. It's a most impressive performance."[47] To a voter-cum-drama critic, the skill of the handler would indeed be more interesting than the views and expertise of the candidate covered up in the alley.

In the same spirit, media commentary after the three debates centered on which candidate seemed the most relaxed, the most likable, with the best one-liners, as though the election were to result in the selection of a dinner guest, not a President. Networks and wire services asked debate coaches to judge the candidates on style and presentation. It was a landmark in the development of politics as a spectator sport. Media values had almost completely supplanted the values of governing.

The ascendancy of commercial media values would not be as troubling if voters had other means to get the political information they need. Energetic national parties, for example, could convey policy proposals and information about the candidates. But the American national parties, though revitalizing in some ways, are not yet able to rival the reach of television and newspapers.

Another source of political information are the campaigns themselves, which speak to the voters directly through advertising and personal appearances.

But the campaigns faced a steady drumbeat of criticism, from commentators and voters, that the candidates were not talking about the big issues. Without doubt, that is a difficult task. To address a huge audience, a speaker needs a simple and compelling message. It is much simpler and more compelling to focus on the murderous Willie Horton than to discuss the complexities of balancing public safety against the need to rehabilitate criminals.

Symbolic appeals, in short, fit naturally into presidential campaigns. Despite the pleas for more on "big issues," voters respond more intensely to symbolism, and to their general sense of a candidate's ability and style, than to substantive policy concerns. When the CBS News/New York Times poll asked prospective voters whether "the issues" or the candidate's competence were more important to their voting decision for President, only 19 percent chose the issues; 67 percent chose competence. In the words of Dukakis's communication director Leslie Dach, "You're not going to win because you have a slightly better plan to address day care or to address health care. You're going to win because the proposals demonstrate to voters that you're a leader who'll take charge on the issues they care about."[48]

Even for a public underwhelmed by "the issues," the 1988 campaign was awash with symbolic appeals. Perhaps symbols such as the Pledge of Allegiance became so prominent because the real problems of the nation—the deficit, toxic wastes, declining productivity—are so complicated and intractable. And perhaps the symbols offered some genuine insight to voters. Ads featuring Willie Horton and the ACLU did suggest that George Bush associated himself with a different vision of crime and punishment than did Michael Dukakis.

But the costs of that insight were extremely high. For one, a campaign based on symbolism almost requires that its candidate be insulated from reporters' questions. When reporters are free to probe at will, there is the risk that they will report the symbolic theme in a different context from the one the campaign intends, or ignore it altogether. After he was nominated, Bush permitted very few opportunities for reporters to question him. Although Dukakis was more accessible at first, he soon learned that it was self-defeating to be the one presidential candidate responding to media questions; that diverted press coverage from the message he wanted to convey. He also learned, after limiting his accessibility, that there is no downside to avoiding the press.

Another failure of a symbol-laden campaign, for a democracy, is that it permits both campaigners and citizens to ignore the realities of the candidates' abilities and the nation's needs. Although 1988 began as the year of the "character issue," with reporters eagerly tracking Gary Hart's sexual adventures, it ended with little serious attention paid to the records and expertise of the two men who won their party's nominations. Both George Bush and Michael Dukakis had spent decades in public life: decades of political decisions, learning experiences, successes and failures. The audiences of the commercial media saw and heard little of this storehouse of information about the candidates' records, even though many might have found it relevant to their voting decisions.

The nation's most serious challenges, too, got lost amid the thicket of flags and furloughed criminals. In the last month of the campaign, David Broder wrote that by not talking about the budget deficit, Bush and Dukakis "will not face the reality that we are crippling the ability of this nation to make the investments it needs to guarantee its future." The yearly interest payment on the national debt is the fastest-rising element of the federal budget. "When Ronald Reagan became president," Broder pointed out, "79 cents of every income-tax dollar was available to pay for military salaries, weapons and all our domestic needs. When his successor takes office, only 63 cents of every tax dollar will be there after the interest bill has been paid"—a bill that adds up to two-thirds of what the federal government now spends on education, training, employment, and social service programs.[49]

The campaigners and the media are not the only ones who bear the blame for avoiding issues of such seriousness. It has long been a principle of American politics that voters want more and better government services for themselves, and lower taxes. It is not easy to explain that trying to achieve both these goals at the same time produces budget deficits; Walter Mondale's proposal for a tax increase hung like the ghost of Christmas past over the 1988 campaign.

But good teachers have explained difficult concepts before. The problem is not just the difficulty of the issues. The problem lies in the structure of incentives for candidates and reporters to deal with these issues. The 1988 campaign suggested that there are no incentives at present for campaigners and the media to address the tough problems of governance; the incentives all lead toward the use of symbols, and the creation of artificial drama through the emphasis on polls and strategic moves. The question remains whether it is possible to create different incentives: forces encouraging campaign debate that enriches voters' choices among candidates. For when the 1988 presidential campaign came down to a choice between Willie Horton and the Pledge of Allegiance, the only people enriched were the campaign consultants.

Notes

1. "The Democrats' Week," *Washington Post*, 24 July 1988, C6.

2. Maralee Schwartz, "Dukakis Camp Awaits 'Soft-on-Crime' Wave," *Washington Post*, 24 July 1988, A20.

3. Robert W. Merry, "Post-Reagan GOP: Faded Glory or a Fresh Start?"*Congressional Quarterly Weekly Report* 46 (13 August 1988): 2243.

4. The data are from Rhodes Cook, "Current Democratic Advantage Could Evaporate by November," *Congressional Quarterly Weekly Report* 46 (11 June 1988): 1578.

5. Rhodes Cook, "Long a Republican Province, West Takes a Look at Dukakis," *Congressional Quarterly Weekly Report* 46 (14 May 1988): 1317.

6. On political symbolism, the classic work is Murray Edelman, *The Symbolic Uses of Politics* (Urbana: University of Illinois Press, 1964).

7. See Everett Carll Ladd, *Where Have All the Voters Gone?* 2d ed. (New York: Norton, 1982), 37-45. An early version of the argument can be found in Kevin P. Phillips, *The Emerging Republican Majority* (New York: Doubleday, 1970).

8. Peter T. Kilborn, "A Fight to Win the Middle Class," *New York Times,* 4 September 1988, 1, sec. 3.

9. Morris P. Fiorina, *Retrospective Voting in American National Elections* (New Haven: Yale University Press, 1981).

10. Irwin ("Tubby") Harrison, quoted by Larry Martz et al., "Dukakis's War Dance," *Newsweek* 112 (1 August 1988): 17.

11. Quoted in Maureen Dowd, "Dukakis and Bush Spar on Conservatism," *New York Times,* 8 June 1988, 14.

12. CBS News/New York Times poll, 16 May 1988.

13. Larry Martz et al., "Dukakis by the People Who Know Him Best," *Newsweek* 112 (25 July 1988): 25.

14. Marjorie Randon Hershey, *Running for Office* (Chatham, N.J.: Chatham House, 1984), 96-103.

15. Interview with Mary Alice Williams on CNN, 20 July.

16. Herbert Stein, President Nixon's chief economic adviser, had this response: "That [no tax raise pledge] is like a small boy's declaration that he will never go to the dentist again—sincerely meant but of little predictive value. Mr. Bush's position is generally understood to be that, like Mr. Dukakis, he will raise taxes only as a last resort—but that his last resort would come after Mr. Dukakis's." Quoted in Peter T. Kilborn, "A Fight to Win the Middle Class," *New York Times,* 4 September 1988, 1, sec. 3.

17. David S. Broder, "Dukakis' Big Gamble," *Washington Post,* 24 July 1988, C7.

18. CBS News/New York Times poll, 16 May 1988.

19. See, for example, Norman H. Nie et al., *The Changing American Voter,* Enl. ed. (Cambridge: Harvard University Press, 1979).

20. This meeting was described by Paul Taylor and David S. Broder in "Early Volley of Bush Ads Exceeded Expectations," *Washington Post,* 28 October 1988, A1.

21. An earlier court decision (*West Virginia State Board of Education* v. *Barnette,* 319 U.S. 624 [1943]) had overturned a similar law on the ground that it violated the religious freedom of Jehovah's Witnesses, who are forbidden by their faith to pledge allegiance to any material object.

22. George F. Will, "Texas on the Ticket," *Washington Post,* 17 July 1988, C7.

23. Republican media consultant Doug Bailey, quoted in Lloyd Grove, "Simplicity Credited in Bush Surge," *Washington Post,* 15 October 1988, A1.

24. Quoted in David S. Broder, "Bush KO'd 'Doonesbury'—and Himself," *Washington Post,* 21 August 1988, C7.

25. For a discussion of Quayle's legislative career, see Richard F. Fenno, Jr., *The Making of a Senator: Dan Quayle* (Washington, D.C.: CQ Press, 1989).

26. Quoted in Larry Martz et al., "A Shaky Start," *Newsweek* 112 (29 August 1988): 20.

27. Larry Martz et al., "Dukakis on the Defense," *Newsweek* 112 (5 September 1988): 33.

28. "Nobody Is Perfect," *New York Times,* 12 September 1988, A21.

29. Quoted in John Dillin, "Why the Flag, of All Things, Became an Election Issue," *Christian Science Monitor,* 21 September 1988, 5.

30. Taylor and Broder, "Early Volley of Bush Ads."

31. CBS News/New York Times poll, 22 August 1988.

32. Mark Green, "How Dukakis Can Overcome Bush's 'Slur du Jour,' " *New York Times,* 17 September 1988, 15.

33. Quoted in E.J. Dionne, Jr., "Dukakis Campaign Hones Edges to Combat Slump," *New York Times,* 9 September 1988, 1.

34. Ronald D. Elving, "Democrats Struggle to Define Their Destiny," *Congressional Quarterly Weekly Report* 46 (16 July 1988): 1946.

35. Robin Toner, "Dukakis Camp's Insularity Bemoaned," *New York Times,* 28 October 1988, 10.

36. See John G. Geer, "The Effects of Presidential Debates on the Electorate's Preferences for Candidates," *American Politics Quarterly* 16 (October 1988): 486-501.

37. Bernard Weinraub, "Campaign Trail," *New York Times,* 23 September 1988, 13.

38. George F. Will, " 'Never Give a Child a Sword,' " *Washington Post,* 7 October 1988, A23.

39. CBS News/New York Times poll, 6 October 1988.

40. Peter Bragdon, "Quayle Faces the Challenge of His Young Life," *Congressional Quarterly Weekly Report* 46 (20 August 1988): 2319.

41. John Dillin, "Dukakis Takes Off Gloves for Final Rounds," *Christian Science Monitor,* 30 September 1988, 4.

42. Robin Toner, "Dukakis Denounces Bush's Proposed Tax Break as a Treat for Rich," *New York Times,* 28 October 1988, 11.

43. Quoted in Michael Rezendes, "Bushwhacked on Law and Order, Dukakis Points to His Record," *Washington Post National Weekly Edition,* 24–30 October 1988, 7.

44. E.J. Dionne, Jr., "New Poll Shows Attacks by Bush Are Building Lead," *New York Times,* 26 October 1988, 1.

45. C. Anthony Broh, "Horse-Race Journalism: Reporting the Polls in the 1976 Presidential Election," *Public Opinion Quarterly* 44 (1980): 514-29.

46. A.M. Rosenthal, "We Told You So," *New York Times,* 25 October 1988, 27.

47. Robert Strauss, quoted in Bernard Weinraub, "Democratic View from the Outside," *New York Times,* 23 September 1988, 13.

48. E.J. Dionne, Jr., "Race Reflects Voter Concern with Image Over Substance," *New York Times,* 18 September 1988, 1. See also Arthur H. Miller et al., "Schematic Assessments of Presidential Candidates," *American Political Science Review* 80 (June 1986): 521-40.

49. "Why Cynicism Is Winning by a Landslide," *Washington Post,* 2 October 1988, C7.

4

Public Opinion Trends

BARBARA G. FARAH AND ETHEL KLEIN

George Bush won the 1988 presidential election, not only because he was the heir apparent to a successful Republican administration, but also because he put such values as patriotism, national security, and personal security at the top of his campaign agenda. In so doing, Bush focused attention on the character of the two presidential candidates and what they stood for. He succeeded in getting the American people to know and to like him better than his Democratic rival, Michael Dukakis.

The 1988 campaign was about character and values, and about how the public responded to the issues raised within these contexts. But character and values do not exist in a vacuum. Voters come to any election campaign with certain political orientations imbedded in their partisan affiliation and political philosophy. Both served as lenses through which issues, events, and campaign messages were viewed and evaluated. Added to this political mix was some retrospective judgment of the past administration. In the 1988 campaign, evaluations of Ronald Reagan and his policies contributed to how the voters assessed each candidate.

The public's response to symbols—the flag, tanks, liberals, and criminals—dominated the 1988 campaign. George Bush's ability to shape and control the agenda was evident in his effective use of such issues as the Pledge of Allegiance, national security, and crime and drug control. Bush demonstrated that his values were similar to those held by all Americans, and he convinced voters that he would defend America against all foes, internal and external. Michael Dukakis's response to the Bush values campaign came too late.

For the Democratic candidate, the neglect of the economic climate might be regarded as a lost opportunity in this campaign. At the beginning of the campaign there were anxieties about the economy, the budget deficit, and the future of this nation. Despite the nation's economic woes, issues such as the budget deficit and trade deficit were rarely discussed. The role of economic issues in the 1988 campaign could serve as a reminder of what might have been.

For many political commentators, women's sense of economic vulnerability held the key to the White House.[1] The importance of gender to the 1988 campaign could not be minimized in the spring of this election year. By deflecting the campaign away from the economic issue, Bush was able to win over a majority of men and minimize the loss among women voters. Concentrating on the role of gender in this campaign illustrates how a particular constituency reacted to the issues and evaluated the candidates.

In the final analysis, the election was determined by how committed voters were to their candidate. The campaign revolved around people getting to know the candidates and their values and then making a choice between the Republican and the Democratic candidates. Before election day, voters had to decide which man they liked and which man they did not like. Candidate evaluations ultimately held the key to Bush's electoral victory.

Viewing the election campaign from the perspective of the voters reveals the dynamics of the struggle for control of the Oval Office. Public opinion polls, the prime source used for gauging what voters thought about the candidates and their campaigns, often added confusion rather than enlightenment to the campaign (see chapter 3). Nevertheless, the political "horse-race" figures reported virtually every week of the campaign provided an overview of the struggle for the Presidency.[2]

The Horse Race: An Overview

Pollsters, pundits, the media, and the public focused their attention on the horse race. The movement in public opinion that occurred between May and November is chronicled in the "fever" lines of the presidential horse race (see figure 4.1). Even though George Bush led in the polls from late August until election day, his lead was never so great that the election was considered to be over before the voting. Indeed, at many points in the campaign there was at least some expectation that the gap would be closed or even reversed by election day.

By following the horse-race figures from the beginning of the election campaign to its end, it is possible to see changes in public opinion at critical junctures. The horse-race figures present a summary measure of how each candidate is doing at a particular time in the campaign; they do not reveal what is behind these voting evaluations. Indeed, the criteria for judging candidates at the beginning of a campaign are quite different from those used at the end. A brief overview of the 1988 election campaign can highlight the critical events of the campaign and show the public's reaction to the candidates in light of these events.

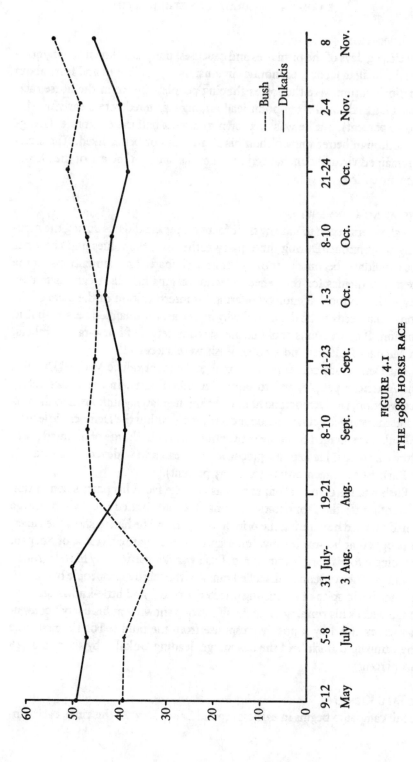

FIGURE 4.1
THE 1988 HORSE RACE

NOTE: Percentages for 19-21 August are from CBS News poll; all others are from New York Times/CBS News polls. Percentages for 8 November are actual results.

PRECONVENTION
In the closing days of the primaries and caucuses, party attachments, judgments
about the Reagan record, economic circumstances, and hopes and fears about
the nation's future were the forces shaping people's choice in the horse race.
Michael Dukakis held a ten-point lead among registered voters early in May
(49 to 39 percent), but he was unknown to almost half the electorate. George
Bush, although better known than his rival, was not better liked. The situation remained virtually unchanged two months later, on the eve of the Democratic convention.

NOMINATING CONVENTIONS
As usual, voters began to narrow their focus on the candidates during the nominating conventions. During these party gatherings, the values and character
of the candidates become part of the political debate. The conventions set the
context and themes for the general election campaign. Each candidate tries
to shape the political agenda by offering his interpretation of the state of the
nation, what needs to be done, and why he is the best-qualified person to lead
the nation. If conventions could be measured in terms of horse-race numbers,
both Michael Dukakis and George Bush were successful.

The Democratic convention had two goals: to introduce Michael Dukakis
to the American people, and to present a united party. In the weeks before
the convention, the Democratic nominee remained largely unknown to the voters, and there was speculation about divisiveness within the Democratic leadership. Dukakis emerged from the convention clearly in charge of a united party
and the campaign. He kept his preconvention lead and widened his advantage
over Bush to seventeen points (50 to 33 percent).

Bush had his own challenges to master as he faced his party's convention
one month after the Democratic meeting: He had to shed the "wimp" image
that had plagued him during the primary season, and he had to show the American people that he was his own man and not merely the shadow of Reagan.

Going into his party's convention, Bush was not particularly liked by American voters. The convention dispelled many of the misgivings people had about
him, and this in spite of his having selected a young and little-known senator,
Dan Quayle, as his running mate. Bush's strong showing at his party's convention was rewarded by a positive response from the public: For the first time
in the campaign, Bush held the advantage, leading Dukakis by six points (46
to 40 percent).

THE FALL KICK-OFF
The fall campaign begins in earnest around Labor Day. At this time, each can-

didate works to consolidate his support base, to hammer home the basic messages of the campaign, and to present himself as a candidate who is competent enough to be President of the United States.

George Bush kept the public's attention on the agenda he had laid out at his party's nominating convention: He challenged his Democratic opponent on his patriotism, his liberalism, and his record as governor of Massachusetts. In early September, Bush maintained his lead in the horse race over his Democratic opponent by 47 to 39 percent.

THE DEBATES

Between mid-September and mid-October, the presidential and vice-presidential candidates met to debate. Each debate enabled the public to judge the character and values of the candidates, as well as the issue positions of these men.

Polls taken after the debates showed some of the impact these events had on people's voting intentions. Dukakis's strong showing in the first debate helped chip away at the lead Bush had held throughout September. The horse race narrowed from a five-point Bush lead to only a two-point lead in favor of Bush (45 to 43 percent). One week later, despite a poor performance by Dan Quayle in the vice-presidential debate, George Bush managed to regain his five-point lead over Dukakis (47 to 42 percent). By the end of October, a few days after the final presidential debate, Bush commanded a thirteen-point lead in the electoral horse race (51 to 38 percent). In large part, this was a reflection of Bush's strong performance in the second debate and his rival's lackluster appearance.

THE FINAL DAYS

Just days before the election, there was still some speculation that Michael Dukakis might be able to fool the pollsters. He had been waging a newly energized campaign during the past few weeks around a populist economic message that encouraged some to think he might squeak by with a victory on election day. The reality showed something very different. In polls conducted less than a week before election day, George Bush was still comfortably ahead of Michael Dukakis. Heading into the home stretch, the Republican presidential candidate held an eight-point lead over his opponent (48 to 40 percent).

Partisanship, Ronald Reagan, and Ideology

Underlying the political discourse of the 1988 election were three issues: partisanship, Ronald Reagan, and liberalism. Each served as a lens through which voters evaluated the candidates, the issues, and the events of the 1988 campaign. Each played a role in determining the electoral outcome.

PARTISANSHIP

All candidates expect that their core supporters—those who identify with the party—will remain in their camp. In the initial phase of any campaign, candidates try to bring their partisan identifiers into the fold. Once they have succeeded in capturing the attention and support of these voters, they can begin to court the nonaligned and those who identify with another party. But while Republicans expected to hold on to most partisan identifiers, they also coveted some Democrats who might be persuaded to break from party ranks, as they had done in 1980 and 1984. The challenge for the Democrats was to hold on to their supporters and minimize the defection (see table 4.1).

TABLE 4.1

CANDIDATE PREFERENCE BY PARTISAN SUPPORT (IN PERCENTAGES)

	9–12 May			8–11 September			8–10 October			2–4 November		
	Rep	Dem	Ind	Rep	Dem	Ind	Rep	Dem	Ind	Rep	Dem	Ind
Bush	79	13	39	85	15	47	82	16	49	84	20	53
Dukakis	13	76	49	8	74	32	10	73	40	9	69	33

	Election Day Exit Poll		
	Rep	Dem	Ind
Bush	91	17	55
Dukakis	8	82	43

The partisans in each camp started the campaign by giving their candidate about the same levels of support (79 percent of Republicans supported Bush, and 76 percent of Democrats backed Dukakis). By the fall, more Republicans were backing Bush (85 percent) than Democrats were supporting their candidate (74 percent). But defections from the Democratic candidate never reached the high levels they did during the election campaign of 1984 when Ronald Reagan ran for reelection.

Along with the party regulars, a key group of voters in any election are those who remain unaligned. In fact, political Independents have proved to be the most troublesome voters for recent Democratic presidential aspirants. Making up about a quarter of the electorate, this group contributed to the large victories that Ronald Reagan enjoyed in both 1980 and 1984. Thus, the Democrats' objective was to try to win over the Independents. Back in May, the Democrats were optimistic that the Independents might side with their candidate this time around; Dukakis had a 10 percent lead over Bush among this group (49 to 39 percent). But the Bush campaign demonstrated how quickly it could turn the situation around. Early in the fall campaign, Bush took the lead away from Dukakis among Independents and maintained a steady advantage from September until late October, when his lead increased to 14 percent. On election day, George Bush received a sizable share of the Independent vote (55 percent). The only consolation for the Democrats was that the margin of victory Bush received from this group of voters was less than half as large as it had been in 1984 for Ronald Reagan.

THE REAGAN FACTOR

Every election is to some degree based on a retrospective judgment of the party in office.[3] Even though there was no incumbent running for reelection in 1988, Vice-President Bush's identification with the Reagan administration was so close that Reagan and his policies could not help but be factors in the political campaign. Early in the campaign, Michael Dukakis tried to remind voters about the Iran-*Contra* scandals and George Bush's role in that affair. Dukakis also mentioned the record-breaking deficits, both budget and trade, that had occurred during eight years of a Republican administration and tried to connect them to Bush's economic program.

Bush played a delicate balancing act during the summer and fall. While not wanting to appear to be eclipsed by the popular President, he nevertheless wanted to get the message across that it was right to "stay the course."

The close correspondence between Reagan's job-approval ratings and Bush's standings in the polls suggests that the outcome of the election was nothing more than another vote for President Reagan (see table 4.2 on page 110). The evidence is indeed persuasive, since both Bush and Reagan experienced the same surge in support following the Republican nominating convention and then a progressive climb in support and popularity until election day. The job-approval ratings measure how well Ronald Reagan is liked and turn out to be very closely associated with partisan attachments: Republicans approve of Reagan's job performance, while Democrats do not.

Reagan's approval ratings were fairly good indicators of how people would vote (see chapter 5), but they do not necessarily reveal why people supported Bush over Dukakis. What seems to have played more of a role in Bush's victory than Reagan himself were Reagan's policies. That is, Ronald Reagan was not being judged by the voters in 1988; instead, the election was a referendum on Reagan's policies.

In early September, only 28 percent of the voters saw their vote as ensuring the continuation of Reagan's policies, while 41 percent were voting to change them. The remaining 23 percent did not consider their vote to be about the Reagan legacy. By election day, slightly more voters regarded their vote as a

TABLE 4.2

COMPARISON OF BUSH'S STANDING IN THE HORSE RACE
AND REAGAN'S JOB-APPROVAL RATING (IN PERCENT)

	Poll standing of Bush	Approval of Reagan
9–12 May	39	49
5–8 July	39	53
31 July–3 August	33	50
19–21 August	46	59
8–11 September	47	55
21–23 September	46	57
8–10 October	47	61
21–24 October	51	60
Election day	53	56

referendum on Reagan's policies (36 percent wanted to "stay the course"); an equal share of voters, 35 percent, voted to change direction. A steady quarter of the electorate claimed that its electoral decision was based on reasons other than Reagan's policies. On 8 November, the two groups of voters who saw their vote as a referendum on Reagan's policies effectively canceled each other's votes.

The deciding ballots were cast by voters who did not regard the 1988 election as a vote for or against Reagan's policies. Instead, these voters insisted that their voting decision had nothing to do with the past administration. These voters gave the winning edge to George Bush by 57 to 41 percent.

No Labels versus Liberals
Michael Dukakis declared that he did not like labels and that his campaign would focus on competence, not ideology; the Republicans put ideology squarely on the campaign agenda. Before the Republican nominating convention, voters' ideological predispositions did not influence their vote choice. Bush was leading among conservatives, in large measure because so many of them were Republican partisans; Dukakis had the backing of liberals and a modest majority of the moderates.

At his party's convention, George Bush hoped to get voters to view the issues and his opponent through a particular ideological lens—that of liberalism. He defined Dukakis as a card-carrying member of the American Civil Liberties Union (ACLU) who was outside the political mainstream. Bush hammered away at the "L word" by showing how Dukakis's attitudes were liberal on crime and national defense. In launching an attack on liberals, George Bush was picking on a relatively small group in the electorate (15–20 percent) and an even smaller segment of his own political party (fewer than 10 percent). He had a lot to gain and little to lose by employing this strategy. By early September the "L word" had become a major theme of the Bush campaign, and the role that ideology was to play in the campaign was evident.

The Bush campaign instilled doubts about Michael Dukakis by equating his being a liberal with not being tough enough. People's perceptions of the Democrat changed dramatically over the course of the campaign as a consequence of the name-calling (see table 4.3). In May, before Dukakis was labeled

TABLE 4.3

DEFECTIONS FROM DUKAKIS AMONG THOSE
WHO CONSIDERED HIM A LIBERAL
(IN PERCENTAGES)

	9–12 May	8–11 Sept.	21–23 Sept.	1–3 Oct.	2–4 Nov.
Bush	50	72	72	66	61
Dukakis	39	22	19	26	30
% of voters saying Dukakis was a Liberal	27	37	36	43	56

with the "L word," 27 percent of the electorate considered him to be a liberal. Among this group, half of them supported Bush and 39 percent said they would vote for Dukakis. By September, after Bush had planted the seeds of doubt about Dukakis's political philosophy, 37 percent of the electorate were calling Dukakis a liberal. The voting intentions of those voters had changed dramatically: Bush was now supported by 72 percent of the voters who considered Dukakis a liberal, while Dukakis held on to only 22 percent of them. Among those who did not consider Dukakis a liberal, a majority supported the Democrat. After the first debate, when Bush again invoked Dukakis's affiliation with the ACLU, the proportion of the electorate who considered Dukakis a liberal increased to 43 percent, and two-thirds of this group planned to vote against him.

The Bush campaign was effective in its use of ideology as a campaign issue; it was able to label the candidate who said the campaign would not be about labels. Bush's aim was to attract the attention and support of political conservatives, who constitute about a third of all American voters and a significantly larger segment of the Republican party (about 50 percent). Bush proved to be extremely successful in his appeals to conservatives — attacking Michael Dukakis as a liberal, using the Pledge of Allegiance as an issue, and declaring his support for the death penalty. In September, two-thirds of all conservatives intended to vote for Bush, an increase of 15 percent in four months (see table 4.4). The outcome of the election showed that eight out of ten conservative voters cast their ballots for Bush, a feat that matched Reagan's score in 1984 (see table 5.5

on page 146). In fact, Bush was also able to win about a quarter of the Democratic conservatives in the process.

Political moderates, who constitute a plurality of the voters (about 45 percent), became key players in an election that revolved around an ideological spectrum. At the beginning of the campaign, when ideology was not an issue, moderates gave an electoral edge to the Democratic candidate. But Dukakis's failure to respond to the ideological name-calling launched by his opponent resulted in a slow but steady erosion of support among moderates. On election day, Bush and Dukakis won a split decision from this group.

TABLE 4.4

CANDIDATE PREFERENCE BY POLITICAL IDEOLOGY (IN PERCENTAGES)

| | 9–12 May | | | 8–11 Sept. | | | 8–10 Oct. | | | 2–4 Nov. | | |
	Lib	Mod	Con	Lib	Mod	Con	Lib	Mod	Con	Lib	Mod	Con
Bush	25	36	52	24	42	67	31	40	66	21	49	64
Dukakis	70	51	37	62	45	24	60	48	26	68	42	24

| | Election Day Exit Polls | | |
	Lib	Mod	Con
Bush	18	49	80
Dukakis	81	50	19

What was the furor over liberalism about? For the past eight years, President Reagan made cutbacks in many federal programs, saying that the country needed a smaller government that provided fewer services. The liberal approach to governing—big government providing more services—was being challenged by a Republican candidate who told everyone to "read my lips—no new taxes."

In the early phase of the campaign, in May, about half the electorate (47 percent) was against the expansion of the federal government, while 41 percent preferred more government provision of necessary services. Those voters who supported bigger government backed Michael Dukakis (60 to 30 percent), while those who wanted to see the federal bureaucracy downsized favored Bush for President (49 to 39 percent). In early October, voters' attitudes toward the federal government had not changed at all; neither had their voting intentions. Bush was still favored by those who wanted a smaller government, but by a wider margin (61 to 31 percent), while Dukakis won only majority support among those who favored expanding the functions of the federal government (53 to 35 percent). This is one issue where campaign rhetoric failed to move voters from one position to another.

Ideology became a critical element in the campaign of 1988. George Bush was effective in targeting liberals and the ACLU. He also attacked liberal policies that called for a bigger government providing more services. In so doing, Bush painted a portrait of a Democratic candidate who did not share the values or aspirations of most Americans.

Whose Values?

Candidates talk about themes and issues in order to give voters a sense of their own values and the direction in which they hope to lead the country. Historically, Republicans have used family, flag, and national security as major themes in their campaigns; Democrats have been better at talking about policies and programs.

Patriotism and security, both personal and national, were the dominant values invoked in the 1988 campaign. The politics of symbols involves promoting a cluster of issues that evoke similar values. George Bush never called Michael Dukakis unpatriotic, but Bush appropriated patriotic symbols by defending a strong military and championing the Pledge of Allegiance. The Republicans also seized on widespread fears of crime, drugs, and violence by calling for the death penalty for murderers and drug pushers, and by promising to take a very tough stance against criminals, in order to address people's need for personal security.

PATRIOTISM AND SECURITY

The question of patriotism arose when Bush grabbed the flag and pledged his allegiance to it at his party's nominating convention, and then promised to strengthen America's defenses. Dukakis's veto of a Massachusetts bill requiring teachers to say the Pledge of Allegiance allowed Bush to raise the issue and implicitly to challenge the Democrat's patriotism. Bush said he loved this country and promised to keep America strong, warning that Dukakis's policies would weaken America's defenses. By early September, the use of patriotic symbols had helped Bush overtake Dukakis in the polls.

Americans thought their presidential candidates were patriotic. Most voters said that Bush and Dukakis were equally patriotic, and these voters split their votes evenly between them. Voters who felt one candidate was more patriotic than the other overwhelmingly supported the candidate they considered to be more patriotic (see table 4.5).

THE PLEDGE OF ALLEGIANCE

On the issue of the Pledge of Allegiance, most people agreed with George Bush

TABLE 4.5

PATRIOTISM, THE PLEDGE OF ALLEGIANCE,

AND NATIONAL SECURITY

(IN PERCENTAGES)

Patriotism Evaluation

Would you consider George Bush and Michael Dukakis very patriotic, somewhat patriotic, or not very patriotic? (8-11 September)

	All	Bush Voters	Dukakis Voters
Bush more patriotic	20	79	15
No difference	66	41	43
Dukakis more patriotic	9	17	76

Pledge of Allegiance

Do you think the Pledge of Allegiance should be an important issue in the presidential campaign, or should other issues be getting more attention? (8-11 September)

	All	Bush Voters	Dukakis Voters
Important issue	31	51	34
Focus on other issues	61	44	44

National Security

If George Bush [Michael Dukakis] were elected President, do you think he would make U.S. defenses stronger, make them weaker, or would he keep defenses at the present level?

	8–11 September			21–24 October		
	All	Bush Voters	Dukakis Voters	All	Bush Voters	Dukakis Voters
Bush stronger	55	65	26	58	71	21
No difference	32	40	48	33	25	59
Dukakis stronger	12	13	74	8	13	72

that the Pledge should be required in schools (70 percent). Despite this agreement, two-thirds of the voters felt that the campaign should focus on other issues that were more important. By championing the Pledge, Bush helped his candidacy gain momentum as he benefited from a 17 percent advantage among nearly a third of the electorate who felt it was an important issue. He succeeded in doing this without creating a backlash among those who felt the campaign should focus on other issues.

NATIONAL SECURITY

Republicans were most effective in shifting public support away from Dukakis by portraying him as a national security risk. Bush promised to strengthen American defenses and increase commitments to the military. He cited Dukakis's inexperience and his lack of commitment to the nation's defense. Insisting that the Democrat would weaken American security, Bush warned voters not to take that risk.

Bush's lead was based on values implicit in keeping America strong, rather than on a policy of increased militarism. In July, when Dukakis was leading in the polls, few people wanted to increase the level of military spending (17 percent). Voters who wanted to increase defense spending or maintain present spending levels divided their votes evenly between the candidates, while those who wanted to decrease spending gave Dukakis a decided advantage (65 to 25 percent).

Three months later, after Bush had attained a comfortable lead, most people still wanted to maintain current levels of spending, and support for spending increases actually declined to 10 percent. Dukakis had retained his advantage among those wanting to decrease spending, but Bush gained a 43 percent advantage among voters who wanted to increase spending and an 18 percent advantage among those wanting to maintain current spending levels.

Voters withdrew their support from Dukakis because they feared he would weaken the nation's defenses. Nothing in the Dukakis campaign made voters think that he would keep America strong. Instead, what voters heard about were all the weapon systems that the Democrat would get rid of and the inexperience of Dukakis in dealing with other nations. The Republicans succeeded in putting the Democrats on the defensive very early in the campaign. By September, over a third of the electorate believed that Dukakis would weaken defenses. This concern persisted. Two weeks before the general election, 41 percent agreed that Dukakis would weaken national security.

Perceptions of Bush's and Dukakis's relative positions on the question of a strong defense had significant electoral consequences. In early September, slightly more than half the electorate felt that Bush would strengthen the nation's defenses more than Dukakis would, and voters gave Bush a strong lead (see table 4.5). A third of the electorate saw no difference between the two candidates and favored Dukakis by a small margin.

National security became increasingly important in shaping the voters' perspective as the campaign progressed. Two weeks before the election, a majority of the electorate believed that Bush would strengthen American defenses more than Dukakis would, and gave Bush a 50 percent advantage. Dukakis's advantage among the third of the electorate that did not see this as a campaign issue increased to 34 percent. Michael Dukakis lost the election because the Republicans convinced voters that he would weaken America and Bush would keep the country strong.

PERSONAL SECURITY
Important to people's sense of well-being is the question of personal security. In 1988, many voters were anxious because they and the people they cared about had little control over their lives. They agonized about what could be done in the face of increasing violence, crime, and drugs.

Bush seized on personal security issues by demanding that laws get tougher on criminals; he supported the death penalty for murderers and drug pushers, and defended citizens' rights to bear arms. By focusing the campaign on these issues, the Republicans were able to portray the Democrats as outside the mainstream. Bush painted Dukakis as soft on crime by focusing on the Massachusetts prison furlough program and on Dukakis's opposition to the death penalty.

Ironically, it was George Bush, not Michael Dukakis, who started out the political season vulnerable on the question of crime (see table 4.6). Before the conventions, voters were more likely to say that Bush, rather than Dukakis,

TABLE 4.6

DEALING WITH CRIME

(IN PERCENTAGES)

Do you think George Bush [Michael Dukakis] would be tough enough in dealing with crime and criminals, or don't you think so?

| | 5–8 July[a] | | | 21–24 October | | |
	Tough	Not Tough	Don't Know	Tough	Not Tough	Don't Know
George Bush	23	49	28	62	24	14
Michael Dukakis	20	36	44	37	49	15

| | Voting Preference | | | | | |
| | 5–8 July[a] | | | 21–24 October | | |
	All	Bush Voters	Dukakis Voters	All	Bush Voters	Dukakis Voters
Bush tougher	18	72	17	43	82	8
No difference	55	39	44	40	36	51
Dukakis tougher	27	17	73	17	5	85

a. Varied wording: *Do you think George Bush [Michael Dukakis] has been tough enough in dealing with crime and criminals, or don't you think so?*

was not tough enough in dealing with crime and criminals (49 to 36 percent). A plurality did not know what Dukakis's position on the question was.

At this early stage, slightly more than half the electorate said the candidates did not differ in how they would deal with criminals. Voters who did not think crime was an issue gave Dukakis a slight (5 percent) edge. Those voters who did see a difference voted for the candidate they thought would be tougher on crime by almost three to one. Dukakis's lead over Bush at this time was due in part to the greater number of voters who believed Dukakis was tougher on crime than Bush was.

Then came the television advertisements and news coverage that took the focus away from Bush and spotlighted the Dukakis record. Pictures of Willie Horton and the victims he raped and beat while on furlough from a Massachusetts prison brought the issue of Dukakis's alleged failure into millions of living rooms throughout the country. This was followed by pictures of the revolving door of justice as prisoners filed into a Massachusetts prison only to file right back out. The message was clear: Dukakis cared more about criminals than he did about innocent people. According to these Republican ads, Dukakis was soft on crime.

The Republicans succeeded in turning the crime issue around. Two weeks before the election, many more voters said Bush would be tougher on criminals (43 percent) than were willing to say Dukakis would be tougher (17 percent). Bush's taking a tough stance on crime helped him overtake Dukakis. Those voters who saw no difference in how the candidates would deal with criminals, and therefore did not think that crime was an issue, gave Dukakis a 15 percent advantage.

Drugs emerged as a key issue early in this election year. Poll after poll revealed drugs to be one of the most important problems facing Americans today. George Bush headed the Reagan administration's war on drugs. Dukakis tried to discredit Bush by pointing to the failures of his efforts and by stressing Bush's alleged links to General Manuel Noriega of Panama. Bush proudly defended his efforts to stop the flow of drugs into the country and promised to get even tougher by favoring the death penalty for drug dealers.

Americans favor the death penalty for drug dealers; in July, however, this preference had no electoral significance. Voters who favored the death penalty were as likely to vote for Bush as for Dukakis (44 to 44 percent). By the end of the campaign, the issue had become highly politicized. Those who favored the death penalty for dealers intended to vote for Bush (59 to 30 percent), while those who opposed it chose Dukakis (57 to 33 percent). Bush had the advantage in pursuing this personal security issue because two-thirds of the electorate agreed with him on the death penalty.

The 1988 campaign was not a rally behind specific policies raised by George Bush. Few voters favored increased military spending (10 percent) or thought the Pledge (31 percent) or the death penalty for drug dealers (16 percent) were important issues that should be the focus of a national campaign. These issues served as symbols of patriotism and national and personal security. They allowed the Republican campaign to portray Bush as closer to people's values.

Economic Vulnerability: The Missed Message

Perceptions of the health of the nation's economy played a strong role in shaping voters' choices. Throughout the campaign, the public's assessment of the economy was mixed. Low unemployment, low inflation, and low interest rates helped the Republicans, but high trade and budget deficits dampened their ability to run on an unassailed record of economic recovery. The Democrats needed to convince people that the "Reagan recovery" had not been without its costs and to point out to people that they were working hard just to "stay in place."

Preconvention media polls and focus-group research told both campaigns that the public was concerned about America's economic future. Although no current fiscal crisis worried the electorate in early spring, there was a sense of public unease, a feeling that America's economy was fragile. People were looking for change. A growing number of voters were concerned that the economy would get worse, and the majority felt that the next generation would be bogged down paying for the current recovery. While voters liked Ronald Reagan, they rejected his administration's policies and were looking for new directions.

The Republicans launched their first effort to frame the discussion of the economy right before the Democratic convention. They started with a strong anti-Carter television spot to remind people of how angry they had been eight years ago. Black-and-white stills of former President Carter were interspersed with pictures of gas lines and unemployment lines; the old song "I Remember You" played in the background. Voters were warned not to take the Reagan successes for granted.

Another commercial featured a seven-year-old girl, sitting on the steps of her suburban home, smiling while she drew in her coloring book. Voters were told that she had known only peace and prosperity throughout her life. An announcer proclaimed that when the Democrats controlled the White House, people could not afford to buy a house or start a family. This was a "feel good" advertisement, aimed at making voters feel secure. Again the message was not to take success for granted, and it underscored the Republicans' point that the Democrats did not know how to manage the national economy. Bush did acknowledge that some people had been left out of the Republican economic recovery. He pledged to sustain the Reagan expansion and at the same time to address some of its inequities. His was going to be a "kinder, gentler nation."

The Democrats did not develop a paid media campaign around the economy, but their convention focused the public's attention on issues of economic vulnerability. Voters were reminded that the Reagan recovery did not help everyone. Democrats framed this election as a fight for America's standard of living.

Dukakis warned Americans against being lulled into complacency by the Republicans. Too many Americans were working hard just to break even. Too many Americans were one paycheck, one divorce, one college tuition, one nursing home, or one day-care-center bill away from being economically strapped. Too many young couples had to borrow the downpayment for their first home from their parents. The threat to the nation's standard of living was a direct result of the astronomical trade and budget deficits created by the Republican administration. The increasing number of Americans who were homeless, hungry, and sick—abandoned without any protections—were the visible casualties of Republican mean-spiritedness. The public was very responsive to this message; support for the Democrats soared after their convention.

After the nominating conventions, the Republicans gained control of the political agenda and shaped the context in which the economy was discussed during the general election. They did this by assuaging people's fears that the country faced a precarious economic future; by raising doubts about the Democrats' ability to manage the economy; and by aggressively moving the agenda away from deficits and domestic priorities. They put the Democrats on the defensive by concentrating on issues of national security and cultural values. Dukakis's failure to address economic problems and set some national priorities to deal with these worries during the early stages of the general election reinforced Republican assertions of his incompetence and cost him a large number of supporters.

Voters who thought the nation's economy was getting better supported Bush, while people who thought that it was getting worse favored Dukakis (see table 4.7). But the outcome of the election would depend on the large number of voters who predicted that the economy would stay the same. In the spring, voters who expected no change in the economy chose Dukakis over Bush (47 to 39 percent). The Democrats lost this advantage by early September, when people who expected the economy to remain stable favored Bush over Dukakis (52 to 34 percent).

These voters were not choosing George Bush because they supported Reagan's economic policies. On the contrary, only a third of those who believed

TABLE 4.7

THE FUTURE OF THE NATION'S ECONOMY (IN PERCENTAGES)

Do you think the economy is getting better, getting worse, or staying about the same?

	9–12 May	8–11 Sept.	1–3 Oct.	10–15 Nov.
Better	21	15	18	14
About the same	42	56	53	60
Worse	34	27	26	24

Economic Future and Voting Preference

	9–12 May		8–11 Sept.		1–3 Oct.		10–15 Nov.	
	Bush	Dukakis	Bush	Dukakis	Bush	Dukakis	Bush	Dukakis
Better	64	25	73	19	74	17	85	15
Same	39	47	52	34	47	41	56	44
Worse	25	65	25	64	23	64	30	70

that the economy would stay the same said that they were voting to continue the Reagan legacy. People were supporting the status quo because they had no sense of where the Democrats would lead them.

After the Labor Day kick-off, the economy was eclipsed by discussions of national security, patriotism, and crime. The Republicans were setting the agenda, and they wanted to keep the focus off the economy. Still, most voters felt that the economy was an important election issue. The majority believed that the condition of the nation's economy in the coming year depended on who was elected President in November. Most voters still agreed with the Democrats' critique of the Reagan recovery, despite their support for Bush.

The Democrats lost their ability to capitalize on economic concerns because Dukakis was unable to convince voters who shared his views that he could address the problems. Seven out of ten voters who were optimistic about the future of the next generation planned to vote for Bush, but only half the pessimists intended to vote for Dukakis. If Dukakis had been as effective as Bush in mobilizing people who shared his views on the economy, the election would have been much closer. His failure to define his economic agenda early in the campaign left many with doubts about his abilities.

By the time Dukakis turned to a populist economic message in the last two weeks of the campaign, it was too little, too late. People still worried that the Reagan recovery was bought at their children's expense, but only half of those concerned with the next generation had enough confidence in Dukakis to support his candidacy. The Democrats campaign theme of "I'm On Your Side" did not convince voters that they would be economically better off under a Dukakis administration. Most people felt that if Bush were elected President, the U.S. economy would stay about the same. In contrast, a Dukakis Presidency was seen as likely to bring change, with more people predicting a change for the worse, not for the better (39 to 24 percent). Voters were also more apt to fear that they personally would suffer if Dukakis became President than if Bush were elected (34 to 20 percent).

On election day, voters who said they were better off today than they were in 1980 (46 percent) supported Bush. Those who said they were worse off (28 percent) planned to vote for Dukakis. Voters who thought current conditions were the same as in 1980, when the nation was in serious economic trouble, should have voted for Dukakis. The majority did, but a substantial number (40 percent) voted for Bush despite this negative assessment. Perhaps these voters believed the Democrats would only make matters worse.

Many voters also left the polls on election day concerned about the nation's economic future. About half were hopeful, but an equal number were concerned. Bush had an advantage over Dukakis in mobilizing his economic base. He was able to motivate 73 percent of the optimistic voters to support his candidacy, while only 65 percent of the pessimists voted for Dukakis. The Democrats made a serious mistake in letting the Republicans take the economic issue away from them.

What Happened to the Gender Gap?

As the 1988 election moved away from the nominating process and on to the general election, the gender gap appeared to be one of the central battlegrounds that would determine the outcome of the campaign in a close election. George Bush was barely holding his own among men and was at a great disadvantage among women voters. In order to win, the Democrats needed to sustain their support among women and gain support among men. In contrast, the Republicans needed to draw more men into their camp and reduce the Democrats' advantage among women, as they had done in 1984. The Republicans succeeded.

GENDER ADVANTAGE: SHIFT FROM DUKAKIS TO BUSH

In May, men's votes were split evenly between the two candidates (43 percent Bush to 44 percent Dukakis), giving the Democrat a negligible 1 percent gender advantage.[4] At the same time, women were clearly siding with Dukakis (53 to 35 percent), resulting in an 18 percent advantage for him.

By September, the Republicans had taken control of the campaign agenda. This led to a shift in the electorate's support, away from Michael Dukakis and toward George Bush. The Republicans were able to activate greater support among men (53 to 37 percent) and reduce Bush's deficit among women dramatically to the point where the women's vote divided almost evenly between Bush and Dukakis (43 to 41 percent). At that point, Bush had a 16 percent gender advantage, based on men's votes. This is a complete reversal of the pattern found in May.

And the shift that became noticeable in September was essentially the pattern that emerged on election day. The Republicans succeeded in getting the majority of men's votes (57 to 41 percent) and women divided their vote evenly between Bush and Dukakis (50 to 49 percent). There was a 7 percent gender gap in 1988, and George Bush won with a 16 percent gender advantage based on men's votes. The Republicans were able to reverse Dukakis's earlier gender advantage by moving the political debate away from the economy, which was potentially a winning issue for the Democrats, and putting the Democrats on the defensive on issues of national and personal security.

THE ECONOMIC VULNERABILITY OF WOMEN

Dukakis's failure to address people's sense of economic vulnerability especially hurt him among women voters. Economic concerns, which include health care and balancing work and family responsibilities, were the driving force behind the gender gap in the early part of the campaign. Women have been absorbed into the labor force, but often in bad jobs at bad wages. More women with young children are working for economic survival today than ever before. Two-thirds of women in the labor force with preschool children are either the family's only wage earner or are contributing to a yearly family income of $15,000 or less.

The Republicans were much more successful in allaying men's fears about the nation's economic future than women's fears. The concerns of men that the economy would get worse decreased from 29 percent in May to 18 percent in October. In contrast, 37 percent of women expressed concern that the economy was getting worse in May; by October, 33 percent continued to be pessimistic.

Dukakis lost his advantage among women voters when he failed to continue championing the economic themes that were raised during the Democratic convention. In the spring, half the women who believed the economy would remain the same rejected staying with the status quo and supported Dukakis (50 to 36 percent). Halfway through the election, the pattern reversed; women who did not expect the economy to change supported Bush (49 to 38 percent). These women, many of them economically vulnerable, shifted their allegiance to Bush because the Democrats failed to address the economic concerns of women.

Dukakis's silence on the economy was less damaging among men. In the spring, men who said the economy would remain the same split their vote between the two candidates (42 to 44 percent). By early September, they had been won over by the Republicans and supported Bush decidedly (57 to 32 percent). In October, they returned to dividing their support evenly between Bush and Dukakis. As these men returned to Dukakis, they helped narrow Bush's gender advantage.

When Dukakis finally campaigned on issues of economic vulnerability, he was able to attract some women toward his candidacy, but it was largely too late. Two weeks before the election, a majority of men (51 percent) and even more women (60 percent) worried that the next generation would be bogged down with the problems that we were creating today. These women gave Dukakis an 18 percent advantage over Bush, while the men divided their support. Still, Dukakis needed to win over many more women (and men) in order to challenge Bush at this late stage.

On election day, George Bush was rewarded by voters who were optimistic about the economy; Dukakis received only tepid support from those who were concerned. Many more men than women (55 to 42 percent) said that they were better off today than in 1980, which is why more men voted for Bush. Women were somewhat more likely (33 to 25 percent) to say they were worse off today, and that is why more women voted for Dukakis. Given the horrible state of the economy in 1980, men and women who said the economy was the same as eight years ago should have supported Dukakis, but they gave Bush a 17 percent advantage because they felt things could be worse under Dukakis.

GENDER AND VALUES: FEELING GOOD
ABOUT AMERICA

By raising patriotic symbols, Bush gained support among both men and women, although men were predisposed to support the Republican, somewhat independent of the question of patriotism. Challenges to Dukakis's patriotism served to erode his support among women.

Men and women who did not think that the 1988 campaign was about patriotism supported different candidates. Men who felt that both candidates were equally patriotic supported Bush (48 to 39 percent), while women favored Dukakis (46 to 36 percent). The Pledge of Allegiance influenced women's vote intention, but not men's. Men who thought the Pledge was not an important issue were as likely to vote for Bush over Dukakis (52 to 38 percent) as those who felt the issue mattered (49 to 38 percent). Women who believed the Pledge was an important issue rewarded Bush (52 to 31 percent); those who felt it was not important favored Dukakis (49 to 37 percent).

National security was the critical issue for men early in the campaign. In September, a majority of both men and women felt that Bush would strengthen the nation's defenses more than Dukakis would. Nevertheless, men who felt Bush was stronger on defense gave Bush a much greater advantage over Dukakis (72 to 23 percent) than women with similar assessments (59 to 29 percent).

The Republicans pressed the issue of national security as the campaign progressed. One commercial showed Dukakis (looking somewhat like Snoopy, the dog in the "Peanuts" comic strip) riding around in a tank as the announcer warned that Americans should not take a chance on Dukakis's inexperience. Another spot began with a portrait of Gorbachev, stressing that the next President would have to negotiate the world's future with this man. In this commercial, George Bush stepped in and shook Gorbachev's hand as the camera froze on their meeting. Again the announcer warned, Americans cannot risk inexperience. The Democrats never managed an adequate response to these ads.

As the campaign came to a close in late October, people were choosing Bush because they were worried about Dukakis weakening the country's defenses. A majority of women (53 percent) and an even greater number of men (63 percent) had sufficient doubts about the Democrat that they planned to vote for Bush. Men and women voters who saw no difference between the nominees or who thought Dukakis would be the stronger candidate on defense went for the Democrat. In the end, the question of national security had a greater impact on men's votes because men were more likely to see Dukakis as threatening national security.

Issues of personal security played a significant role in gaining support for Bush's candidacy among women. Before the nominating conventions, women were more likely than men (27 to 18 percent) to view Dukakis as the tougher candidate on criminals. Men and women who did not think Bush and Dukakis differed in dealing with crime supported different candidates; men split their support evenly between the two, while women gave Dukakis a 13 percent advantage.

Dukakis lost a substantial amount of women's support when he lost the crime issue to Bush. By late October, a plurality of both men and women were convinced by Republican attacks on the Democrat's record on crime that he would not be tough enough in dealing with criminals. Bush received overwhelming support from this group (for men, 86 to 6 percent, and for women, 79 to 10 percent). Men who were not persuaded that the candidates differed in their treatment of crime continued to split their support, but women with similar views gave Dukakis a 25 percent advantage.

In 1988, the gender gap once again proved to be of critical importance to the electoral outcome. By not playing up economic issues and the vulnerability that women felt about the future, Dukakis lost the early advantage he held among women voters. Bush skillfully managed to bring men into the Republican fold by emphasizing patriotism and national security. The negative portrait of Dukakis painted by the Republicans as outside the political mainstream and insensitive to issues of personal security was effective in getting women to rethink their evaluation of Dukakis. Ultimately, Bush succeeded in getting men to like him and women not to dislike him.

Conclusion: *The Voters' Choice*

Unless candidates are incumbents, they tend not to be well known early in a political campaign. The themes and values that each candidate espouses provide voters with a glimpse into the character of the man as the campaign advances. People begin to make judgments about the nominees; they commit themselves to one man and begin to distance themselves from the other nominee. Ultimately, the voters decide on the candidate who conveys qualities of competence and leadership, and who believes in the same basic values that they do.

Tracing the public's impression of the candidates during a long campaign gives us a sense of how well their campaigns are succeeding in framing the character issue. As part of the electoral process, each campaign forces voters to make comparisons between two candidates. People may like or dislike both men, but by election day they will have to make a single choice.

As the campaign progresses, voters begin to align along a continuum ranging from (1) strong Bush supporters who like the vice-president and dislike the Democrat to (2) weak Bush supporters who like Bush but do not know much about his opponent to (3) uncommitted voters who like both candidates, dislike both candidates, or do not know enough about either one to (4) weak Dukakis supporters who like the governor but do not know much about his opponent to (5) strong Dukakis supporters who like Dukakis and dislike Bush.

These evaluations give one a sense of the commitment voters have to their candidates. People who say they plan to vote for Bush (or Dukakis) but have not made a negative judgment about his rival or do not see much difference between the candidates are more likely to change their opinion before election day. The candidate who has the greater proportion of voters strongly committed to him at an early stage in the campaign approaches election day from a much stronger position (see figure 4.2 on page 126).

In May, as the primaries were coming to an end, George Bush was not well liked and Michael Dukakis was largely unknown. Relatively few voters had strong attachments to either candidate, but twice as many of Dukakis's

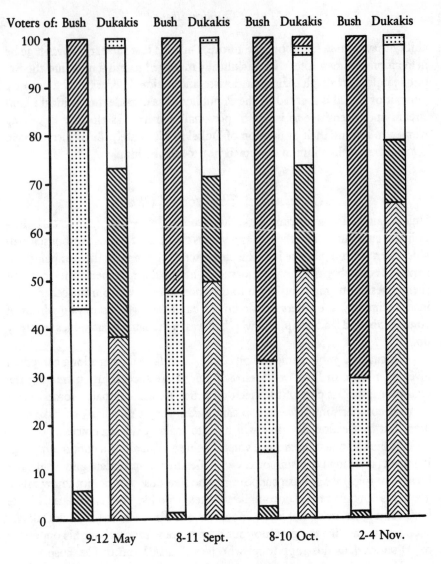

Voters of: Bush Dukakis Bush Dukakis Bush Dukakis Bush Dukakis

9-12 May   8-11 Sept.   8-10 Oct.   2-4 Nov.

FIGURE 4.2

VOTER COMMITMENT TO CANDIDATE

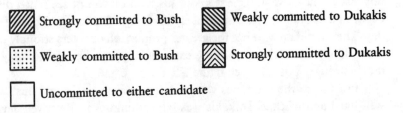

▨ Strongly committed to Bush   ▨ Weakly committed to Dukakis

▨ Weakly committed to Bush   ▨ Strongly committed to Dukakis

☐ Uncommitted to either candidate

supporters felt strongly about their candidate (38 to 19 percent). By Labor Day, George Bush had succeeded in getting people to like him and not to like Michael Dukakis. The Democratic candidate, still largely an unknown to two out of five voters, had as many voters disliking him as liking him. By now, both candidates could count on half their prospective voters being strong supporters; however, the number of strong supporters who were voting for Bush had increased by 33 percent since May, while Dukakis's strong supporters had increased by only 11 percent.

By the beginning of October, the Republicans' verbal assaults on Dukakis had hit their mark: Dukakis's negative ratings slipped to an 8 percent deficit, while Bush held on to a 10 percent advantage in his favorable-unfavorable ratings. In terms of voter support, Bush could count on two-thirds of his voters being strongly committed to him. Dukakis's vote base was much more uneven; only half of it came from supporters, and a quarter of those who would vote for him were still not committed to either candidate.

Four days before the election, Bush was liked by about half the electorate (46 percent) and disliked by only a third. What Dukakis faced as election day approached was just the opposite: a third of the electorate liked him, but 41 percent disliked him. Bush's support base remained intact: 71 percent were strong supporters. Voters strongly committed to Dukakis finally rallied to their candidate's side: Just before election day, Dukakis could count on 65 percent of his voters being strongly committed to him.

Thus, Bush's voters liked him earlier and liked him longer, and there were many more of them than favored Dukakis. Bush gave his supporters something to like about him; he also gave them things to dislike about Dukakis.

Public opinion in the 1988 election reacted to the candidates and the issues they presented. Throughout the campaign, the candidates had the opportunity to present themselves to the American people and make their views well known to them. Early in the campaign, George Bush focused on common American values—patriotism, pride in America, and strength in our national defenses. Bush told the American public what he stood for: the Pledge of Allegiance, the flag, a strong national defense and protection against the criminal element. He also took the initiative and defined his opponent: a liberal, a governor who allowed the pollution of streams and streets and who was too inexperienced to keep America strong.

Michael Dukakis did not find his voice to counter the charges made against him until very late in the campaign. The damage had already been done. The American public had decided they liked Bush, or at least what he stood for. And they did not like Dukakis, at least not for President.

Notes

1. Barbara G. Farah and Ethel Klein, "The Return of the Gender Gap," *Polling Report* 4, no. 12 (20 June 1988).

2. Polls conducted by the *New York Times* and CBS News are used to detail public opinion during the general election of 1988.

3. Morris P. Fiorina, *Retrospective Voting in American Elections* (New Haven: Yale University Press, 1981).

4. The gender gap refers to the differences in voting preferences between men and women; gender advantage refers to the degree to which one candidate is benefiting from the gender gap.

5

The Presidential Election

GERALD M. POMPER

And is this not an honourable spoil?
A gallant prize? Ha, cousin, is it not? . . .
In faith, it is a conquest for a prince to boast of.

Henry IV, Part 1

After enduring campaigns with little to honor, American voters anointed George Bush as their forty-first President.

The incumbent vice-president continued the pattern of national elections that has brought Republicans to the White House in all but one election in the past quarter of a century. Vice-President Bush, and his running mate, Senator J. Danforth Quayle, won almost 54 percent of the popular vote, gaining nearly 48 million votes, compared to over 41 million for the Democratic ticket of Governor Michael Dukakis and Senator Lloyd Bentsen. The winners achieved majorities in forty states, and collected 426 of the nation's 538 electoral votes.

The Republican victory broke some historic ground and provided some new political trivia. For the first time since the Second World War, the same party won three consecutive terms in the White House. Bush became the first sitting vice-president to win a national election since Martin Van Buren, long ago in 1836. And although political folklore asserts that National League success in the World Series brings Democrats to power, Bush imitated the Los Angeles Dodgers in a come-from-behind triumph.

Yet novelty was not the dominant feature of the 1988 presidential election. The most significant characteristic of the voting results was continuity and confirmation of prior political patterns. Instead of being George Bush's victory, it was an electoral valedictory for Ronald Reagan. Michael Dukakis was the loser, but not the cause of the loss. The election was an endorsement

TABLE 5.1
THE 1988 PRESIDENTIAL VOTE

State	Electoral Vote		Popular Vote		Percentage 1988 (two-party vote)		Percentage 1984 (two-party vote)	
	Bush	Dukakis	Bush	Dukakis	Bush	Dukakis	Reagan	Mondale
Alabama	9		809,663	547,347	59.7	40.3	61.3	38.7
Alaska	3		102,381	62,205	62.2	37.8	69.1	30.9
Arizona	7		694,379	447,272	60.8	39.2	67.1	32.9
Arkansas	6		463,574	344,991	57.3	42.7	61.2	38.8
California	47		4,756,490	4,448,393	51.7	48.3	58.2	41.8
Colorado	8		727,633	621,093	54.0	46.0	64.4	35.6
Connecticut	8		747,082	674,873	52.5	47.5	61.0	39.0
Delaware	3		130,581	99,479	56.8	43.2	60.0	40.0
District of Columbia		3	25,732	153,100	14.4	85.6	13.8	86.2
Florida	21		2,538,994	1,632,086	60.9	39.1	65.3	34.7
Georgia	12		1,070,089	715,635	59.9	40.1	60.2	39.8
Hawaii		4	158,625	192,364	45.2	54.8	55.7	44.3
Idaho	4		253,467	147,420	63.2	36.8	73.3	26.7
Illinois	24		2,298,648	2,180,657	51.3	48.7	56.5	43.5
Indiana	12		1,280,292	850,851	60.1	39.9	62.1	37.9
Iowa		8	541,540	667,085	44.8	55.2	53.7	46.3
Kansas	7		552,659	422,056	56.7	43.3	67.0	33.0
Kentucky	9		731,446	579,077	55.8	44.2	60.4	39.6
Louisiana	10		880,830	715,612	55.2	44.8	61.4	38.6
Maine	4		304,087	240,508	55.9	44.1	61.1	38.9
Maryland	10		834,202	793,939	51.2	48.8	52.8	47.2
Massachusetts		13	1,184,323	1,387,398	46.1	53.9	51.4	48.6
Michigan	20		1,969,435	1,673,496	54.1	45.9	59.5	40.5
Minnesota		10	958,199	1,106,975	46.4	53.6	49.9	50.1

Mississippi	7		551,745	360,892	60.5	39.5	62.3	37.7
Missouri	11		1,081,163	1,004,040	51.9	48.1	60.0	40.0
Montana	4		189,598	168,120	53.0	47.0	61.3	38.7
Nebraska	5		389,394	254,426	60.5	39.5	71.0	29.0
Nevada	4		205,942	132,716	60.8	39.2	67.3	32.7
New Hampshire	4		279,770	162,335	63.3	36.7	68.9	31.1
New Jersey	16		1,699,634	1,275,063	57.1	42.9	60.5	39.5
New Mexico	5		260,792	236,528	52.4	47.6	60.3	39.7
New York		36	2,975,276	3,228,304	48.0	52.0	54.0	46.0
North Carolina	13		1,232,132	890,034	58.1	41.9	62.0	38.0
North Dakota	3		165,517	127,081	56.6	43.4	65.7	34.3
Ohio	23		2,411,719	1,934,922	55.5	44.5	59.5	40.5
Oklahoma	8		678,244	483,373	58.4	41.6	69.1	30.9
Oregon		7	517,731	575,071	47.4	52.6	56.1	43.9
Pennsylvania	25		2,291,297	2,183,928	51.2	48.8	53.7	46.3
Rhode Island		4	169,730	216,668	43.9	56.1	51.8	48.2
South Carolina	8		599,871	367,511	62.0	38.0	64.1	35.9
South Dakota	3		165,516	145,632	53.2	46.8	63.3	36.7
Tennessee	11		939,434	677,715	58.1	41.9	58.2	41.8
Texas	29		3,014,007	2,231,286	56.4	43.6	64.1	35.9
Utah	5		426,858	206,853	67.4	32.6	75.1	24.9
Vermont	3		123,166	116,419	51.4	48.6	58.7	41.3
Virginia	12		1,305,131	860,767	60.2	39.8	62.7	37.3
Washington		10	800,182	844,554	48.7	51.3	56.6	43.4
West Virginia		6*	307,824	339,112	47.6	52.4	55.3	44.7
Wisconsin		11	1,043,584	1,122,090	48.2	51.8	54.6	45.3
Wyoming	3		106,814	67,077	61.4	38.6	71.4	28.6
TOTALS	426	112*	47,946,422	41,016,429	53.89	46.11	59.17	40.83

SOURCE: *Congressional Quarterly Weekly Report* 46 (12 November 1988): 3245.

NOTE: *One elector actually cast a vote for Lloyd Bentsen; the vote is recorded here for the actual Democratic candidate, Dukakis.

of the status quo, not a mandate for policy change. In longer perspective, the election demonstrated not the emergence of a new politics but the continued Republican party dominance of a transformed Presidency.

The Results

George Bush's victory, pictured in the map on the inside back cover of this book and detailed in table 5.1, was geographically broad. Winning states in every region of the nation, the vice-president did particularly well in the South and in the Rocky Mountain states. In thirteen states, he won better than three of every five votes; ten of these Republican strongholds were in these two regions.

The victory was broad, but shallow. Almost half of the Republican ticket's electoral votes came from states (depicted with diagonal lines on the map) in which a switch of no more than one in ten votes would have thrown the state into the Democratic column. In such a hypothetical change, Dukakis would have won the election with 313 electoral votes.

Nor was Bush's performance historically impressive. His proportion of the two-party popular vote was relatively low, in fact the lowest of any Republican victor since the beginning of the twentieth century. Even in comparison to three-candidate races, the vice-president's success is underwhelming. With the exception of Richard Nixon in 1968, Bush's margin of victory (in percentage terms) is less than that of any Republican winner since William McKinley narrowly defeated William Jennings Bryan in 1900.

In losing, Dukakis did well—for a Democrat. Winning ten states and the District of Columbia, he captured states in all regions of the nation outside the South, once a Democratic Garden of Eden, but now a paradise lost. The Massachusetts governor's share of the electoral vote was the best of the party's losses in twenty years. But, like four of the previous five Democratic nominees, he lost.

The most impressive feature of the election, geographically, is its continuity with the recent past. George Bush's electoral map is a lighter photocopy of Ronald Reagan's. Bush did well where the outcoming President had scored his greatest triumphs, and did poorly where his mentor had been relatively less successful. Indeed, the statistical correlation of their vote is the highest of any two candidates in American history.* The political significance is the statistical indication that Republicans have achieved a stable, long-lived, and dominant position in presidential politics.

*The correlation is .94, compared to .87 when Reagan's 1980 and 1984 votes are correlated. The figure is matched only when Harry Truman's vote in 1948 is combined with that year's southern states' rights vote and then correlated to the Roosevelt vote in 1940 and 1944.

TABLE 5.2

THE PRESIDENTIAL VOTE BY SOCIAL GROUPS (IN PERCENT)

% of 1988 Total		1988		1984		% Change Republican Vote (1984-88)
		Bush	Dukakis	Reagan	Mondale	
	Party					
35	Republicans	91	8	93	6	−2
37	Democrats	17	82	24	75	−7
26	Independents	55	43	63	35	−8
	Sex and marital status					
34	Married men	60	39	64	35	−4
35	Married women	54	45	59	41	−5
14	Unmarried men	52	47	56	42	−4
17	Unmarried women	42	57	49	50	−7
	Age					
20	18-29	52	47	59	40	−7
35	30-44	54	45	57	42	−3
22	45-59	57	42	60	39	−3
22	60 and older	50	49	52	48	−2
	Education					
8	Not high school graduate	43	56	49	50	−6
27	High school graduate	50	49	60	39	−10
30	Some college education	57	42	61	39	−4
35	College graduate or more	56	43	58	41	−2
16	Postgraduate education	50	49	52	48	−2
	Occupation					
31	Professional/manager	59	40	62	37	−3
11	White-collar worker	57	42	59	40	−2
13	Blue-collar worker	49	50	54	45	−5
9	Teacher/student	46	52	51	48	−5
5	Unemployed	37	62	32	67	+5
10	Homemaker	58	41	61	38	−3
16	Retired	50	49	60	40	−10
25	Union household	42	57	46	53	−4
	Income					
10	Under $10,000	33	64	45	55	−12
17	$10,001-19,999	45	53	56	44	−11
21	$20,000-29,999	51	47	61	39	−10
20	$30,000-39,999	60	39	66	34	−6
32	Over $40,000	62	37	68	32	−6

TABLE 5.2 *(continued)*

% of 1988 Total		1988 Bush	Dukakis	1984 Reagan	Mondale	% Change Republican Vote (1984-88)
	Race and region					
85	White	59	40	64	35	−5
21	East	54	45	57	42	−3
25	Midwest	57	42	64	35	−7
23	South	67	32	71	28	−4
15	West	58	41	66	33	−8
10	Black	12	86	9	89	+3
3	Hispanic	30	69	37	61	−7
	Religion					
48	White Protestant	66	33	72	27	−6
28	Catholic	52	47	54	45	−2
4	Jewish	35	64	32	67	+3
9	White fundamentalist or evangelical Christian	81	18	78	22	+3
	Community size					
12	Large cities	40	58	36	62	+4
55	Suburbs/small cities	54	44	57	42	−3
33	Rural/towns	56	42	69	29	−13

SOURCES: New York Times/CBS News poll, *New York Times,* 10 November 1988, B6; Cable News Network/Los Angeles Times poll, *National Journal* 20 (12 November 1988): 2855.

The same continuity is evident when we turn to votes among social groups. Table 5.2 shows the breakdown of the presidential vote, in 1984 as well as 1988, among demographic groups. A familiar pattern is evident in both years: Republican votes are more common among those groups that are more privileged, more established in society, more traditional and, aside from women, more numerous in America. Both Bush and Reagan were favored more by whites than by blacks or Hispanics, more by men than by women, more by Protestants (especially fundamentalists) than by Catholics or (especially) Jews, more by the middle-aged than by the young or the old. Similarly, the Republicans did particularly well among suburbanites, nonunion members, southerners, the wealthy, those in more prestigious occupations, and the better educated (except for those with graduate schooling).

The continuing pattern of Republican support among the "better elements" disguises some important variations between the elections of Reagan and Bush. Overall, Bush ran about five percentage points below his mentor, garnering

54 percent to the incumbent President's 59. Bush's losses, however, were concentrated among the lowest-status groups, such as those of lower income, lower education, and Hispanics. Racial divisions nationally decreased slightly, but remained enormous. Even after four generations, these divisions continued the bitter heritage of the Civil War.

The 1988 election results, therefore, had more of the character of a class division. The Democratic ticket won majorities among blue-collar workers, persons without any college education, and those below the median family income ($30,000 a year). In contrast, in 1984 Reagan had carried every one of these groups of disadvantaged voters. Dukakis's last-minute populist appeal, "I'm on your side," probably also reinforced class-based support among past party loyalists: women (discussed more fully in chapter 4), the unemployed, union households, Hispanics, and seven of every eight blacks.

The group divisions in the 1988 election reflect the different strategic targets of the two parties. Every candidate's strategy has two simple elements: Secure your own base, then capture part of the opponent's potential vote. While Dukakis secured his own base, he could not expand significantly beyond that vote. In contrast, Bush successfully implemented these campaign axioms.

Dukakis did solidify the Democratic coalition. The party unity he forged at the Atlanta convention continued in the voting booths of the nation. Dukakis won 82 percent of the self-identified Democrats, a larger proportion of party identifiers than any party nominee since 1964, even more than Jimmy Carter gained in his successful presidential campaign in 1976. More than half the Democrats who voted for Reagan in 1984 returned to the party fold,[1] paralleling the increasing class basis of the vote and the pro-Democratic movement among Catholics.[2] Despite the reported disappointment of blacks at the defeat of Jesse Jackson, they barely wavered in their solid support of the party ticket (although black turnout decreased in some critical states).

But, in 1988, "solidarity's not enough. . . . You can't win elections anymore just by holding the Democratic Party together."[3] The most significant meaning of the election is its confirmation that the long-time erosion of the Democratic base has shaped new contours on the landscape of American politics.

Erosion resulted from three related forces: shrinkage, disloyalty, and non-mobilization.[4] First, the Democratic base was smaller than in the past. The unionized section of the workforce was much smaller than in the party's glory years, reflecting the decline of manufacturing. Large cities and the poor, reliable sources of Democratic votes, were diminishing proportions of the electorate. The elderly, whose political memories were rooted in the traumas of the Great Depression of the 1930s, inevitably were passing from the scene. A second source of erosion was changing loyalties. Most dramatically, the southern anchor had been lost in a complete historic reversal, which has been taking shape over a forty-year period. Throughout American history, no Democrat has ever been elected President without winning a *majority* in the region. By 1988, no Democrat seemed likely to win more than a handful of Dixie's electoral votes.

There were many causes for this regional reversal: migration, ideological conservatism, the development of a high-tech economy, and party organization. Still, the most important cause was the racial revolution in the United States.[5] Historically, the one-party system served the cause of white supremacy in the South. As the national Democratic party increased its commitment to blacks, the one-party system lost its traditional justification, opening the region to Republican gains among whites and casting the Republican party in the role of defender of the racial status quo. By 1988, the Democrats could win only one of every three white votes in the South. Among white men, they did even worse—26 percent: "There's not much Democratic support left among the Bubbas and the Billy Bobs."[6]

The Democrats also lost support among other previous loyalists. The northern anchor of the party has been Catholics, especially those in the working class. Catholics remain more likely to vote Democratic than do white Protestants, and the difference in 1988 was similar to that in most recent elections.[7] The combination of social mobility among Catholics and the rise of new social issues, however, has lost the Democrats some of these votes. Losses are also evident among men, the other component of the gender gap; they have come to favor both the Republican party and Republican presidential candidates.[8]

Democratic losses have had a third source: the party's inability to mobilize potential support among nonvoters. In 1988, only half of all adult Americans actually cast presidential ballots, substantially less than in 1984. Nonvoting is most common among groups more loyal to the Democrats than the Republicans, and decreasing turnout over the years has been most marked in groups, such as blacks and the poor, that are most likely to support the Democratic party.[9]

Yet higher turnout would not necessarily help the Democrats. Leading scholarly analyses conclude that increased participation would have few significant effects on national elections.[10] Furthermore, postelection surveys indicate that nonvoters in 1988 favored Bush even more (by 50 to 34 percent) than those who did participate.[11] More votes cast would not inevitably mean relatively more Democratic votes; that result would occur only if the party could change the political environment (analyzed in chapter 1). In today's politics, it has lost these uncast votes, further eroding support where it counts—at the polls.

The obverse of Democratic losses has been Republican gains, successfully reinforced in the 1988 campaign. Bush carried the traditional Republican constituencies and maintained the more recent party gains among southerners, suburbanites, men, and Catholics. Although he could not match the extraordinary vote shares won by Reagan, Bush kept the party majority intact. Particularly encouraging for the future was the Republican lead among the baby boomers, now approaching middle-age, and its observable, though thin, margin among the youngest voters.

These trends hold the promise of extended party dominance. George Bush, an unspectacular candidate saddled with a running mate favored only by comedians, won a clear victory, swept the Republican base, and kept most of the extended electoral gains achieved in President Reagan's two victories. Bush's accomplishment is not the creation of a new party politics; it is the conservation of an inheritance.[12]

The Politics of the Vote

An election-day cartoon captured a dominant mood of the 1988 campaign. Waiting on line at the polls, a voter complained, "I still don't know whether to vote for Willie Horton's liberator and that host of the breakfast club, or Mr. out-of-the-loop and the guy who's no Jack Kennedy."[13] Apparently, many real voters shared these doubts about, respectively, Dukakis, Bentsen, Bush, and Quayle. Voter participation was the second-lowest in the twentieth century. Of those who did cast ballots, as many as one of six waited until election day to make their decisions.[14]

In examining the results, four political explanations are available. We can examine campaign factors and the voters' personal comparison of Bush and Dukakis (as analyzed in chapters 3 and 4). Specific issues, and the Reagan record, were also argued between the two party candidates. Ideological differences between conservatives and liberals add a third dimension. Finally, the election can be seen as a reflection of basic transformations of American politics.

The most obvious, but incomplete explanation is the conduct of the campaign itself. After all, polls during the year showed that Dukakis had begun with a lead of seventeen percentage points in the summer, that Bush had reversed his fortunes and then opened a large margin after the television debates, and that the gap then narrowed before Bush's 54 to 46 percent victory. (See figure 4.1.) Even before election night, political analysts were condemning Dukakis personally for "a campaign that never understood the demands of a general-election battle, that underestimated Mr. Bush and the ferocity of the campaign he would wage, and that seriously miscalculated the effect of sustained negative attacks." In the same vein, Republican strategists were complimented on "the tenacity of the candidate, the adherence to a well-drafted game plan and . . . a campaign designed to paint Mr. Dukakis as a liberal and to argue that Mr. Bush represented a stark contrast."[15]

Campaigners can make a difference, and they did so in 1988, but an analysis of the election results must begin with the recognition of structural conditions favorable to the Bush candidacy. Past elections had seen the emergence of a strong electoral base for his party (see chapter 3). As the candidate of the incumbent party, the vice-president had the advantage of running during a time of seeming peace and prosperity. No significant American involvement in foreign conflict had occurred during the Reagan administration, and the President had successfully negotiated a major step in world arms control. His party could honestly boast about the nation's economic growth, employment, and control of inflation. Problems in the economy also existed: the federal budget deficit, the national trade deficit, unemployment among blacks; but these problems were esoteric or hidden to most Americans. As a result, predictions of the election outcome based on gross economic data would have been quite accurate in 1988.[16]

The vice-president also was able to use incumbency to his personal advantage. Cooperating exceptionally, President Reagan's administration used the powers of office to aid his heir. Although philosophically opposed to it, the President allowed a popular bill requiring notice of plant closings to become law without his signature, and accepted congressional restrictions on arms control policy. Unpopular actions were delayed until after the election, including farm mortgage foreclosures, proposed changes in eligibility rules for social security, and an appeal to the Supreme Court to make abortion illegal. The President pitched in personally with vigorous barnstorming.

Bush began to claim some of the aura of the White House. To demonstrate his command of foreign policy, he represented the United States in a debate at the United Nations. The controversial attorney general, Edward Meese, was persuaded to resign, and Bush's candidate, Lauro Cavazos, was appointed secretary of education, the first Hispanic in the cabinet. The vice-president took on visible and popular ceremonial tasks, such as greeting the returning Discovery astronauts and witnessing the first destruction of American weapons under the INF treaty.

Crucial to the campaign of 1988, as in any campaign, was the Republicans' ability to set the agenda of the election decision. Bush persuasively argued one continuing theme: *Life in America is good.* The theme had multiple variations, positive and negative: A Republican administration has brought peace and prosperity, *but* Democrats bring unrest and inflation; George Bush stands for consensual national values, *but* Dukakis is a liberal and therefore suspicious; the vice-president is experienced and safe, *but* Dukakis is incapable and risky.

As the challenging party, the Democrats needed to argue for change, but failed in three efforts to establish a convincing theme. The initial focus on "competence" implicitly accepted that current conditions were good and needed only improved management. A later effort was made to turn attention from the present to the future, under the slogan "The best America is yet to come." Finally, the Democrats moved to counter their opponent's appeal to voter satisfaction, arguing that Republican policies were unfair to the middle class. Despite, and probably because of, these diverse efforts, Dukakis disregarded Mario Cuomo's early warning: "There has to be a why to a campaign. It's not enough that you're good looking and well-organized"[17] (even if Dukakis was both).

Issue differences between the presidential candidates did exist in the 1988 election, even if the campaign did not center on these differences. There were also issue agreements, particularly the unspoken pact to ignore such problems as the federal budget deficit. But as an influence on the election outcome, issue differences were far less important than simple approval of the past record of Ronald Reagan.

Sometimes these issue differences were obscure. One foreign observer sarcastically summarized what voters had learned about the candidates during the campaign:

> They thought Mr. Bush was too nice. They now know he can be nasty. If they had heard about Mr. Dukakis at all, they thought he was a technocrat. They now know he can be a stubborn smart-aleck. . . . They know that Mr. Dukakis lets murderers out of jail and that Mr. Bush wants to take away old-age pensions. Well, something like that. They have not learned what either man would do to put the economy on a sound footing or to deal with a reformist Russia. . . . The lesson of the campaign was that, to win, you must not say what you would do, nor what people want to hear. You must say nothing at all.[18]

Yet the candidates did speak on issues, in voluminous position papers, in speeches, and in the television debates. While issues constituted only a minority of the debates' content (see table 3.1 on page 90), the candidates did disagree on such substantive matters as health insurance, an antimissile system, the death penalty, abortion, taxation of capital gains, financing college education, and aid to the Nicaraguan *Contras*.

On most specific issues, Dukakis's position won more favor from the voters than Bush's, but elections are not public opinion polls on discrete topics. They are generalized judgments, on men as well as measures. Each election also reflects previous political history, the 1988 contest even more than most. Voters bring their long-term memories to the polls, as expressed in their party loyalties, and they bring their shorter-term memories of the most recent election.

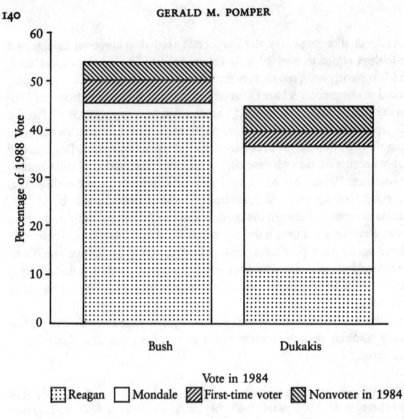

Vote in 1984

::: Reagan   ☐ Mondale   ▧ First-time voter   ▨ Nonvoter in 1984

FIGURE 5.1
CHANGES IN THE VOTE, 1984 TO 1988
(IN PERCENTAGE OF TOTAL 1988 VOTE)

As the heir-apparent of Ronald Reagan, Bush benefited from these memories. The strongest correlate of the presidential vote was approval of the President: Bush won 95 percent of those who wanted "to continue Reagan's policies," and but 8 percent of those who wanted "to change these policies."[19] This general attitude was far more important than voters' opinions on particular issues. Indeed, as we see above, it was at least as important as party loyalty, the most obvious influence on voters.

The vice-president got the bulk of his vote (as seen in figure 5.1) from those who had voted for his mentor four years earlier. These Reaganites provided five of every six votes for Bush. In contrast, Reagan had a wider appeal. When he ran for reelection in 1984, the President gained a third of his support from those who had voted Democratic or had not voted at all in 1980. In one sense, then, Bush could be said to be more dependent on Reagan's electoral base than the President himself.

Beyond particular policy controversies, Bush and Dukakis exemplified the continuing differences between Republicans and Democrats in the interests and philosophies they represent. Concerned with the needs of economic producers, Republicans will restrain government to enhance private goods (such as more restaurants). Focusing on the interests of consumers, Democrats will enlist government to enhance public goods (such as health inspections of restaurants). To one, government threatens; to the other, government protects.

One specific issue in this year's election was illustrative: day care for children of working parents. A majority of mothers of one-year-old children now hold paying jobs. This latest evidence of the national revolution in gender roles makes day care a political necessity. In one of his principal policy initiatives, Vice-President Bush developed a program to provide tax credits for parents of preschool children. Governor Dukakis, in contrast, endorsed a Democratic program in Congress to provide state grants for governmental programs.

The Politics of Values

There is a still more fundamental distinction between the parties' core values: liberty for the Republicans, equal justice for the Democrats. These are also consensual American values, for the United States believes, as the Pledge of Allegiance makes explicit, in both "liberty *and* justice for all." Republicans and Democrats represent the two sides of the nation's continuing internal dialogue about its basic beliefs and the way to reconcile the conflicts between them.

Value differences also underlie party conflict, not only in 1988, on a series of moral issues, ranging from abortion in the privacy of a doctor's office to public rituals of patriotism, such as the Pledge of Allegiance. In contrast to their positions on economic issues, Republicans tend to favor government activity in these areas, while Democrats are more reluctant to invoke the coercive power of the state.

In these matters, Republicans show both theoretic and historic consistency. The classic meanings of conservatism include the belief that the government should not only keep order but also should attempt to develop character and virtue in its citizens. Conservatives see society as more than a collection of private individuals and argue that our public lives are shaped by institutions such as the church and the home. Therefore, matters such as religion or family structure or sexuality are too important to be entirely neglected by government.

Republicans have been the moralistic party in America, which is not necessarily the same as being moral. The party was created to deal with the moral evil of slavery, was closely associated with the temperance movement, and favored constitutional prohibition of alcoholic beverages as late as 1932. Republicans pioneered women's suffrage and the Equal Rights Amendment (endorsed in their 1944 platform) because they viewed women as the carriers of society's moral creed. Today, when feminism undermines rather than supports traditional roles, the party opposes the Equal Rights Amendment.

The party's historic moralism continued in Bush's focus on such issues as pornography, school prayer, and the retributive justice of the death penalty. This attitude is even evident in a favorite anthem at Republican conventions, "The Battle Hymn of the Republic." Originally expressing the party's abolitionist sentiments, the hymn best voices contemporary Republican fervor in the redemptive words of the last verse: "As [Christ] died to make men holy, let us live to make men free."

On moral issues, modern Democrats have adopted a consistent liberal position. Historically, the party was philosophically divided between southern traditional fundamentalists and Catholic workers, the latter more forgiving of worldly sin. Traditionalists favored Prohibition and reading the King James Bible in schools, for example, while Catholics opposed what they regarded as impositions of Protestant morality or a Protestant text.

As southern traditionalists have left its ranks, the Democratic party has come to a more coherent position than before. Democrats now espouse moral liberalism, which makes a sharp distinction between private and public life. In this philosophy, individuals, not society, decide whether and where to pray, whether and when to abort a fetus, whether and how to salute the flag. Emphasizing individualism, Democrats are more tolerant of different life styles, even of eccentricity, sometimes of deviance. When Democrats sing, they praise the diversity and openness of an America "beautiful, for spacious skies . . . [and] good with brotherhood from sea to shining sea."[20]

Given the election returns, the Republican arguments seem more congenial to the voting majority. That success partially resulted from essentially tactical factors, such as Dukakis's failure to answer attacks quickly, or the technical quality of Republican advertisements. The Bush victory has deeper causes, however, rooted in basic values and elementary emotions. These emotional causes were more important than any factual distortions.[21]

When he recited the Pledge of Allegiance, Bush appealed to American patriotism. When he deplored alleged support for child pornography by the American Civil Liberties Union, he touched the nation's love of children. When he attacked the Massachusetts furlough program, he invoked the fear of crime. When his campaign distributed pictures linking Dukakis to Willie Horton, a black escaped convict who raped a white woman, it deliberately stirred the basest racist hysterias. These emotional tones were powerful in themselves; when

TABLE 5.3
SOURCES OF THE PRESIDENTIAL VOTE (IN PERCENT)

	Total Citations	% Voting for Bush	% Voting for Dukakis	Contribution to Vote Bush	Contribution to Vote Dukakis
Positive characteristics of candidates					
Experience	34	97	3	21.2	.6
Competence	27	73	26	12.7	4.6
Cares about people like me	24	23	75	3.8	11.6
Time for a change	18	5	92	.6	10.7
Vision for the future	17	52	46	5.8	5.1
Vice-presidential candidates	13	14	86	1.2	7.2
Dislike own party candidate	10	50	44	3.2	2.8
TV debates	7	54	46	2.4	2.1
Avoiding recession	4	80	19	2.0	.5
More likable	3	52	46	1.0	.9
TOTALS	157			53.9	46.1
Negative characteristics of opponent					
Too liberal	28	94	6	17.3	1.1
Ran dirty campaign	28	30	69	5.5	12.4
Bad judgment	24	46	53	7.2	8.2
Leaves me cold	19	55	43	6.8	5.2
Too risky	15	76	24	7.5	2.3
Close to special interests	13	26	72	2.2	6.0
Too tied to past	10	10	88	.6	5.6
Won't stand up for America	8	65	33	3.4	1.7
Too much of a wimp	7	38	60	1.8	2.7
Won't be elected	4	63	34	1.6	.9
TOTALS	156			53.9	46.1
Issue priorities					
Budget deficit	25	39	60	5.8	9.0
National defense	23	84	15	11.5	2.0
Abortion	20	63	36	7.4	4.3
Crime	18	67	31	7.1	3.3
Government ethics	17	31	67	3.1	6.8
Taxes	15	70	29	6.2	2.7
Drugs	14	41	58	3.4	4.9
Environmental protection	11	28	70	1.8	4.6
Unemployment	10	35	64	2.1	3.9
Foreign trade	5	57	42	1.7	1.2
No issue	12	52	45	3.7	3.2
TOTALS	170			53.8	45.9

SOURCE: Cable News Network/Los Angeles Times poll, *National Journal* 20 (12 November 1988): 2854.

Dukakis voiced no effective response, they became the dominant chords of the election duet.

The effectiveness of the Bush campaign can be seen more precisely in exit polls. Table 5.3 records voter responses to three questions: "Why did you vote for your candidate?" "What did you like least about his opponent?" "Which issues were most important to you?" For each question, in the last two columns of the table, we calculate the contribution made by each response to the Bush and Dukakis vote.[22]

Bush's two advantages are evident in these calculations. First, he established himself as the candidate of the safe status quo. He gained considerable support on the basis of his experience and presumed competence and on his stand against change in the tax structure, as well as fears of the risk involved in a Dukakis Presidency. Second, Bush became the champion of traditionalist values, winning significant shares of the vote through his appeals to conservative attitudes on national defense, abortion, and crime, as well as the negative judgments of Dukakis as "too liberal" or unable to "stand up for America."

The vice-president's stress on these problems was astoundingly successful. Abortion and crime, areas largely outside a President's responsibility, were each cited as important voting criteria by a fifth of the voters. Less than half that number of voters stressed U.S. relations with the Soviet Union, a core concern of any President.[23] But Bush's victory was not personal. He won few votes on the basis of likability or his performance on the television debates, while he lost votes through the campaign he conducted and his associations to "the past" and "special interests."

Dukakis, for his part, hardly aroused personal enthusiasm. Many voters agreed with him that competence was an important criterion, yet most of this group regarded Dukakis as the less competent candidate. The strengths of the governor were not personal. Dukakis gained votes because he came across vaguely as more caring and more oriented toward change, and because he was preferred on many substantive issues.

A novel feature of the 1988 results was the apparent impact of the vice-presidential candidates. One of seven voters cited running mates Quayle and Bentsen as influences on their votes, and the impact was strongly favorable for the Democrats. Indeed, a nasty campaign joke had it that the Republicans were concerned that Bush, if elected, would die in office; the Democrats were concerned that Dukakis, if elected, would live.

Underlying all specific considerations was the electorate's attitude toward the outgoing President. Whatever the issue, those who approved "of the way Ronald Reagan has handled his job as President since 1981" voted for Bush, and those who disapproved voted for Dukakis, as detailed in table 5.4. Of

TABLE 5.4

THE PRESIDENTIAL VOTE, ISSUES, AND REAGAN APPROVAL (IN PERCENT)

Issue	Approve of Reagan			Disapprove of Reagan		
	Citing Issue	Bush	Dukakis	Citing Issue	Bush	Dukakis
Crime	24	89	10	12	23	76
Help middle class	16	64	35	37	5	94
Environment	7	70	27	16	8	91
Prosperity	25	88	11	24	10	88
Budget deficit	10	79	19	16	8	90
Taxes	17	89	10	10	21	77
Defense spending	9	91	8	6	12	85
Soviet relations	9	94	5	2	24	71
Abortion	8	88	10	5	10	78
Vice-presidency	10	57	42	21	5	94
"Liberalism"	23	84	15	31	7	92
Party	13	82	17	16	7	93
Care for poor	6	48	51	26	3	96
Likability	10	81	18	8	8	87
Patriotism	13	93	6	4	28	68
Jesse Jackson	3	76	21	7	4	93
TV debates	8	84	15	6	16	83
Experience	35	97	2	7	49	48

SOURCE: Data recalculated from CBS News poll.

course, attitudes toward Reagan, and toward Bush, were closely related to voters' basic partisanship, but these attitudes were not automatic reflexes of Republican or Democratic loyalty. When it comes to the vote itself, opinion toward the President had as much independent influence as overall partisanship.[24]

Policy preferences favorable to Bush were largely expressive, rather than specific. Yet, if vague, Bush's victory was more deeply rooted than an issue referendum. It was an assertion of basic American beliefs now more closely associated with the Republican party: anticommunism, the uniqueness of the American experience, intolerance of political minorities, distrust of government.[25] To the delight of his partisans and the dismay of his critics, Bush wrapped himself in the Stars and Stripes. But what better clothing is there for an American politician?

Bush's victory, based on conservative values, suggests an ideological interpretation of the election. Certainly Bush framed the electoral contest in these terms, seeking the support of conservatives during and after the Republican convention (see chapter 2) and turning "liberal" into a political epithet. Dukakis tried to avoid the label, and then returned vigorously to traditional liberal themes in the closing weeks of the campaign.

The electorate responded to the candidates. The proportion of liberals and conservatives remain unchanged over the Reagan years, with conservatives outnumbering liberals by 33 to 18 percent. What was different in 1988 was the close correspondence of ideology to the vote. Bush won four of every five conservatives, the same as Reagan, and conservatives were even more important to Bush than to Reagan. While Reagan won a tenth of his votes from self-declared liberals, only one of every sixteen Bush voters would accept the liberal label.

Dukakis did well among liberals, matching Bush's performance among conservatives, and actually did considerably better on the left than previous Democratic candidates have done. The Massachusetts governor also gained an even break among the large group of moderates, nearly a majority in the electorate. Like all recent Democratic candidates, except Jimmy Carter in 1976, he ran badly among conservatives; significantly, Carter is the only Democratic winner in the past quarter of a century. The polarization of the vote made the election an ideological decision, but given the greater number of conservatives, it also made the election a Republican victory.

TABLE 5.5
PARTY AND IDEOLOGY IN THE PRESIDENTIAL VOTE
IN PERCENT VOTING FOR BUSH (REAGAN)

Ideology	Partisanship			
	Republican (35%) Bush (Reagan)	Independent (26%) Bush (Reagan)	Democratic (37%) Bush (Reagan)	Total Bush (Reagan)
Conservative (33%)	95 (96)	77 (87)	34 (44)	80 (82)
Moderate (45%)	87 (89)	51 (59)	18 (24)	49 (53)
Liberal (18%)	73 (75)	26 (40)	6 (12)	18 (28)
TOTALS	91 (93)	55 (63)	17 (24)	54 (59)

SOURCE: Data recalculated from CBS News poll.

Table 5.5 further illuminates the ideological polarization of the election, by showing the distribution of the Bush vote, by both partisanship and ideology, alongside the 1984 Reagan vote. (The second number in each cell is Reagan's vote among the designated group.) Clearly, both factors are important, but Bush benefited from the combination. He won decisively among all varieties of Republicans, even the smaller groups that rejected the conservative label. Dukakis suffered defections from the sizable factions of moderates and conservatives within the Democratic rank and file. The Republican vote was a party vote, reinforced by ideology. The Democratic vote was also a party vote, but one weakened by ideology.*

The Effects of the Vote

For the Republican party, the election results were promising signs, indicating the stabilization of its vote and its likely future dominance of presidential elections. In a campaign of conflicting agendas, the party's stress on basic values became dominant. In an election defined by ideology, the conservative candidate won. In a vote marked by adherence to party loyalties, the Republican candidate won. In a contest without Reagan on the ballot, his tepid successor won.

The party's hopes could be lifted further by voters' self-declared loyalties. Since the time of Franklin Roosevelt, the Democrats had been the dominant party, with leads as great as 2–1 during the 1960s. By 1984, and continuing to 1988, the Republicans had nearly reached parity, even as their national vote fell.[26] Further potential for electoral growth existed in the party's small edge among nonvoters and among those who voted for the first time in 1984 (see figure 5.1).

Together, these trends make 1988 a confirming election, demonstrating the long-term "secular realignment" of American politics toward a Republican presidential majority. This realignment is not a sudden event, occurring in a single "critical election."[27] It is the accumulated result of population changes, weakening party loyalties, innovative campaign methods, and changes in the issue agenda of American politics from economic issues to basic values.[28] Republican power is more than the popularity of particular candidates or Presidents. It is the strength of a party that most voting Americans now believe is better able, as a party, to safeguard their peace, prosperity, and political philosophy.[29]

This party realignment cannot be explained by blaming individual Democratic candidates for conducting poor campaigns. These candidates, after all, were openly chosen by their party and truly represented their party's beliefs. Democrats have lost presidential elections with nominees from the Northeast,

---

*The following table shows the combined distribution of partisan and ideological loyalties in 1988, calculated from the CBS News/New York Times election-day exit poll. Each cell is the appropriate percentage of all voters answering both relevant questions.

	Republicans	Independents	Democrats
Conservatives	19.9%	7.7%	6.7%
Moderates	13.2	14.7	18.4
Liberals	2.0	4.3	13.0

the Midwest and the South, and with nominees from the left, center, and right of their party. The fault is not in the party's stars, but in itself.

Democrats certainly remain a strong party, in control of both houses of Congress, increasingly well financed, and competitive for the Presidency. Capture of the White House will come eventually, if for no other reason than the inevitable swings of the electoral cycle. To bolster their prospects, however, Democrats must do more than wait complacently for the next scandal or recession. They must give more attention to the growing areas of the nation, looking for candidates from the South and West. They must repair their losses among major voting groups such as white southerners, men, and Catholics, and mobilize their potential support among nonvoters.

Most of all, presidential Democrats must understand the value of values. The party's economic and welfare programs remain popular, and an electoral majority can be forged from voters' concerns for equality and social justice. To win this support, however, Democrats must first assure the electorate that they truly endorse its basic and emotional commitments to national defense, public safety, and moral stability. They need not imitate Republicans. Future Democratic candidates must only step over a "values threshold" before they enter the arena of substantive political conflict.

The Republicans' national strength is clear, but it is not sufficiently long lived or sufficiently deep to be invulnerable. Even as Bush won the Presidency, the Democrats made gains in both houses of Congress (see chapter 6) and in state elections. Instead of accepting a new party loyalty, voters became more inclined to split their tickets. This partisan ambiguity was particularly marked among Bush voters; more than a fourth backed Democrats for Congress, compared to a sixth of Dukakis voters who turned around to vote Republican for the House.[30] To many Americans, this split decision is a desirable informal addition to the constitutional scheme of checks and balances.[31]

The divided vote carries important implications in long-run consequences for the character of American government. Behind the different votes may be different views of the nature of these offices. In every political system, the distinguished British commentator Walter Bagehot wrote in 1867, there are two distinct elements:

> First, those which excite and preserve the reverence of the population—the *dignified* parts . . . ; and next, the *efficient* parts—those by which it, in fact, works and rules. There are two great objects which every constitution must attain to be successful, which every old and celebrated one must have wonderfully achieved: every constitution must first *gain* authority, and then *use* authority; it must first win the loyalty and confidence of mankind, and then employ that homage in the work of government.[32]

In the United States, the Presidency has always combined dignified and efficient parts; the President has been characterized as both the chief of state and the chief of government. Increasingly, voters may see the office as the dignified element in our informal Constitution. The President becomes the personification of the common values of the society, the ceremonial prince of the nation more than its political leader. This use of the office was handled masterfully by Ronald Reagan, who was well prepared as a former actor to create political drama: "That which is mystic in its claims; that which is occult in its mode of action; that which is brilliant to the eye; that which is seen vividly for a moment, and then is seen no more; that which is hidden and unhidden; that which is specious, and yet interesting. . . ."[33]

Republicans are more likely to win elections to a dignified Presidency because they are more favored on the basic values that this kind of office embodies. Republicans are seen as more likely to "stand up for America" and to preserve tradition. Issue preferences are subordinated in these elections, at least in tranquil times, because the Presidency is not seen as the office for resolving political conflict.

It then becomes the job of Congress to deal with the particularistic needs of constituents and the distinctive demands of interest groups. Americans call themselves ideological conservatives, but also favor "operational liberalism," endorsing government programs to promote health, education, and civil rights.[34] Because Democrats are more trusted to "care about people like me," or to be "on your side," Democrats continue to control the House and Senate. Divided government is the result of a divided American political mind.

A divided government is unlikely to be an active government, for the Constitution provides no substitute for the Presidency as a continuing source of energy and policy direction. A dignified Presidency is also a weakened Presidency, even though the office certainly carries with it much real power, in the critical areas of foreign policy and nominations to the Supreme Court. As the President becomes ever more the spokesman of the nation's consensual values, however, he becomes ever less able to challenge the nation to new values.

The division of party control of the Presidency and Congress also carries short-run implications for the incoming Bush administration. Faced by increased Democratic strength in Congress, the new President will find it difficult to set off in any new policy directions. Moreover, having campaigned with limited attention to specific issues, he cannot claim a mandate for his policies. Although the Republican campaign issued hundreds of policy proposals, "the politics of incivility remained its dominant tone." Bush won the election "by blackguarding his opponent. The question neither he nor his men had addressed was what he had done to himself"[35]—or to the governmental process.

The vote itself (see table 5.3) cannot be read as an endorsement of Bush's program. Policies toward abortion and crime were important in the Republican victory, but these can be affected little by the President, except possibly through Supreme Court appointments subject to Senate approval. Bush did win votes from persons concerned with national defense. Yet, no meaningful policy mandate can be read from these opinions, since there was little difference between the candidates in this area, and voters did not support an increase in military spending.

The clearest policy mandate in the election returns deals with taxes. Before, during, and even after the campaign, Bush repeated his Clint Eastwood imitation: "Read my lips, no new taxes." Two-thirds of the voters endorsed this position, and the tax issue contributed significantly to the Republican vote. At the same time, the electorate seemed to echo Bush's call for a "kinder, gentler nation" and favored more spending on education and the environment, as well as more attention to the concerns of blacks. How could these conflicting preferences be reconciled with the same electorate's priority concern, the federal budget deficit? Despite their endorsement for tax restraint, fully two-thirds of the voters saw the contradiction, and expected Bush to ask for more taxes.[36]

The election results provide no policy mandate for the new President other than the confining promise of no increase in taxes. The new administration owes its power to the popularity of Ronald Reagan and the electoral coalition he passed on. It inherits the problems, but not the personal support, of its progenitor. George Bush asked for nothing more than to be a substitute for Ronald Reagan. He has his wish.

Notes

1. *New York Times,* 10 November 1988, B6.

2. Polls significantly disagree on changes among Catholics and Jews. Table 5.2 reports the −2 percent and +3 percent shifts recorded by the New York Times/CBS News poll. However, the Cable News Network/Los Angeles Times poll found four-year decreases in Republican support from 59 to 49 percent and 32 to 24 percent.

3. William Schneider, "Solidarity's Not Enough," *National Journal* 20 (12 November 1988): 2853-55.

4. These categories are derived from Robert Axelrod's quadrennial analysis of party voter coalitions. Most recently, see "Presidential Electoral Coalitions in 1984," *American Poltiical Science Review* 80 (March 1986): 282-84.

5. Race, indeed, is the best single, general explanation for the current transformation of American politics. See Edward G. Carmines and James A. Stimson, *Issue Evolution: The Racial Transformation of American Politics* (Princeton: Princeton University Press, 1988).

6. Schneider, "Solidarity's Not Enough,'" 2853.

7. Paul Abramson, John Aldrich, and David Rohde, *Change and Continuity in the 1984 Elections* (Washington, D.C.: CQ Press, 1986), 146.

8. A slight male preference for Republicans, and a larger female preference for Democrats, is evident in party identification. Both men and women largely cast their votes along party lines, but men were slightly more likely both to vote their Republican loyalty and to defect from Democratic loyalty. Independent men gave Bush 58 percent, Independent women 52 percent. See chapter 4, and *New York Times*, 10 November 1988, B6.

9. Frances Fox Piven and Richard A. Cloward, *Why Americans Don't Vote* (New York: Pantheon, 1988), 160-64.

10. Raymond Wolfinger and Steven Rosenstone, *Who Votes?* (New Haven: Yale University Press, 1980), chaps. 4, 6.

11. *New York Times*, 21 November 1988, B16.

12. Using a familiar typology, the election of 1988 should be categorized as a "maintaining" election. See Angus Campbell et al., *The American Voter* (New York: Wiley, 1960), 531-38.

13. Steve Kelley, *San Diego Union*, distributed by Copley News Service.

14. Thomas B. Edsall and Richard Marin, reporting the ABC News poll, *Washington Post National Weekly*, 14 November 1988, 13.

15. *Wall Street Journal*, 8 November 1988, A1; *New York Times*, 12 November 1988, 8.

16. See Steven Rosenstone, *Forecasting Presidential Elections* (New Haven: Yale University Press, 1983), 40-42.

17. *New York Times*, 29 March 1988, A1.

18. "The Perils of Punditry," *Economist*, 5 November 1988, 23f.

19. Equal proportions of the electorate preferred each course. Bush won a critical margin of support (by 57 to 41 percent) among the quarter of the electorate that claimed their vote was "not influenced by Reagan's policies." Data are from the CBS News/New York Times election day exit poll. See also chapter 4.

20. These points are further elaborated in Gerald Pomper, "The Evolving Ideologies of the Parties," *The World & I*, November 1988, 28.

21. Kathleen Hall Jamieson, "Is the Truth Now Irrelevant in Presidential Campaigns?" *Washington Post National Weekly*, 7 November 1988, 28.

22. The contribution of each factor is calculated by multiplying the proportion of people who mentioned the item by the percentage of people who voted for Bush or Dukakis. Since more than one response was permitted, resulting figures are then recalculated on a base of 100 percent. Illustratively, 34 percent mentioned experience as a positive characteristic, and 97 percent of these people voted for Bush. All the responses summed to 155 percent. The contribution of experience to Bush's 53.9 percent of the vote is: $.34 \times .97 + 1.55 = 21.2$ percent.

23. New York Times/CBS News poll, *New York Times*, 9 November 1988, A25.

24. On half the issues listed in table 5.4, the division of the vote is very similar whether we examine approval of Reagan or party loyalty. On the remaining issues, approval ratings are significantly more highly correlated to the vote on five factors: defense spending, Soviet relations, abortion, patriotism, and experience. Partisanship is more closely related to the vote on four factors: helping the middle class, caring for the poor, the vice-presidential nomination, and party itself. Data were recalculated from the CBS

News/New York Times election day exit poll.

25. Michael Robinson saw these advantages early, in "Can Values Save George Bush?" *Public Opinion* 11 (July/August 1988): 11-13, 59-60.

26. Abramson et al, *Continuity and Change,* 209-14.

27. These terms, and the fundamental concepts of party realignment, were originated by V.O. Key, Jr., in "A Theory of Critical Elections," *Journal of Politics* 17 (February 1955): 3-18; and V.O. Key, Jr., "Secular Realignment and the Party System," *Journal of Politics* 21 (May 1959): 198-210. Important later works include Walter Dean Burnham, *Critical Elections* (New York: Norton, 1970); Jerome Clubb et al., *Partisan Realignment* (Beverly Hills: Sage, 1980); and Carmines and Stimson, *Issue Evolution.*

28. Recent studies of trends toward a Republican majority include Everett Ladd, "As the Realignment Turns," *Public Opinion* 7 (December/January 1985): 2-7; Stanley Kelley, "Democracy and the New Deal Party System," in *Project on the Federal Social Role* (Washington, D.C.: National Conference on Social Welfare, 1986); John Petrocik, "Realignment: New Party Coalitions and the Nationalization of the South," *Journal of Politics* 49 (May 1987): 347-75; John K. White, *The New Politics of Old Values* (Hanover, N.H.: University Press of New England, 1988); and Maureen Moakley, *Party Realignment in the American States* (Columbus: Ohio State University Press, forthcoming).

29. A month before the election, voters believed the Republican party was "better able to insure a strong economy" (by 52 to 31 percent) and "more likely to keep us out of war" (by 42 to 30 percent). At this point, doing better than his party, Dukakis trailed Bush by only 50 to 45 percent. See CBS News/New York Times poll, 8-10 October 1988.

30. Adam Clymer, *New York Times,* 14 November 1988, B9.

31. According to an October 1988 NBC/Wall Street Journal poll, 54 percent of voters "think it is better to have different parties controlling Congress and the Presidency"; see *National Journal* 20 (17 December 1988): 3214.

32. *The English Constitution* (London: Oxford University Press, 1928; first published 1867), 4.

33. Ibid., 7.

34. The distinction was originally made by Lloyd Free and Hadley Cantril, *The Political Beliefs of Americans* (New York: Simon and Schuster, 1968), and repeatedly verified in later opinion polls.

35. *Newsweek* 112 (21 November 1988): 116-18.

36. New York Times/CBS News poll; *New York Times,* 27 November 1988, E4.

6

The Congressional Elections

Ross K. Baker

Throughout the presidential campaign, Governor Michael Dukakis tried to convince the American voters to look beyond the peace and evident prosperity and ponder some of the disquieting signs of the future. He asked them to think ahead about the future well-being of their children and to believe that "the best America is yet to come." Dukakis, however, learned to his regret that in American politics the future has a very weak constituency and that the oldest political standard is still the most powerful: What have you done for me lately?

But if Dukakis failed to make the case for a change in times that were tranquil, if not downright quiescent, other Democrats were able to benefit from services rendered. The ranks of Democrats in Congress were modestly strengthened—a net gain for the party of one Senate seat and five House seats. Yet the real story of the congressional elections of 1988 is not one of gains so much as it is one of continuity. The real victor in the congressional elections was not the Democratic party, it was the "incumbent party."

One is almost tempted to make the case that voters were hedging their bets, that they were unwilling to accept Governor Dukakis's anxieties about the future but prudently elected Democratic majorities to both houses of Congress to keep President Bush humble and cautious in his policies. A secondary set of checks and balances might even be read into what the electorate did on 8 November 1988—a line of defense for the cautious voters that reinforces the constitutional separation of powers with a Presidency that is normally Republican and a Congress that is habitually Democratic.

Such a strategic logic on the part of the electorate has never been proven, however. In 100 million disaggregated decisions in 435 House elections and 33 Senate contests, voters responded to appeals that were local and personal rather than national and programmatic. In terms of the outcome, indeed, the presidential and congressional contests might have taken place in different coun-

TABLE 6.1

THE COMPOSITION OF CONGRESS IN 1989

U.S. Senate

100th Congress		101st Congress	
Democrats	54	Democrats	55
Republicans	46	Republicans	45

Democrats		Republicans	
Freshmen	5	Freshmen	5
Incumbents reelected	14	Incumbents reelected	9
Incumbents defeated	1	Incumbents defeated	3
John Melcher, Mont.		Lowell P. Weicker, Conn.	
		David K. Karnes, Neb.	
		Chic Hecht, Nev.	

U.S. House

	Seats	100th Congress		101st Congress		Gain/Loss
		Dem.	Rep.	Dem.	Rep.	
Alabama	7	5	2	5	2	
Alaska	1	0	1	0	1	
Arizona	5	1	4	1	4	
Arkansas	4	3	1	3	1	
California	45	27	18	27	18	
Colorado	6	3	3	3	3	
Connecticut	6	3	3	3	3	
Delaware	1	1	0	1	0	
Florida	19	12	7	10	9	− 2D/ + 2R
Georgia	10	8	2	9	1	+ 1D/ − 1R
Hawaii	2	1	1	1	1	
Idaho	2	1	1	1	1	
Illinois	22	13	9	14	8	+ 1D/ − 1R
Indiana	10	6	4	6	4	
Iowa	6	2	4	2	4	
Kansas	5	2	3	2	3	
Kentucky	7	4	3	4	3	
Louisiana	8	4	4	4	4	
Maine	2	1	1	1	1	
Maryland	8	6	2	6	2	
Massachusetts	11	10	1	10	1	
Michigan	18	11	7	11	7	
Minnesota	8	5	3	5	3	
Mississippi	5	4	1	4	1	
Missouri	9	5	4	5	4	
Montana	2	1	1	1	1	

TABLE 6.1 *(continued)*

	Seats	100th Congress		101st Congress		Gain/Loss
		Dem.	Rep.	Dem.	Rep.	
Nebraska	3	0	3	1	2	+1D/ −1R
Nevada	2	1	1	1	1	
New Hampshire	2	0	2	0	2	
New Jersey	14	8	6	8	6	
New Mexico	3	1	2	1	2	
New York	34	20	14	21	13	+1D/ −1R
North Carolina	11	8	3	8	3	
North Dakota	1	1	0	1	0	
Ohio	21	11	10	11	10	
Oklahoma	6	4	2	4	2	
Oregon	5	3	2	3	2	
Pennsylvania	23	12	11	12	11	
Rhode Island	2	1	1	0	2	−1D/ +1R
South Carolina	6	4	2	4	2	
South Dakota	1	1	0	1	0	
Tennessee	9	6	3	6	3	
Texas	27	17	10	19	8	+2D/ −2R
Utah	3	1	2	1	2	
Vermont	1	0	1	0	1	
Virginia	10	5	5	5	5	
Washington	8	5	3	5	3	
West Virginia	4	4	0	4	0	
Wisconsin	9	5	4	5	4	
Wyoming	1	0	1	0	1	
TOTAL	435	257	178	260	175	+3D/ −3R

SOURCE: *Congressional Quarterly Weekly Report,* 12 November 1988.

tries. The results of the congressional elections show little change in the partisan balance in the two houses of Congress. Table 6.1 illustrates the remarkable continuity in the proportions of Democrats and Republicans from the 100th Congress to the 101st. The absence of dramatic change in the overall party balance is attributable, in large measure, to the ability of incumbents in both parties to prevail.

The Importance of Being Incumbent

The Senate ended up with a Democratic edge in seats of 55–45 over Republicans, a net gain of one seat for the party from the last Congress. That modest increase, however, needs to be qualified. One of the four Democrats who unseated

TABLE 6.2
CHANGE OF PARTISANSHIP IN THE HOUSE AND SENATE, 1954-88

	Total Changes	Incumbent Defeated		Open Seat	
		Democrat to Republican	Republican to Democrat	Democrat to Republican	Republican to Democrat
House					
1954	26	3	18	2	3
1956	20	7	7	2	4
1958	50	1	35	0	14
1960	37	23	2	6	6
1962	19	9	5	2	3
1964	57	5	39	5	8
1966	47	39	1	4	3
1968	11	5	0	2	4
1970	25	2	9	6	8
1972	23	6	3	9	5
1974	55	4	36	2	13
1976	22	7	5	3	7
1978	33	14	5	8	6
1980	41	27	3	10	1
1982	31	1	22	3	5
1984	22	13	3	5	1
1986	20	1	5	7	8
1988	8	1	5	1	1
Senate					
1954	8	2	4	1	1
1956	8	1	3	3	1
1958	13	0	11	0	2
1960	2	1	0	1	0
1962	8	2	3	0	3
1964	4	1	3	0	0
1966	3	1	0	2	0
1968	9	4	0	3	2
1970	6	3	2	1	0
1972	10	1	4	3	2
1974	6	0	2	1	3
1976	14	5	4	2	3
1978	13	5	2	3	3
1980	12	9	0	3	0
1982	4	1	1	1	1
1984	4	1	2	0	1
1986	10	0	7	1	2
1988	7	1	3	2	1

SOURCE: Norman J. Ornstein, *Vital Statistics on Congress, 1987-88* (Washington, D.C.: American Enterprise Institute, 1987), 52, 54.

a Republican, Bob Kerrey of Nebraska, defeated an incumbent who had been appointed to a vacancy held by a Democrat. Accordingly, it would not be inaccurate to call the Senate results a wash.

In the House, the Democrats gained three seats, which gave them an 85-seat advantage (260–175). The election of 1988, moreover, marked the first time in twenty-eight years that the party winning the Presidency failed to gain seats in Congress. While in control of the House during the last four presidential elections, Democrats also lost an average of 13 House seats each time they failed to elect a President (see table 6.2). For Majority House Leader Thomas S. Foley, the Democratic gain was "a clear signal of a deliberate judgment on the part of the American people to keep Democrats in Congress."[1]

A total of 22 of the 26 senators and 402 of the 408 sitting House members prevailed. The 84 percent success rate for incumbent senators was a significant improvement over the 75 percent reelection rate for incumbent senators in 1986. The average incumbent success rate in Senate elections since 1978 has been closer to the 75 percent figure of the Senate class of 1986 than to this year's result. So it was a good, if not great, year for incumbent senators.

Incumbent senators have long been the more vulnerable of the congressional candidates, but this year they showed few conspicuous signs of weakness. Although four incumbents lost, the winning margins for successful Senate incumbents increased handsomely over 1982, when this year's class of senators last stood for election. Only four senators, all Democrats, won by smaller percentages than in 1982 — Byrd of West Virginia, Burdick of North Dakota, Matsunaga of Hawaii, and Sarbanes of Maryland.

It is rare when the percentage of incumbents reelected to the Senate surpasses that of the House. In the post-world War II period, only in 1960 and 1982 has senatorial reelection success been greater than that of the House (see table 6.2).

Some incumbent senators won by margins normally associated with the less competitive House seats. Senator Daniel Moynihan (D-N.Y.) won with 67 percent, and midwestern Republicans John Danforth of Missouri and Richard Lugar of Indiana beat their respective opponents by identical margins of 68–32 percent.

While the House-Senate differences this year were not so pronounced, the senator is simply a more visible figure than the House member and is more apt to be held accountable when things go wrong in the country. The great attention paid to senators by national and local media is associated with their greater prestige compared to House members, but the limelight in which they bask can be treacherous. If a senator says something stupid or controversial or impolitic, the press is there to cover and report it. The obscurity of most

House members gives them freedom from the relentless attention of the press. What little the media say about them often originates with their own press secretaries and is usually flattering. And their districts of roughly 550,000 people permit them to become known personally to a larger percentage of the electorate than a senator, who may represent 30 million people in a state like California.

On the House side, the phrase "incumbent advantage" scarcely describes the success enjoyed by the men and women already holding seats. An "incumbent franchise" might be a more accurate term. The 98.5 percent success rate achieved by House incumbents defending their seats exceeds even the 98 percent attained by sitting representatives in 1986. But at levels as high as these, differences of less than 1 percent are trivial. In no House election since 1974 has the rate of incumbent success been less than 90 percent, and rates approximating 100 percent no longer occasion any amazement (see table 6.3).

A rule of thumb for designating a House seat as "marginal" is one in which the incumbent wins by 60 percent or less. If that standard is applied to the 1988 results, only forty-five House incumbents fell below 60 percent in their reelection bids—slightly more than 10 percent.

House incumbents have always had very high rates of reelection. Beginning in the 1960s, however, the number of House members who won their seats narrowly, the "marginals," dropped.[2] The reasons why incumbents seemed safer was less clear than the fact that fewer seats were competitive than had previously been the case.

There is an obvious political advantage that comes to incumbents through the emoluments of office. House members, for example, receive an allowance that enables them to hire a staff of roughly twenty people. Senators and representatives enjoy the free mail privilege known as the "frank." Incumbents in both Houses use the television and radio studios of Congress to send public service messages back to their states and districts. Although they are forbidden to use these facilities for campaign spots, many local stations look on this thinly concealed self-promoting material as free footage. The House Recording Studio charges members $42 for twenty minutes of studio time that includes the use of two cameras, a TelePrompTer, and a videotape machine. A challenger seeking the same service would pay more than $500.[3]

Incumbency allows officeholders to get what amounts to an easement on a seat through a combination of help to voters or taking credit for federal projects that they are able to secure, taking positions on issues that make them appear to be champions of their constituents, and broadcasting these achievements to constituents.[4] These activities enable incumbents to achieve a degree of positive name recognition. In order to match that name recognition, little-

TABLE 6.3

THE ADVANTAGE OF INCUMBENCY IN THE HOUSE AND SENATE

Year	House				Senate			
	Seeking Reelection	Defeated (primary)	Defeated (election)	Percentage Reelected[a]	Seeking Reelection	Defeated (primary)	Defeated (election)	Percentage Reelected[a]
1946	398	18	52	82	30	6	7	57
1948	400	15	68	79	25	2	8	60
1950	400	6	32	91	32	5	5	69
1952	389	9	26	91	31	2	9	65
1954	407	6	22	93	32	2	6	75
1956	411	6	16	95	29	0	4	86
1958	396	3	37	90	28	0	10	64
1960	405	5	25	93	29	0	1	97
1962	402	12	22	92	35	1	5	83
1964	397	8	45	87	33	1	4	85
1966	411	8	41	88	32	3	1	88
1968	409	4	9	97	28	4	4	71
1970	401	10	12	95	31	1	6	77
1972	390	12	13	94	27	2	5	74
1974	391	8	40	88	27	2	2	85
1976	384	3	13	96	25	0	9	64
1978	382	5	19	94	25	3	7	60
1980	398	6	31	91	29	4	9	55
1982	393	10	29	90	30	0	2	93
1984	411	3	16	95	29	0	3	90
1986	390	1	10	97	28	0	7	75
1988	408	1	6	98	26	0	4	84

SOURCE: *Congressional Quarterly Weekly Report*, 5 April 1980, 908; 6 November 1982, 3302, 3320-21; and 8 November 1986, 2811, 2845.
a. Counting both primary and general election defeats.

known challengers have to spend vast amounts of money. But their ability to secure campaign funds tends to be hampered by the energetic fund raising used widely by incumbents.

Incumbents do not only raise money to conduct a campaign; they raise enough money to deter challenges before they can be mounted. Cash on hand is used to scare off people who covet the incumbent's seat in Congress, and the money is then rolled over and augmented to intimidate future challengers. As Burdett Loomis aptly pointed out, "In 1980, only three House members held a postelection balance of more than $250,000, with none of these hitting $300,000, and in 1982, only seven representatives retained more than $300,000. After the 1983-84 election cycle, 23 House members had accumulated more than $300,000. During the 1985-86 cycle, this number rose to 39, and 54 congressmen had at least $250,000 in the bank."[5]

The advantages enjoyed by incumbents and their ability to wall themselves off from presidential results has given us a Congress that is a virtual carbon copy of its predecessor in terms of partisan balance. Yet the uniformly high rates of incumbent success in the House and Senate obscure certain important differences in the way in which campaigns for seats in the two chambers were fought. In 1988 this was especially true of the connection between national issues and the issues over which congressional campaigns were fought and the role of presidential coattails in House and Senate elections.

The House Races:
The Politics of Insulation

When a Republican presidential candidate wins the popular vote by 54–46 percent and garners 426 electoral votes to his Democratic opponent's 112, but his party loses strength in Congress, one is entitled to be skeptical about the effects of presidential coattails. Republican candidates for congressional seats tried valiantly to paint their Democratic opponents in the same negative hues that Vice-President Bush used on Governor Dukakis, but they were generally unsuccessful. Democratic candidates either embraced Dukakis or distanced themselves from him, depending on their political circumstances. Secure Democratic incumbents were not fearful of being identified with Dukakis, but as one Democrat in a swing district in Michigan mused when a Dukakis field operative came to organize his constituency for the presidential candidate, "I'd be thrilled if they kept that young man out of my hair."[6]

The number of congressional districts that gave a majority of their votes to a presidential candidate of one party and congressional candidates of the other was 196 out of 435 in 1984. That is roughly 45 percent of all districts.

The percentage has risen steadily in the three national elections since 1976. Significantly, the rise of split-outcome districts persisted even in the Reagan landslide of 1980. In that election, where a strong anti-incumbent mood in the electorate gave the GOP not only the Presidency but control of the Senate as well, the percentage of split-outcome House districts adversely rose by more than 4 percent over the previous presidential year. In the Senate, too, there were dramatic examples of discrepancies between the presidential and congressional vote. In the three states where Democrats ousted Republican senators—Connecticut, Nebraska, and Nevada—George Bush triumphed. His winning margin in Nebraska and Nevada was 60 percent.

A major factor contributing to the rise in split-ticket voting is the decline in party loyalty among voters. Voting the "straight ticket" for candidates of the same party from the President down to local officials is no longer common. No modern candidate for Congress would dream of basing an electoral strategy on the strength exerted at the head of the ticket. The coattail effect is also diminished by a trend that exists apart from presidential politics: The number of districts in which presidential coattails might have some impact on the outcome are few in number. The generally accepted figure for House seats that are truly competitive has usually been placed at about 25 percent. That means that real contests occur in only about 100 of 435 districts. This year, the number of competitive seats was even smaller.

Another important ingredient in the ability of House members to insulate themselves from what takes place at the presidential level is the practice of incumbents to become identified in the minds of the voters as apolitical problem solvers. The skill of House incumbents in protecting constituents from bureaucratic breakdowns that jeopardize such government benefits as social security and veterans' programs forms a bond between incumbents and voters that presidential candidates can rarely break.[7] Channeling federal projects and grants into their districts, and publicizing relentlessly their fidelity to the interests of the districts, solidifies that bond.[8] Making frequent trips back to the district and diverting increasing numbers of staff members from Washington to offices in the district completes the picture of members whose careers are dedicated to the welfare of those they represent.[9]

House members enjoy a great deal of autonomy in regard to party leaders in Congress and party campaign organizations. The bulk of members' campaign money and their entire reelection strategy are products of their own energy and inspiration. This has enabled House members to avoid being blamed for the shortcomings of Congress and has reduced the influence of presidential coattails on district outcomes. In order for those coattails to have an effect on the outcome in a congressional district, the margin between the winning and

losing presidential candidates must be large enough for the fractional effect
of the top of the ticket to be felt.

It is estimated that every additional percentage point of the vote won by
a presidential candidate will add about one-third of a percentage point to the
congressional candidates of his party.[10] It would take a tremendous number
of those one-thirds to make a difference in the final outcome of elections that
are typically won by 20 percent or more.

The Senate Races:
Coattails and the "L Word"

The GOP contenders who tried to tie Democratic congressional candidates to
the failing fortunes of Michael Dukakis and hitch on to the rising star of George
Bush were not generally successful. Making the word "liberal" an epithet had
enormous appeal to some Republican candidates and caused nervousness among
Democratic contenders. In Florida's Senate election, for instance, Republican
Connie Mack used the dreaded "L word" to taunt his Democratic opponent,
Buddy McKay, with the slogan, "Hey, Buddy and Mike [Dukakis], you're liberals." The same approach was used by Senator Chic Hecht in Nevada against
his challenger, Governor Richard Bryan. Pete Dawkins in New Jersey, who
sought the Senate seat of Democrat Frank Lautenberg, clung desperately to
Bush in the hope of a coattail effect, but the pattern was not uniform. One
observer of the Senate campaign concluded a few days before the election that
Republican Senate candidates were "pursuing a selective coattails strategy, avoiding linkage in states where the presidential race is close or Dukakis could help
the Democratic candidate for other reasons." One example was in the state of
Washington where tying ultraliberal Democratic Senate candidate Mike Lowry
to Governor Dukakis only served to moderate Lowry's image.[11]

The Democrats' embrace of Michael Dukakis was equally selective. Strong
Democratic Senate incumbents, such as Maryland's Paul Sarbanes, featured
Dukakis prominently in their advertising. But in Mississippi, where Democrat
Wayne Dowdy was fighting an uphill battle against Republican Trent Lott in
a state destined to go for Bush, Dowdy reluctantly admitted that he would vote
for Dukakis, but then discreetly changed the subject. Less tactful was Florida
Democrat Buddy McKay, who said wistfully, "I'd be a hell of a lot better off
if Bush was running unopposed."[12]

The easy victory of Ohio's Senator Howard Metzenbaum, who had once
been considered among the most vulnerable of the Democrats, illustrates both
the limitations of liberal baiting and the power of incumbency. In July, the
Capitol Hill newspaper *Roll Call* had rated the Ohio senatorial contest a toss-

up and the perceived liberalism of Metzenbaum a serious problem. Metzen-baum dealt with the problem by turning the liberal tag to his advantage. In his television advertising, he defined liberalism as a kind of benevolence and warmth. Republicans were openly envious of Metzenbaum's campaign spots; they gave the irascible and temperamental Metzenbaum a personality face lift by showing him holding small children on his lap and discussing major social issues. Metzenbaum, moreover, could point to projects and jobs that had come to Ohio, for which he could take credit.[13]

What can be said of the effect of coattails in the Senate elections? It is probable that in Florida, a twenty-two point advantage by George Bush helped the cause of Senate candidate Connie Mack, and in Mississippi a Bush margin of equal size helped Trent Lott; in these instances, presidential coattails were so capacious as to be a factor. But these two contests were open-seat races, and so no candidate enjoyed the advantage of incumbency. In three of the other four open-seat Senate races—Wisconsin, Washington, and Vermont—Dukakis won narrowly (Wisconsin and Washington), or Bush's margin of victory was slender (Vermont). In Virginia, the best that could be said of Maurice Dawkins, chosen by GOP voters to oppose a popular former governor, Chuck Robb, is that he gamely played his role as sacrificial lamb.

Sorting out the winners and losers of 1988, one is tempted to ask what attributes other than the obvious factor of incumbency separated the winning candidates from those who lost.

What It Took to Win in 1988

After the election of 1980, the conventional wisdom held that thirty-seven Republican House members and nine Republican senators elected at the same time as Ronald Reagan were the product of a Republican tide running in the country. But "a closer look at the winning Republican challengers indicates that success was critically dependent on the quality of the candidates and the availability of campaign resources."[14] Specifically, in seats narrowly won by Democrats in the previous congressional elections (1978), the Republican challengers who won in 1980 tended to have held previous elective office and been able to raise a substantial amount of campaign money. To use a phrase coined in 1985 by Senator John F. Kerry, chairman of the Democratic Senatorial Campaign Committee, the Republicans had been on the right side of the "stature gap."

Holding previous major office or having a high-visibility occupation (e.g., actor, TV journalist, astronaut) or being a member of a prominent political family confers on a candidate something that less-well-known people spend hundreds of thousands of dollars to develop and perhaps do not fully achieve: name recognition. With name recognition comes a greater likelihood of campaign money and a higher probability of success.

Early in the 1988 campaign, the Republicans hoped to field a team of stars to take on incumbent Democrats: They had former Heisman Trophy winner and army general Pete Dawkins challenge Lautenberg in New Jersey, Cleveland Mayor George Voinovich take on Metzenbaum in Ohio, and the popular farm broadcaster Conrad Burns run against Melcher in Montana. But they failed to prevail upon well-known personalities to run against Moynihan in New York and James Sasser in Tennessee. On their side, the Democrats came up with Congressional Medal of Honor winner and former governor Bob Kerrey in Nebraska to challenge the Republican incumbent. "In all, the Democrats recruited five current and former governors, two lieutenant governors, two attorneys general, and one secretary of state. The Republicans . . . lined up about the same number of House members but [could] claim few proven statewide vote-getters among their . . . challengers."[15]

Quality candidates, whether long-time members of Congress, holders of other statewide office, or simply people with high name recognition share a tactical advantage that sets them apart from the novice: the ability to raise money. And in Senate races in particular, where television and direct mail are mandatory, the cost of running a campaign keeps out all but the most indefatigable and successful fund raiser. Money spoke eloquently in 1988. Preliminary figures from the Federal Election Commission indicate that candidates for both houses of Congress in 1988 raised almost $360 million. Contestants in the 33 Senate races raised almost $158 million, and 435 House candidates raised $202 million.[16]

Incumbents do not always come out on top in congressional elections, but never bet against them. The worst recent year for House incumbents was 1974, the year that the Watergate scandal took its toll on Republicans. Yet even in that election, 88 percent of all incumbents were successful. The previous blowout of incumbents came in 1966 when the artificially large number of Democrats elected in the Lyndon Johnson landslide of 1964 were winnowed out. Yet, as bad as that year was for Democrats, 88 percent of all incumbents successfully defended their seats (see table 6.3.)

A third of the money raised by House and Senate candidates came from political action committees (PACs). These organizations, typically associated with interest groups who seek to influence legislation in Congress, provided 40 percent of the money for House candidates and about 25 percent of the campaign funds for senators. Because of their greater visibility, senators have the ability to raise money nationally from individual contributors; House candi-

TABLE 6.4
PATTERNS OF PAC CONTRIBUTIONS, 1987-88
ELECTION CYCLE (AS OF 30 JUNE 1988)

Percentage of Contribution to:

Congressional incumbents	84.4
challengers	8.6
open seats	9.0
Congressional Democrats	64.9
Congressional Republicans	35.1
House candidates	64.4
Senate candidates	35.6
Senate Democrats	60.1
Senate Republicans	39.9
House Democrats	67.6
House Republicans	32.4
Senate Democratic incumbents	75.9
challengers	13.2
open seats	10.9
Senate Republican incumbents	76.4
challengers	12.5
open seats	11.1
House Democratic incumbents	87.5
challengers	7.7
open seats	4.8
House Republican incumbents	92.2
challengers	2.9
open seats	4.9

SOURCE: Federal Election Commission.

dates, known best to "insiders," rely more heavily on PAC contributions. PACs raise money through contributions from ordinary citizens and from officers and employees of corporations; PACs use this money to support candidates friendly to their interests or cause. The pattern of PAC contributions heavily favors incumbents because PACs and their parent lobbies have established relationships with congressional committees and their members. The ultimate committee assignment of a successful challenger is unknown before election day.

The strong pro-incumbent bias of PACs is illustrated in table 6.4. The groups most generously endowed by PACs are House incumbents of both parties; the percentage of PAC money going to challengers of both parties is pathetically small. Although PAC money to Senate candidates is considerably less than what flows to House members, there is a strong pro-incumbent bias here as well. Roughly three-quarters of all PAC money flowing into Senate campaigns goes to incumbents of both parties. PACs seem to be somewhat more willing to support Senate challengers and open-seat candidates of both parties, with about 25 percent of PAC money going to these nonincumbents.[17]

Generally speaking, Senate and House incumbents in both parties have little trouble raising money from both individuals and PACs; challengers, unless they are of unusually high quality, have to scramble. And even the few challengers (particularly in the House) who manage to raise unusually high amounts of money often find themselves outgunned.

In the "swing state" of Connecticut, with its six House seats evenly divided between Democrats and Republicans, all of them being defended by incumbents, only one challenger was able to get close to the $250,000 generally regarded as the minimum amount required to be competitive in a House race. That challenger was Glenn Carberry, a thirty-three-year-old Republican attorney from Norwich, who challenged a four-term incumbent Democrat, Sam Gejdenson.

Gejdenson is an unlikely congressman to represent an eastern Connecticut district that is full of Republican Yankees. "Conservatives must be infuriated that this typical American district continues to elect a congressman who takes outspokenly liberal positions on national and international issues," wrote the authors of *The Almanac of American Politics*. Indeed, the sense that Gejdenson was "out of step" with his district enabled Carberry to raise $200,000. Just how unusual a feat this was can be seen in the fact that Carberry raised an amount equal to that of the other five challengers in Connecticut combined.[18]

No doubt buoyed by this campaign chest, Carberry was quoted as saying, "I certainly recognize that there will be only 10 or 12 challengers in the whole country who will win, but my job is to be one of them."[19] Carberry was wrong on both counts: Only six challengers were victorious, and he was not one of them. Gejdenson, with a $400,000 war chest, defeated Carberry 64–36 percent.

This example illustrates that even an incumbent who is very different ideologically from his district can prevail over a challenger whose views are more nearly in line with those of the voters. The power of incumbency—more than candidate quality or money—conferred a conspicuous advantage in 1988.

What It Took to Lose in 1988

Only ten incumbents in a two-house Congress consisting of 535 members failed to win reelection. There is no more eloquent testimony to the absence in 1988 of any overriding policy current. Those who lost fell into three categories: the unlucky, the inept, and the venal.

In the first category, Representative Jack Davis held a seat that was not strongly Republican. His margin in 1986 was only 52 percent against a twenty-eight-year-old Democratic accountant with no previous political experience. This time, the Democrats nominated George E. Sangmeister, who had served ten years in the state senate. Sangmeister had run unsuccessfully for lieutenant governor in 1986, but the race had given him additional name recognition. This contest in Illinois reaffirmed the importance of candidate quality in mounting challenges to incumbents.

Senator Lowell Weicker of Connecticut was also unlucky. A theory of the senatorial life cycle holds that the third defense of a Senate seat ought to be the easiest for someone representing a two-party state. By the time senators from states with parties of fairly equal strength are ready to run for their third reelection, "Their chances of success are as good as those from one-party states."[20] Weicker had won his first seat in 1970; his third defense of it was in 1988. Even the most comforting theories are no substitute for luck.

Weicker was an able but cantankerous liberal Republican who took on controversial causes (he was an outspoken champion of civil rights and supporter of liberal abortion policies), but he was never very good at tending to political matters within the state. Yet he always managed to outflank the Democrats who ran against him. This time Attorney-General Joseph Lieberman accomplished some political sleight-of-hand by running a substantially conservative campaign. Lieberman managed to hold on to his Democratic base while undercutting Weicker among conservative Republicans, including the columnist and author William F. Buckley, who publicly supported Lieberman.

In the inept category were Mac Sweeney of Texas, Chic Hecht of Nevada, and John Melcher of Montana. Sweeney's 14th Congressional District had been represented for twenty-two years (until 1978) by Democrat John Young. But in 1976 Young was charged with sexual impropriety by a member of his staff and was defeated in a runoff election by Joe Wyatt. Shortly after defeating Young, Wyatt was arrested for sexual misconduct and declined to seek another term. He was succeeded by a Democrat, Bill Patman, son of a former House Banking Committee chairman, Wright Patman. Patman was defeated in 1984 by Sweeney, whose activities as an incumbent were a synthesis of venality and ineptitude.

Sweeney misrepresented his résumé, made false charges against Patman, and was revealed to have compelled a congressional staff member to work on his campaign—a federal offense. Sweeney also was negligent in answering constituent mail and his campaigns were studies in financial mismanagement. His one-time opponent Bill Patman said of Sweeney, "He'd be a Chinese Communist if it would further his cause. I don't think you can be in politics long without some measure of integrity, and I think he has none." The voters of the Texas 14th Congressional District evidently agreed. After giving Sweeney a narrow victory over lawyer Greg Laughlin in 1986, they gave the seat to the same opponent in 1988.[21]

Senator Chic Hecht's problems were of the head, not the heart. First elected in 1982 by defeating the incumbent Howard Cannon, Hecht gained a reputation for ineptitude that found him at the bottom of every list of senators when ranked for effectiveness. He was unable to protect his state from being selected as the site of a nuclear waste repository (Hecht was heard to refer to it as the "nuclear waste suppository") and sponsored little legislation. Although his record showed he had served as an officer in U.S. Army Intelligence, he could never get straight the difference between *covert* and *overt*. In a debate with his opponent, Governor Richard Bryan, he asked a reporter to refresh him on the content of the First Amendment. He claimed at the time that he was not a lawyer, implying that only lawyers would know such trivia.

Senator John "Doc" Melcher, a two-term Montana Democrat, displayed much of Lowell Weicker's cantankerousness but little of his courage. Known as an obstructionist, Melcher had little to show in legislative accomplishment and often tried to position himself on both sides of an issue. Under challenge in 1982, Melcher capitalized on his reputation as a veterinarian by running television spots featuring talking cows. He resorted to this commercial again in 1988, but lost to an underfunded political newcomer, Conrad Burns.

Finally, there were the venal members who lost. In Georgia, it was Republican House member Pat Swindall, who had been indicted shortly before the election. His indictment came on federal perjury charges arising out of his alleged lying to a grand jury in a case involving the laundering of drug money. He was defeated by Democrat Ben Jones, who played the role of "Cooter" in the television series "The Dukes of Hazzard."

In New York's 20th Congressional District, one of the most expensive House races in the country pitted incumbent Republican Joseph J. DioGuardi against former New York Assistant Secretary of State Nita M. Lowey. The incumbent's loss was attributable in part to the basically liberal and Democratic nature of the electorate—an uncomfortable position for a Reagan admirer. Democrats outnumber Republicans in the district by about 6000. Such margins are usually no problem for resourceful incumbents from the minority party; however, three weeks before the election DioGuardi was reported in the local press to have received an illegal campaign contribution from a local automobile dealer. This "October surprise" probably cost DioGuardi the election.[22]

The two most important victims of venality were Representatives Fernand St. Germain (D-R.I.), who had served as chairman of the House Banking Committee, and Bill Chappell (D-Fla.). In Congress for twenty-eight years, St. Germain had been accused of underreporting his assets and was accused by the Justice Department of "serious and sustained misconduct."[23] Chappell, chairman of the Defense Appropriations Subcommittee, was not charged formally with any wrongdoing. Nevertheless, newspaper reports linked Chappell and some staff members to questionable business relationships with some defense contractors.

Casualties in the ranks of incumbents were low, and all could be explained by factors that were idiosyncratic rather than structural. It is impossible to read policy implications into these results, and the returns undercut any effort by Bush to claim a mandate and make him a less formidable figure to those on Capitol Hill.

Congress After the Elections

The 101st Congress will have some new faces, some old faces in new places, and some conspicuous absences. In certain policy areas, accordingly, there will be changes of direction or emphasis.

The policy area most profoundly affected by changes in congressional personnel is banking and monetary affairs. Senate Banking Committee Chairman William Proxmire stepped down at the end of the 100th Congress, and House Banking Committee Chairman Fernand St. Germain was defeated. What makes this policy area particularly important in the 101st Congress is the difficulty being experienced by the Savings and Loan Industry. Because of unwise lending practices by S & Ls in Texas, a wave of failures has struck the industry, and a massive infusion of funds may be required to prop it up. Proxmire had been highly skeptical of practices in the Savings and Loan Industry, and the scrutiny he exercised is likely to be duplicated by his successor. The Senate Banking Committee, moreover, has a relatively strong contingent of members.

Because of the overbearing and dictatorial nature of St. Germain on the House committee, abler representatives tended to avoid the panel. Accordingly, the committee heads into a crucial period lacking in depth and experience. St. Germain's successor, Henry Gonzalez of Texas, has a reputation for being quixotic and temperamental, yet he enjoys the backing of Speaker Jim Wright and was not challenged.

Other major changes also took place in the fiscal policy area with the retirement of the Senate Appropriations Committee chairman, John Stennis. His replacement, former Majority Leader Robert C. Byrd, long used his seat on the spending committee to backstop his power as Democratic chief. More active than Stennis and shrewd in parliamentary maneuvering, Byrd will certainly look out for his own economically depressed state of West Virginia. Byrd will also be a major player in budget negotiations with the White House on the overarching issue facing the 101st Congress: the budget deficit.

The chair of the Budget Committee in the Senate also became vacant at the close of the 100th Congress when Florida's Lawton Chiles retired. The two most senior senators on the committee, and hence in line to assume the chairmanship, declined to seek the post. Ernest F. Hollings of South Carolina elected to remain as chairman of the Commerce Committee, and Bennett Johnston passed up the Budget chair to run for the post of Majority Leader. Johnston also chaired the Energy and Natural Resources Committee, a key slot for a senator who represents the oil- and gas-producing state of Louisiana. The new chairman, third in line, is the newly reelected James Sasser of Tennessee, who was not known as a particularly aggressive budgeter in his first two terms in the Senate.

But if Sasser is an unproven leader on the Senate side of budget policy, the new House Budget Committee chairman, Leon Panetta of California, has a long history of being a major player in fashioning congressional budgets. He had run unsuccessfully for the post against William H. Gray III (D-Pa.) who has now stepped down after having served the maximum of two terms. Gray was elected chairman of the Democratic Caucus, the first black member of Congress to serve in that post.

Another dramatic change took place on the Judiciary Committee when Chairman Peter Rodino of New Jersey decided not to seek another term in Congress. Rodino had seen his job as chairman as the Democrats' first line of defense against the social agenda of conservative Republicans. A staunch opponent of school prayer and abortion restrictions, Rodino was usually successful in bottling up conservative constitutional amendments. His successor, Jack Brooks of Texas, is one of the most colorful and combative leaders on Capitol Hill. He formerly served as chairman of the Government Operations Committee, which enjoys broad powers of legislative oversight over the agencies of the executive branch, a jurisdiction that often brought Brooks into conflict with administration officials. Brooks and Rodino both served on the Iran-*Contra* Committee, and while Rodino adopted a somewhat legalistic and deferential approach to questioning witnesses, Brooks was likely to call an official "a lying son of a bitch."[24] Described by colleague Mike Synar as "the best chairman in the House," Brooks will probably be no friendlier to the conservative social agenda than was his predecessor, but he is likely to take a more active role in scrutinizing certain practices in the business community.[25]

Continuity and Change in Congress

The number of black members of Congress increased by one, to twenty-four, when Donald Payne was elected to fill the seat of retiring Peter Rodino in New Jersey's 10th Congressional District. But blacks in Congress were gaining influence that was more significant than their modest increase in numbers. William H. Gray III, as chairman of the House Democratic Caucus, now holds the fourth-ranking party leadership position in that chamber. Blacks, moreover, who constitute only 5 percent of the membership of the House, enjoy an influence far beyond their numbers. They chair a quarter of all standing and select committees.

The number of women in Congress increased by two, both in the House. There are now twenty-five women in the House and two in the Senate. Although their numbers are comparable to those of blacks, the influence of women is not nearly so great. No standing or select committee is chaired by a woman. Indeed, the last woman to chair a standing committee of the House was Leonor K. Sullivan, who headed the Merchant Marine and Fisheries Committee in the 94th Congress (1975–77).

Changes in the Senate were more dramatic. With Senator Robert Byrd's decision to step down from the post of Majority Leader and assume the chairmanship of the Appropriations Committee, Democrats were faced with finding a successor. On 29 November, they chose George J. Mitchell of Maine, the least senior of the three senators contending for the post.

The nod to Mitchell, a liberal, does not suggest a leftward move on the part of Senate Democrats. The choice of a party floor leader in the Senate is more a product of the internal politics of the chamber than an expression of national trends. Frustrated by cumbersome procedures and unpredictable schedules, Democrats wanted to improve the quality of their working lives, and the serious, energetic Mitchell convinced them that he could bring about reforms. But even though the desire to have an effective national party spokesman did not play a very important role in the Democrats' choice, in George Mitchell they have a presentable and effective public figure.

Mitchell moved swiftly to establish himself as an innovator. In a gesture to younger senators, he asked Thomas A. Daschle of South Dakota to share with him the chairmanship of the Democratic Policy Committee, which sets party policy. Dividing the chairmanship was an effort by Mitchell to parcel out more equally the rewards of leadership. The new leader also moved quickly to heal any feelings that might have been hurt during the campaign for the party post by supporting defeated rival Daniel K. Inouye of Hawaii for the chairmanship of the Steering Committee, which makes Democratic committee assignments. Mitchell also gave his nod to John B. Breaux of Louisiana to be chair of the

Democratic Senate Campaign Committee. Breaux's home-state colleague, J. Bennett Johnston, was the other claimant for Mitchell's leadership post.

The Republican side in the Senate offered few surprises. Bob Dole was reelected Minority Leader and found himself looking down Pennsylvania Avenue at the man who defeated him in the Republican primaries. The circumstances under which George Bush prevailed in the critical New Hampshire primary raised questions about the future of the relationship between the new President and the man responsible for his legislative program in the Senate.

Never the best of friends, the estrangement between Bush and Dole became complete in the period between the Iowa caucus and the New Hampshire primary. Having finished third in the Iowa contest (behind Dole and Pat Robertson), Bush took off the gloves in New Hampshire. With the help of Governor John Sununu, Bush attacked Dole fiercely for his alleged hedging on controversial issues, most notably the Intermediate Nuclear Force (INF) treaty. Dole was angered at Bush's successful efforts to depict him as "Senator Straddle." When a news anchor interviewed the two men during campaign appearances in different parts of New Hampshire, Dole was asked by the moderator if he had any message for the vice-president. "Yeah," Dole replied, "Tell him to stop lying about my record."

When Bush appointed Sununu to the critical post of chief of staff in the White House, it might have been read as a calculated affront to Dole. But Bush moved swiftly to quell those speculations by going to Capitol Hill to meet with Dole and arrange a joint appearance at which Dole pledged his support of the President-elect. Few believed, however, that this truce would result in Bush and Dole becoming the best of friends. Dole is a proud and touchy man who believes firmly that he is the person best qualified to be President. Relations with Dole will be a test of President Bush's tact and diplomacy.

The Bush Agenda and the 101st Congress

The atmosphere of reconciliation and goodwill that George Bush sought to establish in the weeks after his election were a welcome antidote to the rancor of the presidential campaign. No Democrats publicly swore revenge for the alleged bashing of liberals by the Bush campaign, and there were no threats to derail the new President's program. People in politics are remarkably pragmatic; they realize that today's adversary may be tomorrow's ally. Nevertheless, the skeptical smiles that played across the faces of leading congressional Democrats when asked about the likelihood of a major improvement in the federal deficit without a corresponding rise in taxes spoke more eloquently than words about problems to come.

Interviewed on election night, shortly after the networks had declared Bush the winner, House Ways and Means Committee Chairman Dan Rostenkowski did speak out. He dismissed the campaign pledge of the vice-president to lower capital gains taxes by suggesting that that could be accomplished only by raising the marginal tax rate for all taxpayers.

The most consistent Democratic line about the steps needed to deal with the deficit was that "everything must be on the table." That is Washington shorthand for saying that new taxes as well as cuts in the federal budget must be on the agenda in any negotiations between the White House and Congress. In view of George Bush's categorical admonition, "Read my lips. No new taxes," congressional Democrats were not about to take the initiative and preferred to wait for the President to make the first move.

As with controversial policy issues in the past, the most eagerly desired objective on the deficit issue will be political cover. That will mean de-partisanizing the issue and dividing the responsibility meticulously between Democrats and Republicans. With a Republican in the White House and Democrats in control on Capitol Hill, one is less likely to see profiles in courage than profiles in cover.

The device for inoculating an issue is usually some kind of bipartisan commission. This approach has been taken in recent years with the Kissinger Commission on Central America, which was unsuccessful in finding a peace formula for that troubled region, and with the Greenspan Commission, which successfully resolved a dispute over how to rescue the Social Security Trust Fund from insolvency in 1982. Other controversial issues, such as which obsolete military bases should be closed and congressional pay raises, also have been placed in the hands of bipartisan commissions. The National Economic Commission, created in 1987 to deal with the budget deficit, is the device that many in Washington expect to be asked to find a way out of the nation's fiscal problems.

Such approaches signal the failure of normal political processes to handle the nation's most controversial issues. As one member of the House remarked, there is such "intense pressure from so many interest groups out there on one side or other of any particular issue that unless we can take the question outside the political arena, we find ourselves unable politically to come up with a proper and good response."[26] Acknowledging that the use of bipartisan commissions is an abnormal approach to solving thorny questions, the head of a public interest group conceded, "It's certainly political cover, but it's also one of the routes of getting decisions put on the resolution rail than just postponed forever."[27]

The results of the congressional elections of 1988, with their almost seamless continuity raise other fundamental questions about whether the in-

stitutions of American government are performing, in this constitutional bicentennial era, in a manner that the Framers would approve.

Conclusion

The remarkable success of incumbent members of both houses to retain their
seats in Congress raises a fundamental question about the nature of political
responsiveness. Is the insulation of members of Congress from political accountability a source of concern?

Some reformers have expressed concern about the low turnover, arguing
that the House, in particular, is in danger of being mummified in its present
state. From the left there is a concern that "something's out of whack," and
from the right that "freezing the status quo means you only get one side of
the debate" and that side is the liberal side.[28] Others say that the fear of an
oligarchy is unfounded. They point out that the Congress is far more open
than it was thirty years ago when a handful of powerful chairmen from single-
party districts who were never defeated built up enough seniority to dominate
Congress. Some experts even argue that a great deal of turnover is not good
for Congress because it would undercut the ability of the legislative branch
to deal with complex problems by removing incumbents with experience and
expertise.[29]

Moreover, responsiveness in one of its forms seems to be thriving. We have
representatives who really do represent. They defend vigorously the interests
of those who send them to Washington and intervene effectively in behalf of
constituents caught in the toils of the bureaucracy. But the legislators' success
in these apolitical activities can divert voters from the question whether members of Congress are responsive in policy terms.

Perhaps voters are satisfied with the policies of the federal government;
at least, they are not so alienated as to take revenge on incumbents. Voters are
capable of sending messages to those in Washington when they want to make
broad changes in the course of the government. They sent a message in 1974
and again in 1980. Should they decide once again to register their disapproval,
even the most imposing weapons in the arsenal of incumbents may be insufficient to stave off the assault.

Notes

1. David E. Rosenbaum, "Democrats Take Solace as the Party Defies History and Adds to Majority," *New York Times,* 10 November 1988.

2. See David R. Mayhew, "Congressional Elections: The Case of the Vanishing Maginals," *Polity* 6 (1974): 295-317.

3. Walter Pincus and Dan Morgan, "Using Public and Campaign Funds, Senators Beam Selves Back Home," *Washington Post,* 4 November 1988.

4. Mayhew, "Congressional Elections."

5. Burdett Loomis, *The New American Politician* (New York: Basic Books, 1988), 189-90.

6. David S. Broder, "A Declaration of Independence," *Washington Post National Weekly Edition,* 31 October-6 November 1988.

7. See Morris P. Fiorina, *Congress: Keystone of the Washington Establishment* (New Haven: Yale University Press, 1977).

8. See David Mayhew, *Congress: The Electoral Connection* (New Haven: Yale University Press, 1977).

9. John Johannes, *To Serve the People* (Lincoln: University of Nebraska Press, 1984), 211; and Richard F. Fenno, Jr., *Homestyle* (Boston: Little, Brown, 1978), 31-51.

10. John A. Ferejohn and Randall L. Calvert, "Presidential Coattails in Historical Perspective," *American Journal of Political Science* 28 (1984): 127-46.

11. Helen Dewar, "GOP Senate Candidates Rush to Tie Opponents to Dukakis," *Washington Post,* 4 November 1988.

12. Ibid.

13. Susan F. Rasky, "L Word to Metzenbaum Is Ticket to Re-Election," *New York Times,* 1 November 1988.

14. Gary C. Jacobson and Samuel Kernell, *Strategy and Choice in Congressional Elections,* 2d ed. (New Haven: Yale University Press, 1983), 75.

15. Helen Dewar, "The Democrats Have Lined Up Big Guns for the Senate Races," *Washington Post National Weekly Edition,* 22-28 February 1988.

16. *New York Times,* 7 November 1988.

17. Ross K. Baker, *The New Fat Cats: Members of Congress as Political Benefactors* (New York: Twentieth Century Fund, forthcoming).

18. Nick Ravo, "Six U.S. Incumbents Favored to Win in Connecticut," *New York Times,* 27 October 1988.

19. Ibid.

20. Donald R. Matthews, *U.S. Senators and Their World* (New York: Random House, 1960), 241.

21. Michael Barone and Grant Ujifusa, *The Almanac of American Politics 1988* (Washington, D.C.: National Journal, 1987), 1167-68.

22. James Feron, "Lowey Says Westchester Voters Didn't 'Believe in' DioGuardi," *New York Times,* 10 November 1988.

23. *New York Times,* 10 November 1988.

24. "A New Breed of Chair Waits in the Wings," *Current American Government* (Washington, D.C.: Congressional Quarterly, Fall 1988), 78.

25. Richard E. Cohen, "The New Congress: Ready for Battle," *National Journal* 46 (11 November 1988): 2859-70.

26. Kirk Victor, "Commissionism," *National Journal* 20 (22 October 1988): 2694.

27. Ibid.

28. Julie Rovner, "Turnover in Congress Hits an All-Time Low," *Congressional Quarterly Weekly Report* 46 (19 November 1988): 3362-63.

29. Ibid.

7
The Meaning of the Election

WILSON CAREY MCWILLIAMS

> Yet some men say in many parts of England that King
> Arthur is not dead. . . . but rather I will say: here
> in this world he changed his life. — *Morte D'Arthur*

A quarter of a century ago, John F. Kennedy was assassinated, and the American Camelot began to evanesce into the mists of a political Avalon. Three years earlier, in 1960, Michael Dukakis had been caught up in the enchantment of Kennedy's New Frontier; in 1988, he sought to call it back. He failed. The time for Camelot has passed, even for a candidate with more magic than Michael Dukakis possessed.

In 1988, the Democrats came back to the "Boston-Austin ticket" that had succeeded in 1960—a Massachusetts liberal with ethnic credentials paired with a moderate Texan. Electoral logic now works against a northeasterner at the head of such a ticket however; in 1988, Democrats suspected (with reason) that they could have won with Bentsen as their presidential nominee. In 1960, the combination of Lyndon Johnson and traditional party loyalty was strong enough to enable Kennedy to carry most of the South. In 1988, Bentsen's presence on the ticket was insufficient to win even one southern state.

Race and economics have reduced Democrats to a minority of southern whites, an unreliable constituency, sufficient to win in coalition with black voters, but one that requires special cultivation.[1] Locally, biracial coalitions are frequent and often decisive in the South, as they were in 1986; but no Democratic presidential nominee other than Jimmy Carter has assembled such a majority since the federal protection of voting rights transformed southern politics. For Democrats, this trend is probably crucial: Southern votes were essential to three out of their four postwar presidential victories, and in the fourth, LBJ's 1964 landslide, Democrats carried all but the deep South.[2]

177

These days, moreover, the Democrats have no support to spare; Michael Dukakis did a good job of bringing Democrats home (see chap. 5), only to discover that this was not enough. Conservatives outnumber liberals; Dukakis did not approach Kennedy's appeal to Roman Catholics; the political weight of the cities and industrial states—"the last Democratic trench"—is in decline.[3] Even the good news for the Democrats in 1988, their gains in the Midwest and West and their ability to stall or roll back Republican gains among the young, only emphasized the decreased importance of the Northeast and the party's heritage. In 1987, Robert Shrum gave the Democrats good, if unheeded, advice: "The Democratic party has lived off the legacy of John F. Kennedy for twenty-eight years. The torch will go out unless it finally passes to a new generation. We need to invent a new legacy."[4] The "Kennedy business" did not help Dukakis, A.M. Rosenthal wrote at the end of the campaign, because "the young do not vote for the dead."[5]

And yet, Rosenthal is right only in a very narrow sense. Yesterday's events shape today's allegiances, language frames thought, and dead kings and citizens do live on, shadowy, in the body politic.[6]

A century ago, in *A Connecticut Yankee in King Arthur's Court,* Mark Twain described another effort to update Camelot. Sent back in time, Hank Morgan, the Connecticut Yankee, tries to bring Arthur's Britain into the nineteenth century through a combination of technological mastery and showmanship. In 1988, each of the Yankee candidates—no one was deceived by Bush's pose as a Texan—had his technical credentials—Bush's Washington experience set against Dukakis's managerial miracles—but neither was much for flair. Bush, guided by his media "handlers," did better than his rival (although Hank Morgan would probably have called Bush's posturings the "magic of fol-de-rol"), and inevitably, many Democrats incline toward the argument that Dukakis's defects as a campaigner cost them the election.

It may be so. But in Twain's story, for all his gifts as a performer, Hank Morgan fails to transform Britain. The Connecticut Yankee relies on technology and material progress to produce a republic; but the Church, the Yankee's nemesis, keeps control of birth, marriage, and death, the events that punctuate the life of the human spirit. Hank Morgan's politics fail because he neglected the soul. His catastrophe can serve as a cautionary tale.[7] The election of 1988 sent an urgent signal that something is wrong with the political soul of American democracy.

Public Life and Private Media

The campaign was more than "negative." It was a year when civility "took it on the chin," one in which, on talk shows as in politics, nastiness "became a commodity."[8] Even so, it had precedents.

In 1888, President Grover Cleveland, who had survived considerable tarring four years earlier, faced smears and distortions at least the equal of 1988.[9] His former opponent, James G. Blaine, charged that Cleveland had appointed to office 137 convicted criminals, including 2 murderers, 7 forgers, and several brothel keepers. Mrs. Cleveland was forced to deny the rumor that the President beat and abused her. It was said that Cleveland was a dogmatic liberal (of the nineteenth-century variety) and the equivalent of a "secular humanist" because he was reported to have said, "I believe in Free Trade as I believe in the Protestant religion."

Most notoriously, Matt Quay, the Republican boss of Pennsylvania, engineered a scheme by which a Republican supporter, posing as a former British subject, wrote to the British ministry, asking which candidate would best advance Britain's interest. The minister, Lionel Sackville-West, injudiciously replied that Cleveland's free trade sympathies made him preferable, and Republicans exultantly portrayed Cleveland as unpatriotic and, especially in Irish wards, as the tool of British imperialism.[10]

Nevertheless, there is something new and alarming about the incivilities of the presidential campaign in 1988. In the first place, the electronic media give greater force and currency to scurrilities, just as television makes innuendo visible: Blaine's attack on Cleveland's appointments had nothing like the impact of a glowering Willie Horton, illustrating Republican claims that Dukakis had been "soft on crime," or of pictures of garbage afloat in Boston harbor. Moreover, contemporary voters are more exposed to and dependent on mass media.

In Cleveland's day, the press could still be described, in the terms Tocqueville used earlier, as a form of political association. There was a mass press, but the great majority of newspapers were local, the voices and guardians of community. Information from national campaigns and leaders reached most voters only through local editors, leaders, and opinion makers who interpreted it and passed on its propriety and authenticity.[11] In 1988, the media spoke to more and more citizens directly, without intermediaries; gatekeepers could not protect us when the fences had been trampled or pulled down.

In 1888, American politics was still dense with associations, and for both parties, the presidential candidate was only the chief figure in a campaign made up of a myriad of local campaigns in states and wards. Cleveland, in fact, did not campaign at all, considering huckstering beneath the dignity of his office, and Benjamin Harrison's more active office-seeking was very limited by our standards.[12]

Law and technology have combined to create a centralized presidential politics dominated by national media and party committees. In campaigns, as in voting, congressional and local elections are sharply distinct from the presidential contest, so much so that it seemed anomalous, on election night, when candidates for governor and U.S. senator in Montana received about the same percentage of the vote as their party's nominee for President.[13]

The "nationalization of the electorate" has been a major political theme of the century, the result of an effort to "open" politics to individual citizens, freeing them from the control of local elites. Progressive reformers, advocates of the primary system, were also inclined to celebrate the mass media, just as their successors urged "a more responsible two-party system."[14] In one respect, the breaking down of racial barriers to political participation, the process has been pure gain. It has become increasingly clear, however, that the grand design of the reform tradition has failed.

Despite prolonged campaigning, despite vast expenditure of money (in which, in 1988, the two parties were virtually equal), despite the advice of experts and the easing of rules for voter registration, turnout fell — as it has, with the exception of the New Deal years, throughout this century (see chap. 1). This "demobilization" of the electorate is too profound and too persistent to be explained by the requirement of registration or other barriers to voting.[15] In 1988, the fraction of adult Americans who went to the polls was almost 20 percent lower than it was in 1960, when racial discrimination still kept masses of black Americans off the electoral rolls. In Todd Gitlin's axiom, "As politics grows more professional, voting declines."[16]

The affective distance between citizens and public life is great and growing. When they vote for President, voters must evaluate candidates, whose characters they know only superficially, for an office in which character is crucial.[17] We lack the "peer review" that, in earlier years, was provided by party leaders and opinion makers who controlled nominations and guided campaigns. In 1884, the discovery that Grover Cleveland apparently had fathered an illegitimate child provoked the response that such private failings, then as now the focus of media attention, are not the most important indices of *political* character, and Cleveland won the election.[18] In 1988, by contrast, while Gary Hart's derelictions shattered his candidacy, voters did not appear to notice that, after all his years in the Senate, Hart was endorsed by only one incumbent Democratic senator. Judgment by peers is yielding to an "audition" by the media, and private proprieties may now outweigh public virtues.[19]

Be that as it may, citizens *are* dependent on mass media for news and for the interpretation needed to make sense out of the bewildering ravelments of contemporary life.[20] At the same time, the media are great concentrations of power, remote and distant "private governments" that decide who will speak to us and on what terms.[21] In the media's version of deliberation, citizens have no voices; one cannot "talk back" to a television set, and citizens can assert their dignity only by refusing to listen.[22] Of course, a displeased viewer can also change channels, but this "receiver control" is almost entirely negative, given the media's tendency toward a homogenized message.[23]

Yet media decision makers know that, while the power of the media as a whole is overawing, any *single* medium is vulnerable, its position still more precarious because media domination invites resentment. Changing channels is as easy as it is because national television has no organic relation to our lives; a local newspaper or radio station is part of, and often indispensable to, the day-to-day life of a community, but there is no reason why I should prefer ABC to NBC or CBS. The older media, especially the local press, had a position that permitted them to offer "cue giving"—guidance as well as protection—and evaluation was an integral part of their reporting. The electronic media are more anxious to "resonate"; more fearful of giving offense, they cultivate nonpartisanship and a professional neutrality.[24]

Better than the Democrats, the Republicans have understood that this desperate neutrality makes it easy to neutralize the media. Fairly consistently, Republican candidates criticize the media, appealing to the public's fear of "hidden persuaders" and joining its resentment of media power. George Bush virtually began his campaign with a contrived faceoff with Dan Rather, and he continued to fault the media's coverage of the election. This "media bashing" takes the form of asking for fair play or "balanced" treatment, but its real aim is to insulate a candidate—or a President—from criticism, Teflon-coating its beneficiaries.

The success of this strategy was evident in the media response to this year's presidential and vice-presidential debates. After the first debate, the media pronounced the exchange a draw, a defensible stance even if a plurality of viewers thought Dukakis had edged Bush. Even John Chancellor's astonishing claim that Dan Quayle had done well, despite Lloyd Bentsen's one-sided victory, might be explained as a too-rigid refusal to take sides. But television newsmen showed no reluctance to declare that Bush had won the second presidential debate. Taken as a whole, these comments suggest that if the media did not approach Republican candidates "on bended knee"—Mark Hertsgaard's description of the Reagan years—they did bend over backward.[25]

Even at its best, however, television reporting (and increasingly, all reporting) shies away from evaluating the substance, or even the accuracy, of what is said in campaigns (see chap. 3), preferring to discuss the strategy and process of campaigning.[26] Nominally neutral, this emphasis on stratagems effectively tells citizens that the *public* side of politics—and, especially, those questions being argued—is of secondary importance. Even pure quantities, like results of polls and elections, need to be interpreted in the light of "momentum" and "expectations." In this implicit teaching, "real politics" is covert, "a business for professionals" that can be approached only through "inside" information supplied by the media.[27]

Parties and candidates, of course, struggle to control the process of interpretation, bypassing the press whenever possible and controlling "photo opportunities" through carefully contrived events. In 1988, for example, the Dukakis campaign, after beginning with relatively frequent press conferences, followed the Republicans' example in shielding the candidate from the press.[28] Similarly, both national conventions were transparently staged to avoid any appearance of conflict and to project optimism, harmony, and concern for "family values." Ironically, the 1988 conference of the Communist party of the Soviet Union featured heated debate, resembling an old-style American party convention as much as the 1988 American conventions called to mind the traditional, totalitarian gatherings of the Communist party.[29]

"Packaging," however, only redefines the role of the media; by pushing debate and decision offstage, it makes citizens even more dependent on the media to search what is said in public for clues to the real deliberations behind the scenes. Public life, increasingly, is mirroring the media's art; portrayed as trivial or superficial, political events become lifeless and shallow, arguments for cynicism and indifference.[30]

Inherently, the electronic media emphasize the private, self-protective, and individualistic side of American culture at the expense of citizenship and public life. Traditional politics, like older forms of entertainment, drew citizens into public places; the media bring politics to individuals in private retreats. In those settings, private concerns are naturally uppermost, making it harder than usual —and it is always difficult—to appeal to public goods and goals.[31] Politics is dramaturgical: It asks us to step beyond the day-to-day, to see the present in the light of the possible, judging practice by theory. Great politics, like great theater, requires a special space, a precinct for its particular sort of fantasy, from which we reemerge into everyday life. Such distinctions hone and heighten experience; by blurring fantasy and reality so pervasively, television weakens reality's force and fantasy's charm.[32]

Above all else, television is a visual medium, confined to what can be seen and hence to externalities. Sight is our quickest sense, but it is also superficial, and the media's discontinuity of image and affect encourages emotional detachment, adaptation rather than commitment. A politics of the visible comes naturally to, and teaches us to be, a "world of strangers."[33]

At the most fundamental level, politics is about invisible things. A political society can be symbolized—for example, by the flag, George Bush's talisman in 1988—but it cannot be *seen*. Especially in a polity as diverse as the United States, political community is not a matter of outward semblance but of inward likeness, common ideas and ideals. In this sense, television almost necessarily distorts politics, since it is forced to visualize and personalize things that are impalpable or objective.[34] When events suit the medium, as in television's coverage of the southern civil rights movement, it speaks with unique power, but more often it is apt to be misleading, silly (Dukakis's tank ride), or mischievous.

To classical political theory, speech, not sight, is the most political of the faculties because it is in and through speech that we discover the boundaries and terms of political community.[35] But political speech—and, especially, *listening* to political speech—is a skill and pleasure that must be learned; it demands an extended span of attention, the capacity for critical reflection, and that art of hearing that lets us separate meaning from its disguises. Always difficult, that command of rhetoric is harder to cultivate in a society as supersonic as ours, and the electronic media actually undermine the arts of speech and hearing.[36]

Preoccupied with holding their audience, television programmers shun anything that might bore us (the Republican argument, this year, against more than two presidential debates), a logic that tends toward the lowest common public denominator.[37] The 1988 debates were question-and-answer sessions in which no comment could run longer than two minutes; in 1960, Kennedy and Nixon began their debates with eight-minute opening statements. In the 1970s, the average "sound bite" allowed a public figure was 15 to 20 seconds, and the President was given as much as a minute. Pretty thin at best. But in the 1980s, the figure has declined to 10 seconds for *all* public figures.[38] It symbolizes the decline of speech that George Bush, admiring the refrain, made "Don't Worry, Be Happy" into a campaign song, either ignoring the words or trusting that American voters would not notice their very contrary lesson.[39]

"Almost the only pleasure of which an American has any idea," Alexis de Tocqueville wrote, "is to take part in government and to discuss the part he has taken," and even women "listen to political harangues after their household labors."[40] More recently, Frank Skeffington, Edwin O'Connor's fictional mayor, spoke of politics as America's "greatest spectator sport," in which performers could, at least, rely on a critical mass of knowledgeable fans, but Skeffington was already sounding "the last hurrah."[41] In 1988, public speech seemed to be degenerating into shouted incivility, the tough talk of playground squabbles, at best a preface to politics.

The Parties and the Nominations

The primaries worked, in a sense, although the nominating process was too long, too costly, and too much influenced by unrepresentative electorates (see chap. 2). The cost in time and dignity helped keep out some of the most attractive Democratic possibilities, but the primaries sorted out a number of flawed candidates, and the eventual nominees were sensible and able. The electorate, however, did not like the choice, with some reason. Democratic party discontent has a special point, since the primary system puts the party at a strategic disadvantage in presidential politics.

Contested primaries, the rule for Democrats, are associated with defeat in presidential elections. In the last quarter-century, the only Democratic victories occurred in 1964 and 1976, when Republicans had their own bitter internal struggles.[42]

In any election, candidates of the center have a tactical advantage, since they have the best chance of making themselves "acceptable" to a broad coalition. In primary elections, this edge is not always decisive: Candidates "win" primaries by coming in first, and they do not need majorities. In 1988, Dukakis received 42 percent of all Democratic votes cast in primaries, but until the Pennsylvania primary he was under a third, and his victory in Texas, crucial to his eventual nomination, was won with just less than 33 percent of the vote. The primary victor, consequently, can be, like Goldwater or McGovern, the candidate of party militants, who are more likely to participate in primaries. In a contest for the nomination, a centrist is usually the best a party can hope for.

Nevertheless, a candidate who stands in the center of his or her party will be considerably to the right or left of center in relation to national opinion. Primaries pull candidates away from the national center, especially since primaries deemphasize economic issues, about which parties agree, and emphasize intraparty disagreements on foreign policy and social issues, the rallying points of party militancy.[43] Michael Dukakis is a centrist Democrat and no hero to liberals in his own state, but, as George Bush happily observed, Dukakis was forced by the logic of the primaries (especially in Iowa and New Hampshire) to stress his liberal credentials, his membership in the ACLU, and his devotion to peace. These sincere convictions, identifying Dukakis as substantially left of center, indicated his vulnerability. Before his contests with Jackson and rise in the polls induced temporary blindness, it was clear that Dukakis, unable to stir voters anywhere, was too liberal to win even moderate conservatives. Dukakis, James Reston wrote, would "lose the South and bore the North," and so it proved.[44]

For Republicans, it was a near thing: A shift of 7300 votes in New Hampshire would have made Senator Dole the victor in that state, at least lengthening the contest and, given Dole's gift for vituperation, raising the possibility of a donnybrook. As it was, the Republicans avoided a prolonged primary campaign, and they wound up with a candidate at least moderate and possibly better described as part of the party's liberal wing. Beginning with the nominee closer to the center of national opinion, the Republicans enjoyed an advantage that could be countered only by a superior Democratic campaign.

That campaign, of course, did not materialize, for which the primaries also bear some limited responsibility. The effort to capture a nomination establishes habits that persist, in the candidate and his or her staff, in the campaign proper. Part of Dukakis's primary success derived from his refusal to be drawn into intraparty conflict; his reliance on vague, liberal, but relatively unprogrammatic appeals; and his rejection of negative campaigning. Part temperamental, part calculation, Dukakis's tactics within the party foreshadowed his failure in the national campaign.[45]

The problem posed by the primaries is bad news for Democrats, since their party is much less cohesive than the GOP. Republicans declare themselves the party of individual liberty and opportunity, which translates broadly into a defense of property and profit; the Democrats' standard is "equal justice," a much harder term to define. Democrats require deliberation and tests of strength to work out the terms and frame of party coalitions.

There is some balm for Democrats in the offing. Blessed with an incumbent President, the Republicans will probably be able to avoid a primary battle in 1992, though even that is no sure thing. "Main Street" Republicans—the ideological right, buttressed by the party's growing evangelical wing—are almost certain to be frustrated and enraged by the "Wall Street" cast of the Bush administration. That partisan fault line, already rumbling, seems likely to shake Republican foundations, in 1996 if not sooner.[46]

Democrats cannot afford to be much comforted. For the immediate future, Democrats must expect primaries shaped by the candidacy of Jesse Jackson, based on Jackson's support among blacks and the white, middle-class left, the "Peugeot proletariat."[47] Jackson's vote is remarkably stable—from Super Tuesday to the end of the primary campaign, Jackson's percentage of the Democratic vote rose only from 26 to 29—but numbers are not the whole story. Jackson inspires negative coalitions; race injures him with many voters, and by most, he is perceived as too radical, possibly anti-Semitic, and certainly unelectable. Consequently, unless another candidate can dent Jackson's support in either of his two constituencies, the primary campaign is likely to be defined by the effort to establish which candidate is the alternative to Jackson. And that goal, obviously, will exaggerate the already disproportionate influence of the early primaries.[48]

It makes matters worse for the Democrats that money plays so decisive a role in primary campaigns. In general, Democratic money comes from liberal donors, which accentuates the pressure on candidates to establish their ideological bona fides. Since the material interests of liberals often run counter to their political commitments, they have no reason to value an electoral success that is not a victory for principle. Republicans also have their ideologues, of course, but in general, Republican donors see an economic interest in victory that moderates their zeal for pure doctrine. Nevertheless, even Republicans know the problem: The primaries displace those who live "off" politics in favor of those who live "for" politics, which imposes a strain on the political center.[49]

In what has become a quadrennial ritual, the Democrats will tinker with the nominating process. (In fact, they began to do so at the 1988 convention where Dukakis made important concessions to Jesse Jackson.) But the primaries are almost certainly too well established to permit a return to a nomination controlled by professionals, and more modest reforms have so far proved ineffective.[50] For example, "superdelegates," introduced to strengthen the role of professional judgment, have been pretty much irrelevant. Largely elected officials, they are bound to be leery of opposing any candidate who leads after the primaries, even if they think him a loser. In a democracy, it is never safe to resist the "people's choice," and the interest of superdelegates in doing so is lessened by the fact that their own chances of election seem so independent of the national ticket (see chap. 6). There is something to be said for Robert Beckel's suggestion that 60 percent of the delegates be chosen by primaries and the rest by state parties, but that proposal almost certainly offends too many interests to be adopted.

Democrats can and may do something to establish a national campaign staff, independent of the retinues of candidates, which can make plans for a campaign against the Republicans while the primary season is still going on. Such a planning staff might lessen an important Republican advantage: It might attract senior Democrats, who are disinclined to commit their time and prestige to the uncertainties of a primary campaign.[51] Even the shrewdest and best-designed reforms, however, will only better the ability of Democrats to cope with their inherent disadvantage in the nominating process and the difficulty it implies for the campaign.

Politics and Memory

In one important sense, the Democrats, as the "out party," began the campaign one-up on the Republicans. The party in power must defend the whole of its record; the opposition can choose the aspects of that record on which to base its challenge. The "outs" can promise to continue the popular aspects of the administration's program while correcting its flaws; if the "ins" pledge to do likewise, they will be asked why they have failed to act before. Discontent and the desire for change were the foundations of Dukakis's early lead (see chap. 4) and shaped his strategy of limiting criticism of Reagan and his policies, in favor of the "upbeat" theme, "The best America is yet to come."[52]

But the choice between change and the status quo is never the whole story. The appeal to political memory may allow the party in power to present a different choice: not what they promise as opposed to what *we* have done, but what *they* did as contrasted with what we have done. Fear or resentment of the past wars with hope for the future in our judgment of the present.[53]

Until recently, memory was a Democratic fortress, recalling the Great Depression and the Second World War, the glory years of the Roosevelt era—and in the South, where memories faded more slowly than in the North, nursing the straight-ticket heritage of Reconstruction. Now those old remembrances are quieting into whispers, losing their connection to contemporary partisanship, especially since, wounded by change and the media, our political memory is growing shorter.[54] Even the Kennedy years, so important to Dukakis, were only a flickering of the Democrats' candle of memory, obscured by the dark years that followed.

Increasingly, the focus of American political retrospection is Vietnam and the turbulence of the 1960s, permissive morality, stagflation, and the decline of America's imperium, the "greening of America" turned overripe. Out of that half-remembered experience, conservatives—but preeminently Ronald Reagan—have shaped a new, mythic history epitomized by the "L word," liberalism identified with the Carter years, but also with all the excesses of the late 1960s and the 1970s.[55] Ironically, Republicans also benefit from the New Left's critique, which, by portraying liberals as hypocritical and lukewarm, helped build the image of liberalism as morally soft. It is part of Reagan's art, moreover, that implicitly he ran against Nixon as well as Carter, appealing to the distaste for government reinforced by Watergate, assimilating Nixon's era to the "night" dispelled by Reagan's "morning." Where Democrats once ran against Hoover, in 1988, Republicans ran against McGovern, and George Bush argued repeatedly that "neighborhood Democrats" should prefer him to a leadership dominated by "the remnant of the '60s."[56]

Up to a point, Democrats recognized the problem and sought to correct it. Dukakis emphasized work rather than welfare and party leaders insisted on a shortened platform, unburdened by many controversial planks. The Democratic convention featured the author and folk-hero Garrison Keillor, surrounded by children; and Jimmy Carter, praising past Democratic candidates, asked,

"Wouldn't Ed Muskie have made a wonderful President?" Symbolically, Carter was reversing the verdict of 1972, attempting to write George McGovern out of Democratic history. In the same spirit, Michael Dukakis, despite his supposed disregard for symbols, was careful, early in the campaign, to invoke Harry Truman and to make a pilgrimage to Lyndon Johnson's birthplace, and it was Truman's liberalism with which he identified himself toward the end of the contest.

Yet to overcome the Republican version of the past, Dukakis needed a vision of the future, a language of the common good. He never articulated one, and the lack was more noticeable because the appeal to "community" in his acceptance speech was the rhetorical high point of the campaign.[57] More was involved than Dukakis's too-apparent shortcomings as an orator. He betrayed an uneasiness with the idea of community in both the infrequency and artificiality of his references to his ethnicity (despite its obvious political potential) and his choice to respond legalistically to slurs on his patriotism.[58]

It cost him. After the convention, Dukakis's severest losses were among Catholics, a decline most visibly linked to his views on crime, but most fundamentally to the emphasis, in Catholic teaching, on the idea of political society as a moral order.[59] The second presidential debate, his last real chance, was a disaster. Asked what his reaction would be were his wife raped and murdered, he responded with an abstract—and rehearsed—statement of his views on crime; portraying himself as able to make "tough choices," he declined to say what taxes he would raise should it become necessary, refusing to deal with the possibility, even as a hypothesis.[60] Dukakis was unwilling or unable to find words that, validating personal experience, would subordinate it to citizenship, bridging the distance between private feeling and the public good. But that is what his campaign required.

Michael Dukakis came of age in the 1950s, the silent decade, when politically interested students were preoccupied with totalitarianism and McCarthyite repression, and intellectuals elevated the "separation between facts and values" into a dogma, convinced—wrongly—that it leads logically to tolerance.[61] Ideology was "unmasked" to reveal its roots in the interests of groups and classes, and social scientists discerned its impending end.[62] Politics, in these terms, could be reduced to "brokerage," the arrangement of compromise between groups, perfected by able management and skilled administration.

Political science helped make "interest-group liberalism" into "the new public philosophy."[63] A political generation learned to cultivate "realism," a pragmatic "tough-mindedness" that scorns sentiment in favor of "hard fact." That teaching lies behind Michael Dukakis's extraordinary assertion that the issue between him and George Bush was "competence"; it was also the weakest side of the Kennedy years, the illusion of "the best and the brightest."[64]

For all his faults, however, John Kennedy retained a certain Irishness: He set his pragmatism to a poetry that sent hopes dancing. Yet Kennedy was surely no ideologue: suspect on civil liberty and no enthusiast for civil rights, he often seemed to the right of Nixon on issues of foreign policy. In this sense, George Bush's charge was appropriate: Michael Dukakis is a liberal, at least when compared with his hero, and the campaign in 1988 could not be a replay of 1960.

In one critical respect, however, George Bush is more akin to Michael Dukakis than either is to the great Presidents. Bush gave little indication of any idea of public purpose beyond an individualist's devotion to the private sector, the "thousand points of light." His hope for a "kinder and gentler America," consequently, seems to amount to no more than a promise to administer and broker private initiatives so as to moderate conflict. Bush, wrote George Will in disgust, "skitters like a waterbug on the surface of things," and James Skillen observed that both Bush and Dukakis are fundamentally "managerial coordinators" who use language to "buy time" rather than articulate an idea of the common good.[65] The candidates in 1988 reflected the fears and hesitancies of the contemporary public mind, but not the ability to lead or elevate it, and in the end, they confirmed the electorate's disenchantment.

Liberalism, Politics, and Economics

Republican success in attacking the "L word" obscured the fact that political liberalism, more broadly defined, was a world-beater in 1988. Modern liberalism grew up as the advocate of the Positive State, exemplified by the New Deal, urging the use of government, "the common instrument of political democracy," to meet human needs and take on problems that, as individuals, we are too weak to address.[66] In 1988, regulation and intervention were climbing back into favor, and active government commanded broad support.[67]

The Republican platform did not advocate the elimination of a single government program, and George Bush plumped for day care and youth employment. Nevertheless, economic policy was basically a Democratic talking point, and Michael Dukakis scored when he talked about such economic programs as nationwide health insurance. The Republicans gained the whip hand, however, because they were more willing to extend the positive state into foreign policy—Dukakis was hurt by his questions about the Grenada invasion and by a fear that he would endanger "peace through strength"—and into social life.

Bush moved ahead by advocating public support for "values" in civic education, most visibly in his zeal for the Pledge of Allegiance and his defense of school prayer.[68] His stance on abortion also helped, although his waffling entailed some embarrassing moments. Having expressed sympathy for a "Right to Life" amendment, Bush upheld abortion in cases of rape and incest, or to protect the life of the mother, and once he had "sorted out" his views, advocated criminal penalties only for the doctors performing illegal abortions, not for the women who obtain them. Yet even this moderate—or muddled—persuasion favored more government intervention than Dukakis's position in favor of a woman's "right to choice." Bush rejected abortion on demand, as Dukakis did not, and Bush's vacillations put him squarely in the center of American opinion.[69]

Most important, Bush succeeded in portraying himself as the champion of stronger law enforcement, chiefly by arguing for the death penalty for "cop killers" and "drug kingpins." This deprived the Democrats of what had looked to be a major asset. The Democrats began with an unwonted claim on the social issue because the administration looked weak on drugs: "Just Say No" failed to make use of state power, and the government seemed compromised and craven in its dealings with Panama's Noriega. Dukakis, however, offered no distinctive antidrug program, and his views on the death penalty, together with Willie Horton's infamous furlough, helped establish the image of Dukakis as a militant civil libertarian and soft on crime. In this, as in so many things, it seemed a bad year to oppose big government and public power.

That conclusion, however, is one-dimensional. Our culture has always been divided between the individualism of philosophic liberalism and the communitarian strain most powerfully expressed by biblical religion.[70] It is not surprising, consequently, that Americans look to government for more services but also regard it suspiciously and support it grudgingly, demanding tough laws but distrusting public authority, recognizing their own vulnerability but clinging to private liberty.

Modern America magnifies the reasons for skepticism. Government and politics are baffling and frustrating, especially at the national level. To enter public life is to be convinced of one's unimportance; political life forces a confrontation with indignity, even when it hints that the "arts of association" may hold the key to another sort of honor. Private life, by contrast, affords an illusion of control, especially in relatively prosperous times.

John Kennedy's grace helped give a charm to politics, but Kennedy's assassination (and those of Dr. King, Malcolm X, and Robert Kennedy), together with disillusioning experience, emphasized dangers and limitations, weakening the personal attractions and moral claims of public life. Dan Quayle, as Lloyd Bentsen observed, is no Jack Kennedy; today, the rich and the would-be rich, the bright and the handsome, are apt to gravitate toward private pursuits. Shrunk to the measure of the yuppie, Kennedy's image is caricatured by Donald Trump and Alex Keaton.

So much of government's recent record, after all, seems to tell against it. Lyndon Johnson, so forceful and adroit, overreached in Vietnam and over-promised in the War on Poverty. Nixon, despite his reputation as a Machiavelli, stumbled into Watergate; and Carter, who profited from mistrust of government, proved a marplot, additionally cursed with bad luck. For a time, the public thought Ronald Reagan had "taken charge," but the Iran-*Contra* affair revealed him to be feckless, ill informed, and indecisive, a virtual figurehead whose best defense was that he did not remember, or had never known, what was going on. Reagan retained his popularity, but the electorate, forced to recognize his shortcomings, received another jolt to its confidence in government and its judgment of political leaders.

Paradoxically, Reagan's pratfall may have helped George Bush. Bush was a *safe* candidate, a known quantity. Many voters felt that Michael Dukakis might be a great President, but prodded by the Republican campaign and Dukakis's own missteps, they came to fear that he might be terrible. Given the recent record of failed Presidencies, most such voters preferred not to take the chance. Dukakis's vagueness only made matters worse, since it left voters without a clear sense of what he would do.

Moreover, Dukakis's appeal to his "competence," like Bush's own managerialism, may have fed the suspicion that democratic politics, including the Presidency, no longer controls the nation's destiny. In the first place, we know that American life is more and more affected by events and decisions in foreign countries over which the U.S. government has only a measure of influence. We bluster, but we are becoming accustomed to the limits of American power.

Second, in the sphere that does remain to government, bureaucracy plays an often esoteric but increasingly central role. Authority has everywhere a tendency to pass downward, "into the body of the organization."[71] The Executive Office burgeoned in order to help the President control the executive branch; now the agencies of the Executive Office enjoy a sometimes startling independence from presidential control. For years, political scientists have warned that the President is in danger of being made a captive of his own machinery, and while the best modern Presidents have fought that tendency, the drift is there.[72]

Harry Truman insisted that "the buck stops here" precisely because he understood, following *The Federalist,* that the price of presidential authority—and, especially, of the "inherent power" of the prerogative—is a willingness to be held accountable for mischances and the misdeeds of others.[73] The diffusion of power, however, makes it seem more and more inappropriate to think of the President in terms of rule and unfair to hold him strictly responsible for execution. By contrast, it is now common to refer to the President as a manager, a coordinator of policies initiated and carried out elsewhere.

When John Kennedy accepted responsibility for the Bay of Pigs, he meant that it was his decision and that he held himself accountable for the plan, its execution, and its failure. When Ronald Reagan declared himself "responsible" for the Iran-*Contra* imbroglio (and before that, for the bombing of the Marine barracks in Beirut), he meant that he was *legally* accountable, but he went to some lengths to disclaim *personal* responsibility, and his language— "Mistakes were made"— directed the blame to a subjectless organizational process. Reagan's preposterous innocence made it easier for him to make such arguments; Lyndon Johnson could never have persuaded us that he did not know the details of the Iran-*Contra* policy. Nevertheless, Reagan indicates the direction of things: Accountability is shrinking into a thin political fiction.

Kurt Vonnegut saw it more than thirty-five years ago, imagining a future America in which government had become separate from politics, and hence from civic deliberation and direction. In Vonnegut's fantasy, the President was a former actor—"he had gone directly from a three-hour television program to the White House"— and his job amounted to a kind of media show:

> All the gorgeous dummy had to do was read whatever was handed to him on state occasions: to be suitably awed and reverent, as he said, for all the ordinary, stupid people who'd elected him to office, to run wisdom from somewhere else through that resonant voicebox and between those even, pearly choppers. . . . Just as religion and government had been split into disparate entities centuries before, now, thanks to the machines, politics and government lived side by side, but touched almost nowhere.[74]

The doubt that politics makes, or can make, more than a trivial difference to our lives calls into question the possibility of self-governance and hence the basis of the American republic. This evidently concerns all parties and all citizens, but it should be particularly disquieting to Democrats, since theirs is preeminently the party of the state, the champion of "citizenship values against market values."[75]

Democrats need to remind themselves, moreover, that this "civic ethic" holds, in principle, that economic interests are subordinate and do not deserve to rule, in the country, in the self, or in the party. For Democrats, this is not an entirely comfortable teaching. Divided between the most culturally modern and most traditional groups in America, Democrats would prefer to avoid "social issues" and broader questions of value; scarred by Bush, the Dukakis campaign hoped to "drive such questions off the political agenda and replace them with economic concerns."[76] In general, most voters did see the Democrats as the defenders of their interests, and Dukakis's late campaign—"I'm on your side"— drew most Democrats home. It was not enough. Economic concerns will blot out everything else only when economic problems are overwhelming, as they were in the Great Depression. They could not do so amid the relative prosperity of 1988.

In any case, economic interests are clearly inseparable from questions of foreign policy, just as social concerns are linked to economic phenomena like the two-wage-earner family. In fact, the need to shore up our economic culture —pride in work, commercial rectitude, and willingness to save—is probably the most important economic issue confronting the republic.[77]

The "American Century" is ending in a mood of dread; Americans worry about the country's future even when they are more or less confident about their personal fortunes. Conservative cheerfulness seemed forced—"Be Happy," the Bush theme song, is eerily parallel to the Depression favorite, "Ain't We Got Fun"—and a great many Americans voted for Bush not so much because they believed he could avert the day of reckoning but because they expected him to postpone it.[78]

Debt towers. In eight years, America has changed from the largest creditor to the largest debtor nation, and public and private borrowing has become an economic way of life. To alarm Americans with memories of the Carter years, George Bush did not refer to the magnitude of inflation; he recalled the sky-high interest rates of Carter's last year, imposed in the (successful?) attempt to drive inflation down. Implicitly, Bush realized that Americans do not mind paying dearly if they can borrow cheaply, but the public is never quite able to forget that we are discounting the future to pay for the present.

Americans are also uneasily aware of the trade deficit and the apparent decline of American products in the international economy. They see foreigners buying U.S. assets, and suspect it is "on the cheap."[79] Long accustomed to something like economic autarky, Americans are still uncomfortable with our increasing dependence on foreign economic decisions, even though our new vulnerability is subtler and easier to ignore than the oil shortages of the 1970s.[80] And as Paul Kennedy argues, political power tends to follow the path of economic decline.[81] Pridefully, Americans used to quote Berkeley's vision of America's future, "Westward, the course of empire takes its way." No more: American preeminence seems to be passing, like that of the ancient empires, moving further west across the Pacific.[82]

About their personal economic prospects, Americans are mostly optimistic, but there are reasons for disquiet. Poverty, although increasing, is still distant from most, but they are disturbed by homelessness, its most visible form.[83] More and more Americans sense—and many know by experience—that upward mobility, the opportunity celebrated by Republicans, is becoming difficult, and even a middle-class standard of living is harder to attain. Jobs are less secure, and the preponderant evidence indicates that the new jobs being created are not "good jobs at good wages." From 1980 to 1986, average personal wages fell 2 percent (discounting inflation), and household incomes rose 10 percent only because of women entering the workforce, a resource now substantially spent.

Americans have long been accustomed to achieving a middle-class standard through borrowing, a strategy made even more necessary by the fact that college costs are rising faster than families' ability to pay. Young Americans, however, are likely to find this burden heavier, and perhaps unsupportable, because future gains in prosperity are likely to fall short of expectations. Over the succeeding decade, the wages of a thirty-year-old worker in 1950 increased 58 percent, and in 1960, 44 percent; by 1977, the figure had fallen to 21 percent.[84] "It is a true rule," John Winthrop argued, "that particular estates cannot subsist in the ruin of the public."[85] He was right: Our personal economic destinies cannot be separated from the country's shadowed future.

The private centers of power in American postindustrialization, are a source of problems rather than solutions. Americans are unsettled by mergers, "junk bonds," and "leveraged buyouts," and they are troubled by corporate power generally. In a *Washington Post* poll, 66 percent of Republican voters (as opposed to 14 percent of GOP convention delegates) agreed that corporations have "too much power."[86]

In 1932, Berle and Means described the separation of ownership from control, the growing ascendancy of managers over stockholders in the modern corporation. Today, however, managers seem unable to protect themselves against takeovers, even with such innovations as the "poison pill" defense. Finance, always powerful, has become imperial, and it sometimes seems that managerial bureaucracy, displacing politics in public life, is *being* displaced in economic life.[87] On Wall Street, observers note a radically short-term orientation in which wealth and control have become separated from production. At the center of our economic life, a contemporary version of "conspicuous consumption" is undermining the discipline of productivity.[88]

Liberalism, Values, and Community

Yet, discontent with this "conservative permissiveness" in the economy is only part of the broader feeling that society is out of control, falling toward Gehenna. Every day's news—if not everyday experience—testifies to the frequency of disordered families, child abuse, child neglect, and teenage suicide. And for millions of voters in 1988, the drug problem ranked first among political issues.[89]

The difficulty is more fundamental than such tumults; it can be heard even in the silences of contemporary life. American households are radically mobile—

somewhere around 20 percent of Americans move every year—and we learn to be fearful of attaching ourselves to people or places in order to avoid the pain that comes with uprooting. Divorce, now commonplace, underlines that lesson, and even stable families are more and more apt to be limited to two generations (only about 25 percent of American children have a significant relationship with a grandparent), a setting that teaches Americans that important relationships are short term.

Illustratively, in a 1988 television ad, a young girl, separated from her friends by her family's move, complains that she does not make friends easily. A motherly employee of the moving company reassures her, "You've already made one. Me." Yet, obviously, this slight acquaintance with an adult who, because of her job, will also soon be moving on, is no substitute for the intimate ties the girl has lost. The ad offers only the cool counsel that such transient relationships may be the best we can hope for, and as at least one news story reminds us, closer bonds may not be safe. In Wisconsin, two teenage friends, unable to bear the separation when one family moved away, ended a weekend reunion in suicide.[90] Experience cautions Americans to keep their relationships shallow, their liabilities limited, and their obligations minimal.

Shouting that individuals are insignificant, contemporary America also whispers the more seductive lesson that, in consequence, they are free from responsibility and that it is not even legitimate to hold them accountable. Lewis Lapham describes that temptation:

> A man can feel shame before an audience of his peers, within the narrow precincts of a neighborhood, profession, army unit, social set, city room, congregation or football team. The scale and dynamism of American democracy grants the ceaselessly renewable option of moving one's conscience into a more congenial street.[91]

And it is predictable, if unedifying, that the dominant moral doctrine of the media is a version of relativism and the ethic of success.[92]

Despite all that, Jimmy Carter was right to discern a "moral hunger" in the electorate, a yearning attested by the remarkable success of Allan Bloom's *The Closing of the American Mind,* with its appeal to natural right and to the enduring classics of Greek antiquity.[93] Yet America is too diverse and Americans are too accustomed to the benefits of modern commercial society to admit of a return of traditional morality and community, especially since Americans have enough memory of Jim Crow to know that community can be repressive. The past that holds the broadest appeal in popular culture is recent, though stabler: *Who Framed Roger Rabbit?* is likely to be contemporary America's closest approach to the trial of Socrates.[94]

At the same time, civil order—and, especially, a democratic one—does require and rest on shared beliefs and principles.⁹⁵ In regimes that are not democratic, the culture of the ruling elite can be the foundation for political life; democracy presumes a much broader sharing of civic ethics and culture. Democratic debate is possible only about matters we are willing to submit to the judgment of majorities, and so presumes that we are minimally confident in the public's decency and idea of justice. It is the things not in debate that make democratic argument possible, as Tocqueville observed in an older America:

> Thus, in the moral world, everything is classed, adapted, decided and foreseen; in the political world, everything is agitated, uncertain and disputed: in the one is a passive, though voluntary, obedience; in the other an independence, scornful of experience and jealous of authority. These two tendencies, apparently so discrepant, are far from conflicting; they advance together, and mutually support each other.⁹⁶

Tocqueville worried, however, that individualism, embedded in the laws, would eventually eat up those public and private virtues he called "the habits of the heart," and there is evidence that just such an imbalance is developing in American culture. Robert Bellah and his associates found that Americans are losing the languages of biblical religion and civic republicanism, the historic rivals of individualism in our national dialogue. Even when Americans act in terms of these older values, they tend to explain and justify their lives in the language of utilitarianism, calculated self-interest, or "expressive individualism," the appeal to private feeling.⁹⁷ Too many "modern people" have "sadly concluded" that: "greed is the universal motive, sincerity is a pose, honesty is for chumps, altruism is selfishness with a neurotic twist and morality is for kids and saints and fools." ⁹⁸ At the same time, like Glaucon in Plato's *Republic*, they long to be persuaded that it isn't so.⁹⁹

A great deal of Ronald Reagan's abiding popularity reflects his effective appeal to patriotism and "traditional values," but this rhetoric, while important, must be set against a record of symbols and policies that forward individualism.¹⁰⁰ Neither Ronald Reagan nor George Bush has been willing to ask Americans for sacrifice, and where their policies have imposed burdens, they have almost universally fallen on the less fortunate.

In foreign affairs, the Reagan administration celebrated cheap victories, but it shied away from policies that involve significant costs. Verbally firm on terrorism, the Reagan administration hesitated to risk the lives of hostages, pursuing its secret negotiations with Iran. Despite the importance of Nicaragua in Reagan's world view, he preferred covert action to either an open use of prerogative or an all-out, popularity-risking effort to persuade the public.¹⁰¹ And conservatism's social issues, with their challenge to contemporary middle-class life styles, were never high on Reagan's political agenda and probably rank even lower for George Bush.[102]

In part, this reticence derives from the accurate calculation that Americans are unwilling to make more than modest sacrifices. At bottom, however, Republicans are individualists in principle, devoted to the private sector and to private gain. In the second debate, George Bush assailed Michael Dukakis's plans to make tax evaders pay, saying that they would lead to "IRS agents in your kitchen." (Characteristically, Dukakis let slip the chance to call his opponent soft on law enforcement.) On the other hand, Democrats have failed to make clear that they understand that political community is more than "inclusiveness," that it imposes duties as well as rights.

This was the deeper dimension of the argument over the death penalty and law enforcement that hurt Dukakis in 1988. At the Democratic convention, Dukakis's invocation of community spoke, as his citation of John Winthrop indicated, to the biblical elements of the American tradition and to all the resonances in our culture that are older than the individualism of liberal philosophy. Political community, however, presumes, as a ruling principle, some idea of the common—and, ultimately, of the human—good. Communitarianism sees political society as a moral order, and the laws of such a regime, designed to strengthen what is admirable and right, entail penalties for the wicked as well as rewards for the virtuous.[103]

By contrast, philosophic liberalism begins with autonomous individuals, and it rejects the idea of a single human good. Political society, in this view, has no moral mission, no goal to shape the soul. It exists to advance private rights more effectively, and public policy is properly a calculation of utilities.[104] Liberalism is always hesitant to punish because it doubts that, strictly speaking, there is any *wrong:* There are only rights carried to excess, as in the saying "We have a right to do as we please, so long as it does not infringe the rights of others." Obviously, liberals can and do punish, but they are more comfortable with the effort to cure the "underlying conditions" of crime by providing positive incentives to civil behavior.[105]

To ask whether the death penalty "deters," as Dukakis did, is to range oneself on the liberal side of the debate, seeing punishment in terms of utilities and from the criminal's point of view. It also misses the vital communitarian point that decent citizens are not "deterred" primarily by the likelihood of punishment—if that were the case, America would be in even worse straits—but by the idea that crime is wrong.[106]

In a troubled society, citizens look to government to vindicate their decencies and to protect public life from simply private-spirited calculation. Periodically, any political society must call on its citizens to risk their lives, to suffer economic loss, and to disrupt their relationships on behalf of the public good. Citizenship, like civility, begins with a form of self-denial, a willingness to see oneself as a part of a whole. Punishment balances the scale, imposing on vice a homage to civic virtue, and a political society that is too gentle with crime or avarice will find, in the not so very long run, that it has lost its citizens.[107]

Toward Public Renewal

Abler and less hollow than his predecessor, George Bush may be willing to grapple with the nation's deeper problems. Republicans have no immediate interest in tampering with their formula for success in presidential elections (although as memories fade, it will grow harder to run against the late 1960s and the Carter era.)[108] By contrast, Democrats have every reason, at least as a presidential party, to attempt to articulate a view of the common good.[109]

In the first place, Democrats need a more positive, less apologetic foreign policy.[110] This is a matter for delicacy, since Democrats are far more divided than Republicans in their attitudes toward international affairs; in a 1987 poll, Democrats divided almost equally when asked whether the United States should "support anticommunist forces around the world."[111] Even that polarization, however, argues against dovishness and for moderation, and there is a special urgency to the need for a new Democratic perspective on foreign policy.

There are unmistakable signs that the "Vietnam syndrome" is ending. Even more dramatically than the Vietnam memorial, Jane Fonda's apology to veterans signals the war's new place in national remembrance, and the rise of courses on Vietnam in nonelite colleges is a political omen Democrats cannot afford to ignore. This change is an opportunity for Democratic reconciliation, since lines are softening on both sides of the Vietnam divide. The controversy over Dan Quayle's military record established or revealed a new, lower conservative standard, by which patriotism is satisfied by law-abidingness: One did one's duty, George Bush implied, by refraining from burning draft cards or flags.

This is as clear a portent as Ronald Reagan's divorce was in social policy: Conservatism is adapting, and opinion in contemporary America, while not dovish, is also not on the side of the hawks.[112] If Ronald Reagan can become an apostle of arms control, it should be possible for Democrats to lose their reflex against the use of military force, avoiding their recent tendency to overgeneralize the "lessons" of Vietnam. (Senator Bill Bradley has already set an excellent example.) Perhaps some Democrat may even observe that both those who fought in Vietnam and those who resisted the war filled a fuller measure of patriotism than those who merely obeyed the law.

In any case, Democrats surely need to offer some examples of "toughness," some instances of willingness to punish and to enforce standards of civil conduct, if they are to be credible advocates of political community. Locally, even very liberal Democrats, like Assemblyman Jack O'Connell in California, are apt to support stricter sentences, including the death penalty, and Congress was wise in voting to enforce child-support payments.[113] Beyond particular policies, Democrats have a special reason to demonstrate that their party has a vertebral moral identity. The Democratic party cannot weaken in its advocacy of racial and gender equality; it is probably committed to a pro-choice position; and the list goes on. Committed to change in so many areas of life, Democrats must demonstrate to the electorate that, more than weathervanes, they have some principles that do *not* change.[114]

This is nowhere more evident than in relation to race, the "dirty little secret" of the election of 1988.[115] Actually, it was not much of a secret. There is more and more willingness to speak about the drift of whites away from the Democratic party, and not only in the South. Among Democratic candidates since Franklin D. Roosevelt, only Lyndon Johnson received the support of a majority of whites, and Johnson's revolution helped persuade a large number of working-class white voters that, in the last analysis, Democrats will prefer the interests of blacks to their own.[116]

At the same time, it is harder to overcome such feelings by an appeal to guilty consciences. Legal segregation is a hazy memory, and for the most part, overt racism has yielded to subtler forms. For example, in the media—and hence in the view of most Americans—race is visible largely in relation to crime and the sleazier forms of interest-group politics.

Philosophic liberalism offers little help. The primacy of individual rights in the liberal tradition implies that equality, "before the law" and in politics, exists to protect earned inequalities in economic and social life. Enforced integration of low-income housing runs against property rights; busing menaces plans to give one's children the benefit of superior public schools; affirmative action seems to endanger the basic principle of equal opportunity, that jobs should be awarded on the basis of demonstrated ability. Liberal doctrine does recognize the claim of minorities to compensation for past injuries, but its individualism, rejecting the idea of collective guilt, argues that I am responsible only for my own deeds, not those of the past. Policies to promote racial equality are increasingly likely to be seen, in these terms, as "reverse discrimination," violations of the unequal prerogatives of private achievement.

Democrats cannot counter that persuasion, let alone overcome it, without a language of collective obligation. In the biblical view, for example, membership makes citizens participants of the whole of a political society's life, including its heritage. When citizens say that in 1776, "we" declared our independence from Great Britain, they identify with the American past, but this appropriate pride also entails guilt: Our Constitution included slavery, and our society perpetuated racism. "In Adam's fall," the Puritans taught their children, "we sinned ALL."

In that understanding, all Americans have an obligation to make those sacrifices that are necessary to atone. The burdens this involves should be shared as equally as possible: Working-class whites in cities like Yonkers should not be expected to welcome low-income housing when rich, neighboring cities like Scarsdale are left alone. However, when individual Americans suffer some loss in the interest of racial equality, it is no different in principle from conscription, which may call some to serve in time of war while leaving others at home. Every citizen has a civic calling to repay his or her debt to the common life.

Implicitly, by pledging "equal justice," the 1988 Democratic platform went beyond pluralistic inclusiveness. Equality makes its own discriminations. We are not equal in the way we look or in what we have achieved; since equality rejects the testimony of such appearances, it points politics toward the soul. Moreover, a politics founded on the belief in equality excludes racism and relativism, for it holds that what is human is more important than biology or culture.[117] There is also a contemporary truth in the promise of just equality, with its suggestion that equality can be unjust.

America cannot be an ancient Greek *polis* or a homogenous community; political life must find room for our diversities and our privacies, just as prudence must acknowledge the impact of technology and economic change. American democracy needs, and can stand, only so many stanzas of epic poetry; contemporary politics calls for the more prosaic effort to protect and rebuild locality, association, and party, the links between private individuals and public goods. Even such limited goals, however, presume policy guided by a ruling principle, that middle term between repression and relativism whose better name is citizenship.[118] For both Republicans and Democrats, the election of 1988 indicates the need for a new civility, and for the kinds of word and deed necessary to affirm, for the coming century, the dignity of self-government.

Notes

1. Harold W. Stanley, William T. Bianco, and Richard Niemi, "Partisanship and Group Support Over Time," *American Political Science Review* 80 (1986): 969-76; E.J. Dionne, " 'Solid South' Again, but Republican," *New York Times*, 13 November 1988, 32; John Herbers, "A Few but Sturdy Threads Tie New South to the Old," *New York Times*, 6 March 1988, E1.

2. Paul Abramson, "Measuring the Southern Contribution to the Democratic Co-

alition," *American Political Science Review* 81 (1987): 569.

3. The phrase is from E.J. Dionne, "Political Memo," *New York Times*, 20 October 1988, A1.

4. *New York Times*, 12 May 1987, 16.

5. "On My Mind," *New York Times*, 4 November 1988, A35.

6. Ernst Kantorowicz, *The King's Two Bodies* (Princeton: Princeton University Press, 1957).

7. Doubly so, since the proximate cause of disaster in Twain's story is a stock-market crunch engineered by Sir Lancelot.

8. Lena Williams, "It Was a Year When Civility Really Took It on the Chin," *New York Times*, 18 December 1988, 1ff.

9. R.W. Apple recalled Cleveland's experience in relation to the Hart fiasco (*New York Times*, 8 May 1987, 1ff), and Charles Paul Freund invoked it in comparison to the campaign (*Washington Post National Weekly*, 7–13 November 1988, 29-30).

10. Matthew Josephson, *The Politicos* (New York: Harcourt Brace, 1938), 426; Allan Nevins, *Grover Cleveland: A Study in Courage* (New York: Dodd, Mead, 1932), 428ff; and Allan Nevins, ed., *The Letters of Grover Cleveland* (Boston: Houghton Mifflin, 1933), 183-84, 188-89.

11. Alexis de Tocqueville, *Democracy in America* (New York: Schocken Books, 1961), 1:204-15; Sally Foreman Griffith, *Home Town News: William Allen White and the Emporia Gazette* (New York: Oxford University Press, 1988).

12. Josephson, *Politicos*, 423-24, 427.

13. Jeffrey R. Abramson, F. Christopher Arterton, and Gary R. Orren, *The Electronic Commonwealth* (New York: Basic Books, 1988), 11-13; Joseph Schlesinger, "The New American Party System," *American Political Science Review* 79 (1985): 1152-69.

14. Laura L. Vertz, John P. Fendress, and James L. Gibson, "Nationalization of the Electorate in the United States," *American Political Science Review* 81 (1987): 961-66; William J. Crotty, *Political Reform and the American Experiment* (New York: Crowell, 1977); Committee on Political Parties of the American Political Science Association, *Toward a More Responsible Two-Party System* (New York: Rinehart, 1950).

15. *Providence Journal*, 10 November 1988, A11.

16. Todd Gitlin, "The Candidate Factory," *Boston Review* 13 (August 1988): 6. Implicitly, critics acknowledged the point when they faulted Dukakis's campaign for being "too thin"—too centralized and too little inclined to reach out to local party leaders—and overreliant on "experts." See *New York Times*, 12 November 1988, 8; and Michael Barone, "Those Dukakis Ads Just Don't Work," *Washington Post National Weekly*, 17-23 October 1988, 29.

17. James David Barber, "How to Pick Our Presidents," *New York Times*, 8 March 1987, E23, observed that within broad limits, "the man makes the office."

18. Since James G. Blaine, Cleveland's opponent, combined private rectitude with public sleaziness, Moorfield Storey argued that "we should elect Mr. Cleveland to the public office he is so admirably qualified to fill, and relegate Mr. Blaine to the private life he is so eminently fitted to adorn." Mark DeWolfe Howe, *Portrait of an Independent* (Boston: Houghton Mifflin, 1932), 151.

19. Michael Arlen, "The Candidates Deserve Each Other," *New York Times*, 28 September 1988, A27; it is doubtful that JFK—and possibly even Franklin Roosevelt or Dwight Eisenhower—would have met the media's moral test for the Presidency.

20. W. Russell Neuman, *The Paradox of Mass Politics: Knowledge and Opinion in the American Electorate* (Cambridge, Mass.: Harvard University Press, 1986).

21. Paul Corcoran, "The Limits of Democratic Theory," in *Democratic Theory and Practice*, ed. Graeme Duncan (New York: Cambridge University Press, 1983), 19; *The Nature of Politics: Selected Essays of Bertrand de Jouvenel*, ed. Dennis Hale and Marc K. Landy (New York: Schocken Books, 1987), 44-54.

22. Richard Sennett, *The Fall of Public Man* (New York: Knopf, 1977), 283. Of course, many Americans do talk back to the television set—my father-in-law was particularly eloquent—in a response that is probably healthy but certainly futile.

23. Abramson, Arterton, and Orren, *Electronic Commonwealth*, 15, 46-49; Todd Gitlin, *Inside Prime Time* (New York: Pantheon, 1985), 325-35.

24. Abramson, Arterton, and Orren, *Electronic Commonwealth*, 13.

25. Mark Hertsgaard, *On Bended Knee: The Press and the Reagan Presidency* (New York: Farrar, Strauss and Giroux, 1988).

26. Kathleen Hall Jamieson, "Is the Truth Now Irrelevant in Presidential Campaigns?" *Washington Post National Weekly*, 7-13 November 1988, 28.

27. Gitlin, "The Candidate Factory," 23.

28. Eleanor Randolph, "Now There Are Two 'Stealth Candidates,'" *Washington Post National Weekly*, 26 September–2 October 1988, 14.

29. James North, "While the Soviets Debated, We Poured on the Pablum," *Washington Post National Weekly*, 5-11 September 1988, 25.

30. Eugene J. Alpert, "The Media and the Message," *Political Science Teacher* 1 (Summer 1988): 13; John Chancellor, "Putting Zip, Juice—Interest—into Campaigns," *New York Times*, 29 November 1988, A25.

31. Abramson, Arterton, and Orren, *Electronic Commonwealth*, 177; Gitlin, *Inside Prime Time*, 330, 332; Daniel Boorstin, *The Americans: The Democratic Experience* (New York: Random House, 1973), 393.

32. Barbara Lippert, "Ronald Reagan and Michael Jackson—Together at Last," *Washington Post National Weekly*, 5-11 September 1988, 24; Robert Brustein, "Can Bush as Bush Steal the Show?" *New York Times*, 21 August 1988, E25.

33. Gitlin, *Inside Prime Time*, 248.

34. T.W. Adorno, "Television and the Problem of Mass Culture," in *Mass Culture*, ed. Bernard Rosenberg and David Manning White (New York: Free Press, 1957), 435.

35. Aristotle, *Politics*, 1253a, 9-18.

36. Marc Landy and I made a similar argument in "On Political Edification, Eloquence and Memory," *PS* 17 (1984): 203-10.

37. Dorothy B. James, "Television and the Syntax of Presidential Leadership," *Presidential Studies Quarterly* 18 (1988): 737-39.

38. Gitlin, "The Candidate Factory," 7. Hoping to encourage more substantive discussion, Michael Woo, a Democratic member of the Los Angeles City Council, sensibly suggested legislation requiring political ads on television to be purchased in longer blocks of time. *New York Times*, 13 November 1988, E3.

39. *New York Times*, 14 October 1988, A14.

40. Tocqueville, *Democracy in America*, 1:293.

41. Edwin O'Connor, *The Last Hurrah* (Boston: Little, Brown, 1956), 70; cf. Frank Kent, *The Great Game of Politics* (New York: Doubleday Doran, 1935).

42. Martin P. Wattenberg, "The 1988 and 1960 Elections Compared: What a Dif-

ference Candidate-Centered Politics Makes" (paper presented at the annual meeting of the American Political Science Association, Washington, D.C., 1–4 September 1988).

43. Byron Shafer, "Scholarship on Presidential Selection in the United States," *American Political Science Review* 82 (1988): 962.

44. *New York Times*, 4 April 1988, A21.

45. Dukakis and his staff may have mistaken for positive support what was only antipathy to Jackson, especially since the voters who rejected Jackson as "too liberal" would obviously be vulnerable to later Republican appeals. Scot Lehigh, "Michael Dukakis: The Unmaking of a President," *Phoenix's The NewPaper*, 10 November 1988, 4; *New York Times*, 27 April 1988, A24.

46. Philip Weiss, "The Cultural Contradictions of the GOP," *Harpers* 276 (January 1988): 48-58. In Iowa, Robertson did better than Dole among younger voters and three times better than Bush.

47. The phrase is from Richard Marin, "Jackson's White Support Is the 'Peugeot Proletariat,' " *Washington Post National Weekly*, 2–8 May 1988, 37.

48. Since Jackson's nomination was not a real possibility, his candidacy meant—and probably will mean—that black voters have only a negative influence on the Democratic nominee. Juan Williams, "How Jackson Is Jeopardizing the Influence of Blacks," *Washington Post National Weekly*, 15 June 1987, 23.

49. The distinction derives from Max Weber, "Politics as a Vocation," in *From Max Weber: Essays in Sociology*, ed. Hans Gerth and C. Wright Mills (New York: Oxford University Press, 1946), 77-128; on the contemporary aspects, see Thomas Byrne Edsall, *The New Politics of Inequality* (New York: Norton, 1984).

50. James Lengle, "Democratic Party Reforms: The Past as Prologue to the 1988 Campaign," *Journal of Law and Politics* 4 (1987): 233-73; David Broder and Paul Taylor, "The Democrats' Problem," *Washington Post National Weekly*, 14-20 November 1988, 12.

51. *New York Times*, 12 November 1988, 8.

52. David Broder, "For Dukakis, the Glass Is Half Full," *Washington Post National Weekly*, 2–8 May 1988, 4; and "An Uncertain Electorate Is Tilting Democratic," ibid., 4–10 July 1988, 12.

53. Morris P. Fiorina, *Retrospective Voting in American National Elections* (New Haven: Yale University Press, 1981).

54. John Garvey, "Age of Distraction," *Commonweal* 114 (25 September 1987): 420.

55. Michael Wallace, "Reagan and History," *Tikkun* 2, no. 1 (1987): 13-18; Seymour Martin Lipset, "Americans Sneer at Liberalism, Why?" *New York Times*, 28 October 1988, A35.

56. *Washington Post*, 29 October 1988, A17; Paul Taylor, "Bush Has Dukakis Trapped in a Time Warp," *Washington Post National Weekly*, 10–16 October 1988, 13.

57. Lehigh, "Michael Dukakis: The Unmaking of a President," 6.

58. David Broder, "What Dukakis Should Have Said," *Washington Post National Weekly*, 19–25 September 1988, 4; Edward Walsh, "An Immigrant's Kid for the Immigrants," ibid., 6–12 June 1988, 7.

59. E.J. Dionne, "Political Memo," *New York Times*, 20 October 1988, A1.

60. On the second debate, see *New York Times*, 12 November 1988, A1ff.

61. Steven D. Stark, "The Mandate in the Gray Flannel Suit," *Washington Post National Weekly*, 6-12 June 1988, 24-25; Leo Strauss, *Natural Right and History* (Chicago: University of Chicago Press, 1953), 35-80.

62. Daniel Bell, *The End of Ideology: On the Exhaustion of Political Ideas in the Fifties* (Glencoe, Ill.: Free Press, 1960).

63. Theodore J. Lowi, *The End of Liberalism: Ideology, Policy and the Origins of Public Authority* (New York: Norton, 1969).

64. Bruce Miroff, *Pragmatic Illusions: The Presidential Politics of John F. Kennedy* (New York: McKay, 1976); Robert Gaines, "Cursing the Darkness," *Phoenix's The New-Paper*, 10 November 1988, 1ff.

65. George Will, "A National Embarrassment," *Washington Post National Weekly*, 3–9 October 1988, 33; James Skillen, *Public Justice Report* 12 (October 1988): 6.

66. Robert Kuttner, *The Life of the Party: Democratic Prospects in 1988 and Beyond* (New York: Viking, 1987), 13. The classic statement of modern American liberalism is John Dewey, *The Public and Its Problems* (New York: Holt, 1927).

67. By almost 2 to 1 (60 to 33 percent), Americans responding to a poll late in 1987 rejected any cut in government services. *New York Times*, 1 December 1987, B24.

68. Michael Robinson, "Can Values Save George Bush?" *Public Opinion* 11 (July/August 1988): 11-13, 59-60.

69. On George Bush's early statement of his views, see Robert Zwier, "George Bush," *Public Justice Report* 11 (January 1988): 4. On 1 December 1987, the *New York Times* reported that an identical percentage of Republicans and Democrats (37 percent) favored the existing system of abortion rights, while 40 percent of Republicans *and* 43 percent of Democrats favored limiting abortion to cases of rape, incest, and protecting the life of the mother (p. B24). Abortion divides both parties, but it is more polarizing to Democrats who, on both sides of the issue, appear to feel more strongly than Republicans. See Lewis Bolce, "Abortion and Presidential Elections," *Presidential Studies Quarterly* 18 (1988): 815-27. Of course, Bush's position is an administrative nightmare: Would a woman be entitled to an abortion merely by claiming rape or incest? If she is required to substantiate the charge, what would the standard of proof be? And could a decision be reached within the first trimester, or even the period of gestation?

70. Michael Kammen, *People of Paradox* (New York: Knopf, 1972).

71. John Kenneth Galbraith, "Coolidge, Carter, Bush, Reagan," *New York Times*, 12 December 1988, A16.

72. Edward Corwin, *The President: Office and Powers* (New York: New York University Press, 1957), 300-304.

73. *The Federalist*, No. 70.

74. Kurt Vonnegut, *Player Piano* (New York: Dell, 1952), 118-19.

75. Kuttner, *Life of the Party*, 15; in what follows, I am indebted to Kuttner, *Life of the Party*, 205-47.

76. E.J. Dionne, "Political Memo," *New York Times*, 29 September 1988, A1. On Democratic divisions, see Bolce, "Abortion and Presidential Elections."

77. Amitai Etzioni, "The Party, Like Reagan's Era, Is Over," *New York Times*, 16 February 1987, 27; Michael Lerner, "Neo-Compassionism," *Tikkun* 2 (November/December 1987): 12.

78. Benjamin Friedman, *Day of Reckoning: The Consequencess of American Economic Policy under Reagan* (New York: Random House, 1988); Marie Natoli, "Campaign '88," *Presidential Studies Quarterly* 18 (1988): 714.

79. John Berry, "The U.S. Trade Deficit Won't Vanish Overnight," *Washington Post National Weekly*, 11–17 January 1988, 20.

80. Jeffrey Garten, "How Bonn, Tokyo, Slyly Help Bush," *New York Times*, 21 JULY 1988, A25.

81. Paul Kennedy, *The Rise and Fall of Great Powers* (New York: Random House, 1987); Lester Thurow, "A Briefing for the Next President," *New York Times*, 21 August 1988, F2.

82. George Berkeley, "On the Prospect of Planting Arts and Learning in America" (1752). Berkeley would be as disturbed as most Americans, since he prophesied that America's rise would "close the drama."

83. Tom Wicker, "Always with Us," *New York Times*, 19 November 1987, 27.

84. Frank Levy, *Dollars and Dreams* (New York: Russell Sage Foundation, 1987); Paul Blustein, "The Great Jobs Debate," *Washington Post National Weekly*, 5–11 September 1988, 20-21.

85. "A Modell of Christian Charity," in *Puritan Political Ideas*, ed. Edmund Morgan (Indianapolis: Bobbs-Merrill, 1965), 90.

86. *Washington Post National Weekly*, 15–21 August 1988, 10.

87. A.A. Berle and Gardiner C. Means, *The Modern Corporation and Private Property* (New York: Macmillan, 1934). The vulnerability of managers is not much comfort to ordinary stockholders, although corporate raiders sometimes present themselves as allies of investors, as Gordon Gekko did in the movie *Wall Street*. Even when stockholders make profits, "golden parachutes" (payments to displaced managers) and "greenmail" (payments by management to raiders) indicate the shareholders' basic disadvantage.

88. James Glassman, "The Monster That's Eating Wall Street," *Washington Post National Weekly*, 18–24 January 1988, 23; Etzioni, "The Party, Like Reagan's Era."

89. The phrase "conservative permissiveness" is from Kevin Phillips, "The Reagan Revolution Is Over and the GOP Should Be Grateful," *Washington Post National Weekly*, 17 August 1987, 23. On the general point, see Daniel Goleman, "How Is America?" *New York Times*, 25 December 1988, E12; and Daniel P. Moynihan, "Half the Nation's Children Born without a Fair Chance," *New York Times*, 25 September 1988, E25.

90. *New York Times*, 18 October 1988, A29.

91. Lewis Lapham, "Supply-Side Ethics," *Harpers* 270 (May 1985): 11.

92. Herbert London, "What TV Drama Is Teaching Our Children," *New York Times*, 23 August 1987, H23ff.

93. *New York Times*, 22 November 1987, 37; Allan Bloom, *The Closing of the American Mind* (New York: Simon and Schuster, 1987).

94. Frederic Jameson, "On Raymond Chandler," *Southern Review* 6 (1970): 624-50. In Vonnegut's *Player Piano*, workers displaced by technology do not long for a world without machines, but one in which they are needed to tend and repair machines.

95. Bennett Berger, "Disenchanting the Concept of Community," *Society* 25 (September/October 1988): 50-52; Michael J. Himes and Kenneth R. Himes, "The Myth of Self-Interest," *Commonweal* 115 (23 September 1988): 493-98.

96. Tocqueville, *Democracy in America*, 1:33.

97. Ibid., 2:118-20; Robert Bellah et al., *Habits of the Heart* (Berkeley: University of California Press, 1985).

98. Walt Harrington, "Has Truth Gone Out of Style?" *Washington Post National Weekly*, 4–10 January 1988, 6-7.

99. Plato, *Republic*, 358D.

100. Christopher Lasch, "Traditional Values, Left, Right and Wrong," *Harpers* 273 (September 1986): 13-16.

101. Russell Baker, "Talk So Big, Do So Nothing," *New York Times,* 29 March 1986, A27.

102. Steven V. Roberts, "Reagan's Social Issues: Gone but Not Forgotten," *New York Times,* 11 September 1988, E4.

103. For what follows, I am indebted to Stanley C. Brubaker, "Can Liberals Punish?" *American Political Science Review* 82 (1988): 821-36; see also Michael Sandel, *Liberalism and the Limits of Justice* (Cambridge: Cambridge University Press, 1982), 89-91.

104. Thomas Pangle, *The Spirit of Modern Republicanism* (Chicago: University of Chicago Press, 1988); for a modern example, although one that nominally rejects individualism, see David Truman, *The Governmental Process* (New York: Knopf, 1951), 50-51.

105. Such incentives evidently work in the long term, if at all.

106. Brubaker, "Can Liberals Punish?" 831.

107. "In a good state," Rousseau wrote, "there are few punishments, not because pardons are frequent but because criminals are few. . . . When pardons are plentiful, it is a sure sign that crimes will soon have no need of them, and everyone can see where that leads." Jean Jacques Rousseau, *Social Contract,* bk. 2, chap. 5.

108. Robert Samuelson, "End of the Carter Era," *Newsweek,* 14 November 1988, 59.

109. Kuttner, *Life of the Party,* 210; Bruce Babbitt, "The Democrats' Long Road Back," *New York Times,* 15 November 1988, A31.

110. Mark Shields, "If the Democrats Are to Win in '88," *Washington Post National Weekly,* 11–17 January 1988, 28; A.M. Rosenthal, "On My Mind," *New York Times,* 4 November 1988, A35.

111. *New York Times,* 1 December 1987, B24.

112. E.J. Dionne, "Reopening an Old Wound," *New York Times,* 23 August 1988, A1ff; Fox Butterfield, "Disparity in College Courses on Vietnam," *New York Times,* 27 April 1988, B11.

113. Anthony Kohlenberger, "Jack O'Connell: The Grass-roots Politician," *California Journal* 19 (November 1988): 478.

114. And only ruling principles give the party a claim on those who dissent from its social positions, particularly its stance on abortion. See David Carlin's fine "It's My Party," *Commonweal* 115 (7 October 1988): 521-22.

115. Anthony Lewis, "The Dirty Little Secret," *New York Times,* 20 October 1988, A27.

116. Harry McPherson, "How Race Destroyed the Democrats' Coalition," *New York Times,* 28 October 1988, A31; Edward G. Carmines and James A. Stimson, *Issue Evolution: The Racial Transformation of American Politics* (Princeton: Princeton University Press, 1988).

117. See my essay, "What Will Jackson Do?" *Commonweal* 115 (23 September 1988): 488.

118. Aristotle, *Politics,* 1274b32–1275b24; Robert Dahl, *Dilemmas of Pluralist Democracy* (New Haven: Yale University Press, 1982).

Appendix

Inaugural Address of President George Herbert Walker Bush

Mr. Chief Justice, Mr. President, Vice-President Quayle, Senator Mitchell, Speaker Wright, Senator Dole, Congressman Michel, and fellow citizens, neighbors, and friends.

There is a man here who has earned a lasting place in our hearts and in our history. President Reagan, on behalf of our nation I thank you for the wonderful things that you have done for America.

I've just repeated, word for word, the oath taken by George Washington 200 years ago, and the Bible on which I placed my hand is the Bible on which he placed his. It is right that the memory of Washington be with us today, not only because this is our Bicentennial Inauguration but because Washington remains the father of our country. And he would, I think, be gladdened by this day. For today is the concrete expression of a stunning fact: our continuity these 200 years since our government began.

We meet on democracy's front porch, a good place to talk as neighbors and as friends. For this is a day when our nation is made whole, when our differences for a moment are suspended. And my first act as President is a prayer—I ask you to bow your heads.

"Heavenly Father, we bow our heads and thank You for Your love. Accept our thanks for the peace that yields this day and the shared faith that makes its continuance likely. Make us strong to do Your work, willing to heed and hear Your will, and write on our hearts these words: 'Use power to help people.' For we are given power not to advance our own purposes nor to make a great show in the world, nor a name. There is but one just use of power and it is to serve people. Help us remember, Lord. Amen."

I come before you and assume the Presidency at a moment rich with promise. We live in a peaceful, prosperous time but we can make it better. For a new breeze is blowing and a world refreshed by freedom seems reborn; for in man's heart, if not in fact, the day of the dictator is over. The totalitarian era is passing, its old ideas blown away like leaves from an ancient, lifeless tree.

A new breeze is blowing—and a nation refreshed by freedom stands ready to push on. There's new ground to be broken and new action to be taken. There are times when the future seems thick as a fog; you sit and wait, hoping the mist will lift and reveal the right path.

But this is a time when the future seems a door you can walk right through —into a room called Tomorrow. Great nations of the world are moving toward democracy—through the door to freedom. Men and women of the world move toward free markets—through the door to prosperity. The people of the world agitate for free expression and free thought—through the door to the moral and intellectual satisfactions that only liberty allows.

We know what works: Freedom works. We know what's right: Freedom is right. We know how to secure a more just and prosperous life for man on earth: through free markets, free speech, free elections, and the exercise of free will unhampered by the state.

For the first time in this century—for the first time in perhaps all history— man does not have to invent a system by which to live. We don't have to talk late into the night about which form of government is better. We don't have to wrest justice from the kings—we only have to summon it from within ourselves.

We must act on what we know. I take as my guide the hope of a saint: In crucial things, unity—in important things, diversity—in all things, generosity.

America today is a proud, free nation, decent and civil—a place we cannot help but love. We know in our hearts, not loudly and proudly but as a simple fact, that this country has meaning beyond what we see, and that our strength is a force for good.

Have we changed as a nation even in our time? Are we enthralled with material things, less appreciative of the nobility of work and sacrifice? My friends, we are not the sum of our possessions. They are not the measure of our lives. In our hearts we know what matters. We cannot hope only to leave our children a bigger car, a bigger bank account. We must hope to give them a sense of what it means to be a loyal friend, a loving parent, a citizen who leaves his home, his neighborhood, and town better than he found it.

And what do we want the men and women who work with us to say when we're no longer there? That we were more driven to succeed than anyone around us? Or do we stop to ask if a sick child had gotten better, and stayed a moment there to trade a word of friendship.

No President, no government can teach us to remember what is best in what we are. But if the man you have chosen to lead this government can help make a difference, if he can celebrate the quieter, deeper successes that are made not of gold and silk but of better hearts and finer souls; if he can do these things, then he must.

America is never wholly herself unless she is engaged in high moral principle. We as a people have such a purpose today. It is to make kinder the face of the nation and gentler the face of the world.

My friends, we have work to do. There are the homeless, lost and roaming. There are the children who have nothing—no love, no normalcy. There are those who cannot free themselves of enslavement to whatever addiction—drugs, welfare, the demoralization that rules the slums. There is crime to be conquered, the rough crime of the streets. There are young women to be helped who are about to become mothers of children they can't care for and might not love. They need our care, our guidance, and our education, though we bless them for choosing life.

The old solution, the old way, was to think that public money alone could end these problems. But we have learned that that is not so. And in any case, our funds are low. We have a deficit to bring down. We have more will than wallet; but will is what we need.

We will make the hard choices, looking at what we have, perhaps allocating it differently, making our decisions based on honest need and prudent safety. And then we will do the wisest thing of all: We will turn to the only resource we have that in times of need always grows: the goodness and the courage of the American people.

And I am speaking of a new engagement in the lives of others—a new activism, hands-on and involved, that gets the job done. We must bring in the generations, harnessing the unused talent of the elderly and the unfocused energy of the young. For not only leadership is passed from generation to generation, but so is stewardship. And the generation born after the Second World War has come of age.

I've spoken of a thousand points of light—of all the community organizations that are spread like stars throughout the nation doing good. We will work hand in hand, encouraging, sometimes leading, sometimes being led, rewarding. We will work on this in the White House, in the Cabinet agencies. I will go to the people and the programs that are the brighter points of light, and I'll ask every member of my government to become involved. The old ideas are new again because they're not old, they are timeless: duty, sacrifice, commitment, and a patriotism that finds its expression in taking part and pitching in.

And we need a new engagement, too, between the Executive and the Congress. The challenges before us will be thrashed out with the House and the Senate. And we must bring the federal budget into balance. And we must insure that America stands before the world united: strong, at peace and fiscally sound. But, of course, things may be difficult.

We need compromise; we've had dissension. We need harmony; we've had a chorus of discordant voices. For Congress, too, has changed in our time. There's grown a certain divisiveness. We've seen the hard looks and heard the statements in which not each other's ideas are challenged, but each other's motives. And our great parties have too often been far apart and untrusting of each other.

It's been this way since Vietnam. That war cleaves us still. But, friends, that war began in earnest a quarter of a century ago; and surely the statute of limitations has been reached. This is a fact: The final lesson of Vietnam is that no great nation can long afford to be sundered by a memory.

A new breeze is blowing—and the old bipartisanship must be made new again.

To my friends—and yes, I do mean friends—in the loyal opposition—and yes, I mean loyal—I put out my hand. I'm putting out my hand to you, Mr. Speaker. I'm putting out my hand to you, Mr. Majority Leader. For this is the thing: This is the age of the offered hand. And we can't turn back clocks, and I don't want to. But when our fathers were young, Mr. Speaker, our differences ended at the water's edge. And we don't wish to turn back time, but when our mothers were young, Mr. Majority Leader, the Congress and the Executive were capable of working together to produce a budget on which this nation could live. Let us negotiate soon and hard, but in the end let us produce.

The American people await action. They didn't send us here to bicker. They asked us to rise above the merely partisan. In crucial things, unity—and this, my friends, is crucial.

To the world, too, we offer new engagement and a renewed vow: We will stay strong to protect the peace. The "offered hand" is a reluctant fist; but the fist, once made, is strong and can be used with great effect.

There are today Americans who are held against their will in foreign lands, and Americans who are unaccounted for. Assistance can be shown here and will be long remembered. Good will begets good will. Good faith can be a spiral that endlessly moves on.

"Great nations like great men must keep their word." When America says something, America means it, whether a treaty or an agreement or a vow made on marble steps. We will always try to speak clearly, for candor is a compliment. But subtlety, too, is good and has its place.

While keeping our alliances and friendships around the world strong, ever strong, we will continue the new closeness with the Soviet Union, consistent both with our security and with progress. One might say that our new relationship in part reflects the triumph of hope and strength over experience. But hope is good. And so is strength, and vigilance.

Here today are tens of thousands of our citizens who feel the understandable satisfaction of those who have taken part in democracy and seen their hopes fulfilled. But my thoughts have been turning the past few days to those who would be watching at home—to an older fellow who will throw a salute by himself when the flag goes by, and the woman who will tell her sons the words of the battle hymns. I don't mean this to be sentimental. I mean that on days like this we remember that we are all part of a continuum, inescapably connected by the ties that bind.

Our children are watching in schools throughout our great land. And to them I say, thank you for watching democracy's big day. For democracy belongs to us all and freedom is like a beautiful kite that can go higher and higher with the breeze. And to all I say: No matter what your circumstances or where you are, you are part of this day. You are part of the life of our great nation.

A President is neither prince nor pope, and I don't seek "a window on men's souls." In fact, I yearn for a greater tolerance, an easy-goingness about each other's attitudes and way of life.

There are few clear areas in which we as a society must rise up united and express our intolerance and the most obvious now is drugs. And when that first cocaine was smuggled in on a ship, it may as well have been a deadly bacteria, so much has it hurt the body, the soul, of our country. And there is much to be done and to be said, but take my word for it: This scourge will stop.

And so, there is much to do; and tomorrow the work begins. And I do not mistrust the future; I do not fear what is ahead. For our problems are large, but our heart is larger. Our challenges are great, but our will is greater. And if our flaws are endless, God's love is truly boundless.

Some see leadership as high drama, and the sound of trumpets calling. And sometimes it is that. But I see history as a book with many pages—and each day we fill a page with acts of hopefulness and meaning.

The new breeze blows, a page turns, the story unfolds—and so today a chapter begins: a small and stately story of unity, diversity, and generosity—shared and written together.

Thank you. God bless you and God bless the United States of America.

TABLE A.I

Position	Name	Age	Residence	Occupation
President	George H.W. Bush	64	Texas	Businessman
Vice-President	J. Danforth Quayle	41	Indiana	Attorney
Secretary of State	James A. Baker III	58	Texas	Banker
Secretary of the Treasury	Nicholas F. Brady	58	New Jersey	Businessman
Secretary of Defense	John Tower	63	Texas	Professor
Attorney-General	Dick Thornburgh	56	Pennsylvania	Attorney
Secretary of the Interior	Manuel Lujan, Jr.	60	New Mexico	Businessman
Secretary of Agriculture	Clayton Yeutter	59	Nebraska	Mercantile trader
Secretary of Commerce	Robert A. Mosbacher	61	Texas	Financier
Secretary of Labor	Elizabeth H. Dole	52	Kansas	Attorney
Secretary of Health and Human Services	Louis W. Sullivan	55	Georgia	Physician
Secretary of Housing and Urban Development	Jack Kemp	53	New York	Government
Secretary of Transportation	Samuel Skinner	50	Illinois	Attorney
Secretary of Energy	James D. Watkins	61	District of Columbia	Military
Secretary of Education	Lauro Cavazos	61	Texas	Educator
Secretary of Veterans Affairs	Edward Derwinski	62	Illinois	Government
Chief of Staff	John H. Sununu	49	New Hampshire	Engineer
Director, Office of Management and Budget	Richard Darman	45	Virginia	Businessman
Ambassador to the UN	Thomas R. Pickering	57	New Jersey	Diplomat
Special Assistant to the President for National Security Affairs	Brent Scowcroft	63	Utah	Military
Director of Central Intelligence	William H. Webster	64	Maryland	Attorney
Chairman, President's Council of Economic Advisers	Michael J. Boskin	43	California	Economist

THE BUSH ADMINISTRATION (AS OF 20 JANUARY 1989)

Previous Experience	Education
Vice-President	B.A., Yale
U.S. Senator	B.A., DePauw; J.D., Indiana
White House Chief of Staff; Secretary of the Treasury	B.A., Princeton; J.D., Texas
Secretary of the Treasury; U.S. Senator	B.A., Yale; M.B.A., Harvard
U.S. Senator	B.A., Southwestern; M.A., Southern Methodist
Attorney-General; Governor of Pennsylvania	B.S., Yale; LL.B., Pittsburgh
U. S. Congressman	B.A., College of Santa Fe
Special Trade Representative; Assistant Secretary, Agriculture Department	B.S., J.D., Ph.D., Nebraska
Fundraiser	B.A., Georgetown; J.D., Southern Methodist
Secretary of Transportation; Member, Federal Trade Commission	B.A., Duke; M.A., J.D., Harvard
President, Morehouse School of Medicine	B.A., Morehouse; M.D., Boston University, School of Medicine
U.S. Congressman	B.A., Occidental
Chairman, Regional Transportation Authority, Northeastern Illinois	B.A., Illinois; LL.B., DePaul
Chief of Naval Operations	B.S., U.S. Naval Academy
Secretary of Education; College president	B.S., M.S., Texas Tech; Ph.D., Iowa
U.S. Congressman	B.S., Loyola
Governor of New Hampshire	B.S., M.S., Ph.D., MIT
Deputy Chief of Staff; Deputy Secretary of the Treasury	B.A., M.B.A., Harvard
Career ambassador	A.B., Bowdoin; M.A., Fletcher School of Law and Diplomacy, Tufts University
Military Assistant to the President; National Security Adviser	B.S., U.S. Military Academy; M.A., Ph.D., Columbia
Director of Central Intelligence; Director, Federal Bureau of Investigation	B.A., Amherst; J.D., Washington University, St. Louis
Director, Center for Economic Policy Research	B.S., M.A., Ph.D., University of California, Berkeley

Index

Calvert, Randall L., 175
Campaign strategies, 27, 178-83; and debates, 88-96; of Democratic nominees, 38-39; lessons from 1984 and, 78-83; media and, 96-100; political environment and, 74-78; politics of vote and, 137-39. *See also specific candidates.*
Campbell, Angus, 151
Cannon, Howard, 168
Cantril, Hadley, 152
Carberry, Glenn, 166
Carlin, David, 206
Carmines, Edward G., 150, 152, 206
Carter, Jimmy, 1-3, 14, 24, 38, 82, 135, 146, 187, 188, 191, 195; Democratic party and, 21, 33; and economy, 74, 118, 193; repudiation of, 6-8
Catholic vote, 136, 188
Cavazos, Lauro, 138, 212-13
Chancellor, John, 181, 202
Chappell, Bill, 169
Child care issue, 63
Chiles, Lawton, 170
Class issues, 80, 93
Cleveland, Grover, 2, 179, 180, 201
Clinton, Bill, 70
Cloward, Richard A., 151
Clubb, Jerome, 152
Clymer, Adam, 152
Coattail voting, 162-63
Coelho, Tony, 91
Cohen, Richard E., 175
Community, liberalism, and values, 194-98
Congress, composition, 154-55
Congressional elections of 1984, 22
Congressional elections of 1986, 34
Congressional elections of 1988, 25, 28, 153-74; Bush agenda and, 172-74; incumbency effect, 155-60; interpretation, 163-69; results, 169-72
Conservatism: Dukakis's claim of, 77-78; as influence on voting, 111-12, 146; Republican party and, 8-13, 59-60, 65
Cook, Rhodes, 101
Corcoran, Paul, 202
Crime issue, 73, 86, 94, 95-96, 99, 116-18, 124, 190, 197
Crotty, William J., 201
Cuomo, Mario, 37, 48, 69, 70, 139

Dach, Leslie, 99
Dahl, Robert, 206

Danforth, John, 157
Darman, Richard, 32, 212-13
Daschle, Thomas A., 171
Davis, Jack, 167
Dawkins, Maurice, 163
Dawkins, Pete, 162, 164
Death penalty issue, 117, 197
Debates, 88-96; public opinion and, 107
Defense issues, 9, 58, 82, 94, 115-16, 124
Deficits, 76, 100
Democratic party: balance of power with Republican party, 19-20; Carter administration and, 14; delegates, 42-43; effects of vote on, 147-49; and electoral college, 75; electoral considerations of, 49-53; ideology, 198-99; platform, 52-53, 67; presidential nomination, 37-53, 54-55; primaries, 40-43, 184-86; Reagan legacy and, 11, 26-27; values, 141-47; vice-presidential nomination, 49-52. *See also individual candidates;* Nominations; Political parties.
Derwinski, Edward, 212-13
Deukmejian, George, 63
Dewar, Helen, 175
Dillin, John, 102
DioGuardi, Joseph J., 168
Dionne, E.J., 102, 200, 201-4, 206
Dole, Elizabeth H., 212-13
Dole, Robert, 56, 58, 59, 172, 184-85, 203; primary votes for, 60, 61
Dowd, Maureen, 101
Dowdy, Wayne, 162
Downs, Anthony, 69, 71
Drug issue, 117, 190
Dukakis, Michael, 10, 11, 27, 33, 37-39, 44, 49, 54-55, 70, 129, 153, 177, 197, 203; Bush campaign and, 82-83, 85-88; campaign strategies, 77-78, 79-81, 92; and crime issue, 73; delegates, 42-43; as governor, 77; ideology, 48, 66-67, 189; Jesse Jackson and, 46; meaning of defeat, 188-91; media and, 99, 182, 183; nomination, 48; platform, 52-53; primary votes for, 40, 41, 45, 46-47, 184; public response to, 78, 91, 94, 103-4; and tax issue, 79, 101; and vice-presidential nominations. 49-52, 85. *See also* Presidential election of 1988; Opinion polls.
DuPont, Pierre, 56, 58

Economic issues, 35, 94, 95, 103-4, 118-21, 192-94; in Bush campaign, 74, 75-76, 82;